Wake Island Pilot

Potomac's
MEMORIES OF WAR
Series

Outstanding memoirs that illustrate the personal realities of war as experienced by combatants and civilians alike, in recent conflicts as well as those of the distant past. Other titles in the series:

American Guerrilla: My War Behind Japanese Lines
Roger Hilsman

B-17s Over Berlin: Personal Stories from the 95th Bomb Group (H)
Ian Hawkins

Escape With Honor: My Last Hours in Vietnam
Amb. Francis Terry McNamara with Adrian Hill

Hitler's Prisoners: Seven Cell Mates Tell Their Stories
Erich Friedrich and Renate Vanegas

Lieutenant Ramsey's War: From Horse Soldier to Guerrilla Commander
Edwin Price Ramsey and Stephen J. Rivele

Medal of Honor: One Man's Journey from Poverty and Prejudice
Roy Benavidez with John Craig

The Gulf Between Us: Love and Survival in Desert Storm
Cynthia B. Acree with Col. Cliff Acree, USMC

Under Custer's Command: The Civil War Journal of James Henry Avery
Karla Jean Husby and Eric J. Wittenberg

War in the Boats: My WWII Submarine Battles
Capt. William J. Ruhe, USN (Ret.)

White Tigers: My Secret War in North Korea
Col. Ben S. Malcom, USA (Ret.), with Ron Martz

Wake Island Pilot

A World War II Memoir

Brig. Gen. John F. Kinney, USMC (Ret.)

with

James M. McCaffrey

POTOMAC BOOKS, INC.
Washington, D.C.

First Memories of War edition published in 2005
Copyright © 1995 by John F. Kinney and James M. McCaffrey

First Brassey's paperback edition 1999

Map by Albert D. McJoynt

Library of Congress Cataloging-in-Publication Data

Kinney, John F., 1914–
  Wake Island pilot: a World War II memoir / John F. Kinney,
with James M. McCaffrey
    p.   cm.
  Includes bibliographical references and index.
  1. Kinney, John F., 1914– 2. World War, 1939–1945—Aerial operations,
American.   3. World War, 1939–1945—Personal narratives, American.
4. Fighter pilots—United States—Biography.   5. United States Marine Corps—
Biography.   I. McCaffrey, James M., 1946–.   II. Title
D790.K55   1995
940.54′4973′92—dc20
[B]   95-1686
                                                                          CIP

ISBN 1-57488-204-X (alk. paper)
ISBN 1-57488-736-X (paper)

Printed in Canada on acid-free paper that meets the American National Standards
Institute Z39-48 Standard.

Potomac Books, Inc.
22841 Quicksilver Drive
Dulles, Virginia 20166

10 9 8 7 6 5 4 3 2 1

Contents

Preface

This book relates the story of John F. Kinney's love of flying, and how that passion led him into the U.S. Marine Corps. Captured on Wake Island in December 1941, Kinney survived three and a half years in Japanese prison camps before making his escape. He stayed in the Marine Corps after the war and fought again in Korea. Military retirement in 1959 did not mean total retirement for General Kinney. He then went on to a career in civilian aviation for twenty more years.

This book has been a long time in the making. Encouraged by two fellow Marines, Major General Paul Fontana and Lieutenant General Thomas Miller, General Kinney first thought about putting his story down on paper during the waning stages of the Vietnam War. He wanted to hold out hope to the families of that war's prisoners. He wanted them to see that imprisonment in enemy hands did not have to mean the end of a man's productive life. He was living proof.

Mr. McCaffrey's interest was also sparked during the very early stages of the Vietnam War, when he listened to his high school chemistry teacher, Father Euguene Lutz, C.S.V., tell of *his* experiences on Wake Island and in the same Japanese prison camps.

The bases for this book are General Kinney's memories of a long career and the notes a young Lieutenant Kinney made while a prisoner of war. Other sources—books, articles, official reports—have been employed to amplify Kinney's story and to put it into a wider perspective. If Kinney's recollections differ from those of other men who shared his experiences, it is due to, among other things, the heat of battle surrounding some of the events discussed—the proverbial fog of war that prevents any one participant from seeing every aspect of a battle.

We would like to thank Professor Gregory Urwin of the University of Central Arkansas for introducing us to each other and for sharing some of the massive amount of research that he has collected on the Wake Island experience. Bill Taylor, of Provo, Utah—who, like Kinney, was captured on Wake and escaped from the Japanese—made available to us copies of two prisoner diaries as well as a photo of Woosung Prison. We would also like to thank the librarians at the University of Houston–Downtown for providing us through interlibrary loan with so many of the sources consulted.

John F. Kinney
James M. McCaffrey

Foreword

An atoll consisting of three islets—Wake, Wilkes, and Peale—Wake Island was annexed by the United States in 1898. Its three square miles lie in the Pacific 2,000 miles southeast of Tokyo and 2,300 miles west of Honolulu. Used as a refueling stop for Pan American Airways and being prepared as a naval patrol plane and submarine base, Wake Island was strategically important to both the Japanese and the United States at the beginning of World War II.

The Japanese began air raids against Wake within hours of the attack on Pearl Harbor, and on December 11, 1941, they attempted an invasion. They were repulsed, with heavy loses, by four hundred U.S. servicemen and a thousand civilians. Ironically, during all of World War II, this was the only Japanese amphibious operation in the Pacific that was a failure. Stunned, the Japanese detached two of Vice Admiral Chuichi Nagumo's Pearl Harbor attack carriers to a new task force, and on December 23 they tried again. Although they again received heavy losses, this time they were successful. The Americans surrendered on December 23, one day before reinforcements from Pearl Harbor were scheduled to arrive.

One American captured by the Japanese was a young Marine pilot named John F. Kinney. This is his story. It begins with his desire—actually an obsession—to become a pilot, which he does despite vision problems. Kinney describes vividly the physical thrill of learning to fly and of performing aerial maneuvers. As a young Marine just before World War II, he was assigned to Hawaii. He provides a vivid picture of a young Marine's life among the amusements of Waikiki, while all the time war is in the back of everyone's mind. Eleven days before the attack on Pearl Harbor, Kinney's squadron was dispatched aboard the U.S.S. *Enterprise* in order to have aviation assets present at Wake when the Japanese ambassadors were traveling to and from the United States and to reinforce the island.

Kinney is at his best describing how the heroes of Wake Island held out for over two weeks. The island commander was Lieutenant Commander Winfield Scott Cunningham, Major Paul Putnam commanded VMF-211, and Major James P. Devereux was the commander of the Marine defense battalion. Kinney believes that while Major Devereux was worthy of praise, Commander Cunningham never received the accolades he deserved. He also dispels the myth that a Marine had radioed "Send us more Japs!" Upon the fall of

Wake, Kinney was taken prisoner and on January 12 sent to a prison camp in China. The core of the remainder of the book is the story of his life in prison and his never-ending determination to escape.

Life in prison was no picnic, as the Japnaese did not abide by the Geneva Convention. For those politically correct people of the 1990s, Kinney makes it clear that the Japanese guards were not very nice people. Life in the camps for the approximately 1,500 U.S. prisoners of war was hard. Food was scarce and poor, rats, bugs, and mosquitoes were rampant, and sanitation was awful. The prisoners were constantly abused and beaten, yet Kinney never broke. An ingenious engineer, he was even to make life better, fashioning a crystal set radio, a sextant, and other useful electrical and mechanical aids. While he was incarcerated, he kept his mind busy by studying Japanese and, to prepare for his escape, Chinese.

Kinney and some comrades made their move toward the end of the war, and their escape is a thriller. Both Chinese Communist and Nationalist forces saved Kinney's life and led him after a long and scary journey to American authorities. His descriptions of the differences in the organization and philosophies of the two enemies contain interesting insights.

After the war, Kinney continued to fly in the Marines. He served with distinction in the Korean War and eventually prepared the Marine requirement document for a jet attack aircraft. He collaborated in the design of the A4D Skyhawk. Upon his completion of service, he retired with the rank of brigadier general and worked as an engineer with four aircraft companies for another twenty years. Throughout his well-told story, Kinney describes the traits that make a leader, a pilot, and an engineer. His autobiography is one of drive, determination, intestinal fortitude, and will. World War II was won by heroes like John Kinney. If you seek his monument, look around.

Donald M. Goldstein
Pittsburgh, Pennsylvania

Wake Island Pilot

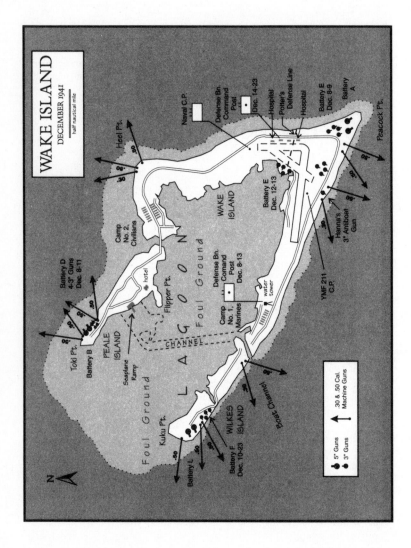

1

Born to Fly

Some people live their entire lives without ever knowing what they really want to do with themselves. They move from job to job, never quite satisfied. Sometimes they even change careers altogether—moving, for example, from engineering to real estate or retail sales. Others, and there are considerably fewer in this class, seem to have an inborn instinct, an unswerving ambition leading them toward a particular profession. I am of the latter group. I wanted to be an aviator.

I have wanted to fly for as long as I can remember; there is just something majestic about being able to soar through the sky like the great birds of prey. Nor was I the first in my family to have this desire. My father's brother, Clair A. Kinney, must have felt this same strange pull, for when the United States entered World War I in 1917, he left his architectural studies at the University of Washington and enlisted in the Signal Corps, which in those days was the branch of the army that oversaw manned flight.

I was still a toddler at the time, too young to understand this great war that the adults all talked about, but I remember being very proud of Uncle Clair when we took him to the train station in Endicott, Washington.

Uncle Clair never came home again. While patrolling the skies over Doulon, France, in the fall of 1918, he and six other American pilots encountered a flight of seventeen German Fokkers. In the ensuing melee, he shot down two of the enemy planes before one of the Germans riddled him and his Spad with machine-gun fire. In spite of his wounds, Clair was able to maintain control of his aircraft long enough to bring it safely to the ground. Unfortunately, he died from his injuries.

Just as I had been too young to understand the war, I was also a little young to grieve for Uncle Clair. Years later, however, I was struck by the irony of the fact that his death provided me with more than just his Distinguished Flying Cross and a legacy of aviation heroism. Since he had gone to war before ever having had a chance to start a family of his own, he had named me and his three other nephews as beneficiaries of his government life insurance policy. My share would later help me pay for college, and my college degree would enable me to qualify for a naval aviation training program.

In the meantime, however, I became more and more interested in flying. As part of the demobilization that followed the armistice after World War I, the army began to dispose of its by-then-surplus air-planes. This allowed civilian aviation enthusiasts to buy these planes at bargain prices. Two young men in my neighborhood, Alvene and Carl Litzenberger, had seen the ads for these Curtiss JN4-D "Jenny" aircraft in 1924 and had somehow come up with the requisite $600 purchase price. The plane arrived in two large wooden packing crates. The fuselage, engine, controls, rudder, landing gear, and pro-peller were in one box, while the other contained the fabric-covered wings and various control wires, pulleys, and miscellaneous fittings. Even though the Litzenbergers were somewhat mechanically inclined, and even though the plane came from the manufacturer with forty-six pages of assembly instructions, they decided to spend a little more money and hire an experienced mechanic to help them put it all together. Before long the three of them somehow got the thing assembled and into the air.

The factory-supplied handbook did not stop with assembly direc-tions; it also contained some five or six pages of helpful hints on fly-ing the Jenny. Some were rather obvious, such as warning the new pilot to make sure he had turned on the switch before trying to start his machine. Another, aimed at those who are never happy unless they are tinkering with something, cautioned them to avoid "tinkeri-tis"—"when the motor is working satisfactorily, leave it alone." Perhaps most disquieting to any pilot, however, was: "Never forget that the engine may stop, and at all times keep this in mind and plan on a safe landing place within gliding distance of wherever you may be."[1]

Maybe it was this last warning that caused the new airmen to use one of my dad's meadows to practice their flying skills. It was rela-tively level and clear of obstructive tree stumps and boulders. Their early flights often occurred within sight of the one-room school-house where I was "imprisoned" in the fourth grade. It was awfully hard to keep my mind on such mundane topics as arithmetic and geography when I could look out the window and see the Litzenbergers flying by in their wonderful machine. I couldn't wait for school to end on these days, and when the bell finally rang I would run all the way to the meadow just so I could get a closer look at the operation.

My daily air shows came to a sad end the following year. Al and Carl, after all, did not have an unlimited supply of funds, and it was sometimes difficult for them to come up with enough money to keep their gas tank full. Planes in those days did not use particularly exotic fuels, so they sometimes siphoned gas from their father's Hudson so they could fly. One evening, while flying with a lady passenger, the plane ran out of gas. It was the possibility of just such an occasion as this that had prompted the advice in the Jenny's manual about always having a safe landing area nearby. In this instance the plane stalled in from a height of about ten feet. The severe emergency landing, even from such a seemingly harmless altitude, caused the passenger to suffer a broken arm, and the plane was a total loss.

My faith in manned flight remained unshaken by such minor setbacks as the Litzenberger brothers' crash. They had simply not been careful enough. They had had bad luck. If *I* ever had the chance to fly an airplane, I hoped to have better luck. My friend Floyd Cook and I decided that we had learned about all we could from observing the Litzenbergers anyway, so we determined to buy our own airplane. *Popular Science* magazine advertised a do-it-yourself kit airplane called the "Penguin," which, like its namesake, had short stubby wings and was flightless. Its sole purpose was to teach flight students to taxi. It did not have enough power to get off the ground. This, of course, was entirely too tame for us, but we took heart from the fact that the ad also assured us that it was a simple matter to bypass the engine's governor, thereby giving it enough power to fly.

As we pored over this ad and dreamed of flying, we realized that there was still the little matter of coming up with the money to pay for "our" plane. It cost only half as much as the Litzenbergers' Jenny, but even $300 was a considerable amount of money in those days. By this time, 1926, the Great Depression was still in the future for city dwellers, but farm families like mine were already feeling the pinch. My dad and uncle, for example, operated our farm on about $600 credit for most of the year. Then, after they sold the crop in September, they used that money to pay off all of the grocery bills for the previous year and started the process all over again. Although wheat and alfalfa were our cash crops, my grandfather tended a garden that produced enough fresh vegetables for the family's needs. My mother's flock of chickens kept us supplied with more eggs than we needed, so she made a little extra money by selling the excess. (And, of course, any of the layers who did not keep up with their expected quota wound up on the dinner table.) We also kept enough pigs on the farm to provide plenty of pork and bacon. We were far from being destitute, but we also did not rub elbows with the Rockefellers.

Getting the $300 from our parents was out of the question, so Floyd and I talked seriously of renting an acre of land and growing potatoes to raise the money. They were selling for a penny a pound, and we thought we could surely make the money that way. I don't think either one of us had any real idea of how hard we would have to work to harvest thirty thousand pounds of potatoes! We would also need about $50 worth of seeds to get started, and there were only a few ways for young boys to earn seed money in those days. The most likely source of earning this money was to hire out to the local farmers to hoe weeds in their fields at certain times of the year. A farmer would space his young helpers at about ten-yard intervals on one side of a field, and they would begin work. When they reached a point about half a mile away—usually after about two hours of backbreaking toil—they would find a supply of cool water waiting for them. After this short rest stop it was back to work again until lunchtime, when the boys would try to find a little patch of shade in which to eat the lunches that their mothers had packed for them that morning. The same process repeated itself in the afternoon, and when the day was finally over the farmer paid each boy the grand sum of one dollar. Looking back, it was probably lucky for us that we were never able to earn the seed money, plant and harvest three hundred bags of potatoes, and buy that plane, for we surely would have killed ourselves within a week.

Despite my longtime infatuation with aviation I entered my teenage years without ever having ridden in an airplane. I had come close a few times. An uncle had bought one of the government-surplus Jennies after World War I, but I was too young to ride with him then. He was also not very proficient. Charles Lindbergh's historic transatlantic solo flight in 1927 generated a tremendous amount of interest all over the world in flying. This fascination with flight was a boon to anyone who could scrape together the cost of an airplane. Sometimes groups of enthusiasts formed flying clubs and pooled their resources in order to experience the exhilaration of flight. And there were the barnstormers. These adventuresome pilot-entrepreneurs traveled the circuits of county fairs and other carnivals selling rides in their wonderful machines to members of the general public. My turn finally came that summer, while visiting my mother's family in Blandinsville, Illinois. We all went to the fair one day, and as soon as I saw the daredevil and his plane I fairly pleaded with my mother to let me go up in it. She consented, and one of my uncles paid the pilot five dollars—a lot of money in those days—to take my cousin and me aloft in his Jenny.

The plane was a two-place, open-cockpit biplane. The pilot flew in the rear seat and any passengers rode just in front of him. Since passenger space was so limited the pilot had replaced the standard seat with a wide plank so he could squeeze two passengers in at a time, thereby doubling his revenue per ride. My cousin and I carefully, but excitedly, scrambled over the side and into the plane. I'm sure the pilot used all ninety of his engine's horsepower to reach its design cruising speed of sixty to seventy miles per hour, and it seemed at the time as if we must be flashing through the sky at an incredible rate. The experience was all I had dared hope for. I *must* fly!

By this time Al Litzenberger—older, and presumably wiser—had moved to Pittsburgh. He was still flying, however, and he flew out to Spokane in his Waco during a transcontinental air race. After the race he came back to Endicott and landed on the high school football field, where my friends and I peppered him with questions about flying. My brief flight back in Blandinsville hardly qualified me as one of Al's peers, but I felt that it did give me a slight edge on some of my equally eager classmates when we discussed flying.

Al's visit seemed to heighten my interest, if that was possible, and after he left I built a mock-up of an airplane cockpit, complete with a stick and rudder controls, in the basement. Then I built a home-made scale model of a Curtiss Hawk biplane from a picture I saw in *Popular Mechanics*, and mounted it on a ball-and-socket joint on the end of a broomstick above my cockpit. I connected the nose, tail, and each lower wing by a system of strings and pulleys to my controls. Then, when I pushed the stick forward, the little biplane nosed down, too. When I applied left rudder, the model also turned left. My younger brother Clair and I would spend hours in make-believe flight to far-off lands. Sometimes we pretended to be in France in 1918, where we came to Uncle Clair's rescue near Doulon by shooting down the rest of the Fokkers.

My interest in flying did not flag all through high school, but I also had begun to have another, perhaps more attainable goal. I wanted to become an engineer. I really enjoyed learning how things worked, whether they were simple telephones or six-cylinder internal combustion engines, and I seemed to have a knack for it. I had already gained a considerable amount of practical experience working for a neighboring farmer, Raymond Darden, during the summers. Not only was the dollar a day he paid me a welcome addition to my college fund, but he also always seemed to have the time and patience to show me how the various pieces of machinery on his place worked. A lot of the other farmers in the neighborhood did not think he devoted enough time to his farming, but I certainly learned a lot from him. I learned to drive his Caterpillar tractor, and when it needed its engine rebuilt I did that, too. I also signed up for a formal automobile mechanics class while I was in college, using my dad's Oldsmobile to practice on. Before long I gained the skill and confidence to completely tear down the engine in the Olds, rebore the block, and install bigger pistons and rings. I performed similar major surgery on the four-cylinder Chevrolet truck we had. Before long I took over all of the basic mechanical maintenance for my dad. A college engineering degree would feed my natural inquisitiveness and might very well help me into a career in aviation. At the very least, it would afford me a good enough salary to be able to afford private flight lessons.

One barrier to my college aspirations was the fact that my small high school did not offer a course in advanced algebra with which to prepare for the college math courses essential to an engineer. Three of my classmates also had hopes of engineering careers, and we were determined not to let this hindrance stand in our way. We went to the principal and asked if he would let us study advanced algebra on our own. Since he had no teacher for such a class, and since he certainly did not want to stifle our intellectual curiosity at such a young age, he agreed. We began our study sessions with the best of intentions, but we found it difficult to maintain the proper focus. Our math discussions often gave way to talking about flying and other subjects of interest to seventeen-year-old boys.

After graduation in 1932, I learned that the army was accepting applicants for pilot training. This seemed like a golden opportunity. The army could teach me to fly, and would even pay me at the same time. This latter was not an inconsequential consideration in the depths of the Great Depression. Maybe I would not need that engineering degree after all.

The greatest immediate obstacle was my eyesight. I had a mild astigmatism and had been wearing glasses since I was eight years old. This did not concern me too much because I figured that I could find some way to memorize the eye charts and fool the army medical men into believing that I had twenty-twenty vision.

Then I found out about another small roadblock, one for which there was no easy solution. Aviation cadets had to have at least two years of college. The cost of a college education was beyond the reach of many young men in 1932. The Depression did not leave most families with any extra money to spend on such things, but I was luckier than most. I still had my Uncle Clair's insurance benefits, and I put them to use by enrolling in engineering classes at Washington State College. Then, in the summer of 1934, armed with two years' worth of formal education and an unfaltering conviction that I would somehow be able to fake my way through the eyesight tests, I reported to Vancouver, Washington, for a preliminary flight physical.

When I arrived, there were so many applicants ahead of me—hundreds—that I could see it very likely would be the next day before my turn came. There seemed to be no point in hanging around indoors, so I went out to soak up a little sunshine while I waited. It was a beautiful warm day and, lying on my back, I was soon fast asleep. I do not remember how long I was out before someone came and got me for my eye examination, but my nap had so relaxed the tiny muscles in my eyes that I was able to pass it with flying colors—even without memorizing the chart ahead of time. Before I could congratulate myself on my good fortune, however, they showed me some pieces of colored yarn and asked me to find the same colors on an adjacent color chart. I was still seeing sunspots and did not do too well on this one.

Next came another examination for color blindness, a devilishly clever test developed by a Japanese man named Ishihara. (This was not the last time I would hear the name Ishihara.) The flight surgeon placed a book in front of me in which the pages were filled with dots of various colors and asked me to tell him what numbers I saw among the dots. The dots were arranged so that some of them formed numbers that were visible only to a person who was not red/green color-blind. I missed a few of them (so did the flight surgeon), but I still was confident that my overall performance was good enough to pass. The army did not share my optimism, however, and informed me that my color blindness had disqualified me from army aviation training.

Of course I was dejected, but I was not ready to give up altogether. Perhaps I could get an appointment to the Military Academy at West Point and go to flight training from there. This route to an aviation career had the additional benefit of allowing me to complete the balance of my college education at government expense. I took the entrance exam, but my score was not as high as the score of the other applicant from my part of the state. Another door closed.

Now I *was* getting a little discouraged, so I returned to Washington State to finish my degree. I had already completed the mandatory two-year Reserve Officer Training Corps (ROTC) program, and now I applied for the advanced ROTC training. The sixteen dollars per quarter that came with it would help defray my other college expenses, and with a reserve commission I might at least be able to get a National Guard assignment as an aerial observer. Then I could try to figure some way to parlay that into a chance to be a pilot.

ROTC cadets were supposed to attend a six-week training camp in the summer between their third and fourth years in college, but that summer my fraternity, Alpha Tau Omega, nominated me to go to the national convention in Memphis. I knew that summer camp was important, but I also knew that a trip to Memphis was not an everyday occurrence for someone in my financial condition. I really wanted to go. I approached Major R. M. O'Day, the professor of military science at Washington State, with my dilemma. Major O'Day was regular army through and through, so he could not very well tell me it was all right to skip summer camp. Unofficially, though, he said that if he found himself faced with the choice between summer camp and a trip to Tennessee he would choose the latter. That was my choice, too.

I had a great time at the convention, but when it was over I was in a hurry to get back to Endicott so I could begin earning money toward the next year's college expenses. When I arrived at the train station at Colfax I still had several miles to go to reach the farm, so I began walking along the road hoping to hitch a ride with a passing motorist. Along the way I saw my old friend Joe Fanzeck working on the small OX-5 Travelair airplane that he and the local butcher owned jointly. I stopped to see what the problem was and to offer my help. He had somehow broken a fuel line, but within a few minutes we had rigged up a suitable repair by borrowing a section of heavy rubber air hose from a nearby gas station. Playing the Good Samaritan had its reward when Joe offered to fly me the rest of the way home.

Having missed summer camp meant that, upon graduation in the summer of 1936, I still owed the army six weeks. I would have to make this time up before I could receive my commission. The nearest camp was at Spokane, but I had already decided to try to seek work in California, so I arranged to put in my six weeks at the Presidio of Monterey. I proudly accepted a commission as a second lieutenant in the United States Army Reserve on July 1, 1936, and began attending weekly drills.

My search for work in California was not quite as fruitful as I had hoped. I made ends meet for quite a while working for the Local Loan Company in San Francisco, calling on delinquent accounts. It was a miserable way to earn twenty dollars per week. The Depression was still a long way from being over, and a lot of people were unable to keep up with their bills. I sometimes spent days trying to locate someone who was behind on a bill only to find that it would work a real hardship on him to come up with even one dollar. These were not deadbeats, for the most part, but hardworking people who were down on their luck. They often promised to pay another dollar the following week, but this almost made me feel guilty because I at least *had* a job.

About the only good thing about this line of work was that I was not tied to a desk, and I managed to knock on a lot of doors during the course of a day looking for more rewarding work. My method of transportation was by nickel streetcar, for which the loan company reimbursed me at the rate of five cents per call. I soon found that not only was I learning the city like the back of my hand, I also could finagle a way to stretch my expense money. By the judicious use of transfer tickets I was able to make three calls for one five-cent street-car fare. At this rate I could clear twenty cents on six calls and have enough for lunch at Woolworth's. My regular lunch was a toasted ham sandwich—ten cents—and apple pie à la mode—another ten cents. Of course, if I ordered both items at the same time I had to pay a penny sales tax, so I waited until after I had paid for and eaten the sandwich before ordering the pie. Money was tight in 1936!

Meanwhile, my search for employment that would cause me less guilt was not meeting with much success. There were not many companies willing to hire a young engineer fresh out of college when there were so many experienced engineers out of work and willing to accept almost any wages. Finally, I heard that Pan American Airways was hiring mechanics. It had recently added passenger service to its regular mail routes from San Francisco to the Far East and needed to keep its three-plane fleet in the air. The planes were the huge thirty-two-passenger Martin 130 seaplanes, although for the long San Francisco–Honolulu flight they carried only twelve passengers because of the weight of the necessary extra fuel. These were the largest commercial airplanes in the world at that time, and I had absolutely no idea what a Pan Am mechanic would be expected to do exactly. But I also knew that whatever it was it could not be so difficult that I could not pick it up very quickly. Besides, a job as an aircraft mechanic would at least get me close to airplanes again. I applied for the job, and, in December 1936, I began work as a twenty-six-cents-per-hour mechanic.

Since Pan Am expected its mechanics to own their own tools I shopped around for some that would last. Sears, Roebuck advertised a set for about $50 that was guaranteed for life, so I took a chance and bought them on the installment plan. (I finally broke one of the sockets fifty years later and Sears cheerfully replaced it, just as it had said it would.) Next I looked around for some form of transportation that would free me from the streetcar schedules, and I spotted a used 1929 Model A Ford coupe for $139. I borrowed $50 from my father for the down payment and then made regular payments of $13 per month until it was paid for.

My initiation into aircraft maintenance was to take a two-foot-long screwdriver and remove the covers from the lower wing fuel tanks on the Martins so I could inspect for saltwater corrosion—a constant problem where aluminum comes into contact with salt water. I then would clean away the corrosion as best I could, repaint the area with zinc chromate, cover it all with a sort of rubberized solution, and reinstall the cover. Another periodic maintenance task was to replace the fabric that covered the tail surfaces and the rear two thirds of the wings. The fabric was good for about three years, but the process of replacing it was so time-consuming that we could never afford to take a plane out of service long enough to do the whole job at one time. Instead, we worked on six-foot-wide sections whenever we could. The old fabric had to come off of six ribs before the new fabric could be stitched into place. Then, just as with scale model airplanes, the entire repair section had to be doped and painted. It took about four days to do just this partial repair.

I soon grew accustomed to the way things were done at Pan American. I enjoyed the work and made several good friends. I was not flying, but at least I was close to airplanes. And it was a lot better than hounding people who had fallen behind on their bills.

Our maintenance work was, of course, tied directly to the flight schedule of the planes upon which we worked. One of the three seaplanes—called "clippers" after the swift oceangoing sailing vessels of the nineteenth century—left from Alameda every Wednesday for the Far East. While it stopped at Honolulu, Midway, Wake, and Guam on its way to and from Manila and Hong Kong, another one headed east across the Pacific, making all the same stops. When the east-bound plane arrived at Alameda we had to make sure we had it in tip-top shape by its scheduled departure time for the return trip. If it was late coming in due to weather or other problems, we might work through the night getting it ready to go back out again on Wednesday. Of course, Pan Am did not expect us to work these long hours for nothing. During weeks when we put in more than forty-eight hours, we got an extra nine cents per hour for the overtime.

One task that really played havoc with the flight schedules was engine replacement. When one of the Martins needed to have one of its four engines replaced it usually took four or five days because each engine's plumbing was handmade, and each line was routed in a different manner. One of my assignments while I held this job was to help devise some method to make engine changes more quickly. I helped design an arrangement of color coding the many tubes carrying oil pressure, fuel pressure, gasoline, oil, antifreeze, and hydraulic fluid so that every engine and firewall would be standardized. Then, when we needed to replace an engine, the spare would already be set up exactly like the one we were taking out. These changes eventually reduced the time it took us to change an engine to about eight hours. A considerable improvement.

Working on the seaplanes was good experience for me, but I wanted to do more than fight saltwater corrosion or replace wing fabric. I wanted to fly. Sometimes bad weather kept a flight from taking off after the mail had already been loaded aboard, and the clipper remained anchored in the water. On those occasions it was necessary for an armed guard to remain in the plane overnight to protect the mail. This duty rotated among the personnel at Alameda, and when I drew the assignment I spent a considerable portion of my time in the pilot's seat pretending to fly. Windy weather heightened the illusion because I could then unlock the controls and actually turn the craft forty-five degrees in either direction. Of course, in my mind I was no longer sitting in the harbor but was high above the Pacific headed for the exotic Orient.

I had not been at Pan Am very long when I ran into a friend and fellow aviation devotee from college, Tommy Sandegren. Tommy not only held a commission as a first lieutenant in the Army Reserve but also was flying for United Airlines. He was surprised, because of our mutual love of flying, that I, too, had not wound up as a pilot with one of the airlines. When I told him about my problem with the color blindness test he suggested that I go to a civilian flight examiner to double-check the earlier finding. I had nothing to lose so I did as he suggested, and I was pleasantly surprised when I received clearance to get a commercial pilot's license. Maybe the army flight surgeon had made a mistake after all. At any rate, I tagged along with Tommy to nearby Hamilton Field to have the flight surgeon there administer the army exam again. This time I passed. Now I was really buoyed up. I was going to fly after all. I submitted another application for army flight training at Kelly Field in San Antonio, but the reply came back saying "our records show that in 1934 you failed an exam because of being color blind. . . . Once color blind always color blind." Down came my spirits again.

This setback did not cause me to give up on flying. It just seemed now that I would have to pay for my own flight training instead of receiving it at government expense. Several of the mechanics at Pan American were qualified pilots and either owned or had access to airplanes. Jack Bridgeman, for instance, was sometimes able to take me up in his girlfriend's Fleet biplane and give me some very basic instruction. Andy Anderson, my roommate for about six months at Alameda, owned a Porterfield, and when he sold it I flew with him to deliver it. Wally Ford agreed to give me formal instruction at no cost since he needed to fly a certain amount of time to maintain his proficiency, but he did not have his own airplane. Therefore even though the lessons themselves would not cost me anything there was still the minor problem of paying to rent an airplane. I finally located a Fleet biplane whose owner was willing to rent it out for seven dollars per hour—about twenty-seven hours' worth of wages for me! Boy, did I want to fly! I could afford only one hour's plane rental per month, but Wally was patient and I was a quick learner. Still, it seemed as if I would never accumulate enough hours to solo.

One day Wally asked if I had tried to get into the navy's new aviation cadet program. It had been in existence for only a few years and was open only to college graduates under the age of twenty-eight.

Men selected for this program would receive a year's flight training, after which they would serve for three years as cadets with the fleet before returning to aviation reserve status. The program had a couple of goals. First, and probably most obvious now, was that it would begin to provide a pool of trained aviators in case the United States found itself pulled into another war. Second, it provided jobs, and jobs in the mid to late 1930s were not easy to find.

The program sounded great to me, and it did not take me long to visit the Naval Reserve station at the Oakland airport to find out more about it. I filled out all the application forms, provided college transcripts, and took yet another flight physical. The navy enlisted medical chief conducting the examination did not find anything wrong with my vision, so maybe I had finally shaken that bugaboo. He then asked if I ever had any trouble when receiving shots with hypodermic needles. I have never met anyone who *enjoyed* getting shots, but I said that one or two did not bother me. If I had to take several at one time, however, I tended to get kind of woozy. That must have been the wrong thing to say. Maybe the navy was looking for human pincushions. Anyway, within a few hours I was found disqualified. No army flying; no navy flying.

The last door to government-sponsored flight training seemed to have closed, so I went back to my one-hour-per-month flight training with Wally Ford. A few months later he again came to my rescue when he told me about a Marine Corps program for aviation cadets. Actually it was part of the same plan that provided the navy with its aviation trainees. I did not know that the Marines even *had* any airplanes, but I certainly was not going to let that stand in the way of my applying for the program. I reported to Captain Richard Mangrum, U.S. Marine Corps Reserve, at Oakland, and I must have made a favorable impression on him. He did not see too many Army Reserve second lieutenants with engineering degrees working as airplane mechanics just so they could be near flying. He accepted me into the program—contingent, of course, on my passing yet another flight physical. I was getting *very accustomed* to these things.

Since the Marines do not have their own medical personnel, they use the navy for looking after their physical welfare. This includes administering flight physicals. Imagine my horror at discovering that the very same navy chief who had washed me out of the navy flight program was going to examine me for the Marines. Luckily, he saw a great number of people during the course of his duties and probably did not have either the time or the inclination to make any mental notes on those who had failed their physical exams and remained civilians. He did not recognize me, and I made darn sure that he thought I could take all the needles anyone could push at me without flinching. I passed, but a few weeks later, as the chief was reviewing his records, he found that I had slipped by him. He sent for me and said, "You son of a bitch, I found your old record where I failed you. If you ever have any trouble or are sick, I'll get you for this." Fortunately I never had to see him again.

I breathed a sigh of relief at having finally passed one of these physical exams, but I knew that I was only over the first of many hurdles that lay between me and the golden wings of a naval aviator. The next step was a thirty-day preliminary training period intended to get rid of those with no real aptitude for flying. After all, the government wanted to make sure that its would-be aviators had what it took before investing a year's training in them. The navy, and by extension the Marine Corps, referred to the Oakland facility as one of its Flight Elimination—or "E"—Bases, and that is where this initial phase was to take place. I was confident that I would succeed, but I nevertheless arranged a leave of absence from Pan Am so that if I washed out I would at least still have my job waiting for me, and reported at Oakland. I discovered that I would have to resign my Army Reserve commission and enter the Marine Corps Reserve as a private first class (pfc). I didn't care. I would much rather have been a lowly pfc with a chance to fly than a desk-bound officer who could only dream of doing so.

I was one of nine eager aviators-to-be who reported for this weeding-out phase of training in May 1938. The other eight were navy seamen second class, and we were all eager for our actual flight instruction to begin. But first things first! This was the military, after all, and we had to absorb some basic facts of military life before we could be trusted in the cockpits of government-owned airplanes. Therefore, a significant part of our "E" Base training consisted of learning such lowly tasks as how to salute correctly, how to tie knots, and how to sweep the dust out of an airplane hangar properly. This was not very challenging. My ROTC training and my stint as a reserve army officer had certainly taught me the basics of military courtesy and chain of command, and it did not take long to master the long-handled broom.

Some of the excitement we experienced at Oakland was due to the fact that the Pacific International Air Races were being held there, and we had ringside seats. The starting line was immediately in front of the hangar that served as our living quarters, and we eagerly helped push some of the racing planes into position for takeoff. I was able to meet some of that day's legendary fliers, men like Roscoe Turner, Art Chester, Steve Whitman, and newcomer Tony LeVier. It was a very heady experience for a young man just beginning his own flight education to be able to mix with these famous aviators.

Activity filled the week preceding the races as work crews erected seating for the thousands of spectators who were expected and set up the pylons that would mark the eight-and-one-third-mile course. Tragically, four days before the races one of these sixty-foot-tall pylons collapsed and killed one of the workers and injured several others. The next day one of the racers making a practice run clipped a dike near the airfield and lost one of his wheels. He was able to land without serious injury to himself, but he and his crew were unable to repair the plane in time for the races.

Saturday, May 28, was the first race day, and the weather was beautiful. There were several preliminary events leading up to the day's feature race. Two acrobatic pilots staged a mock dogfight, finishing up their demonstration with one of them flying upside down and touching his wheels to those of the other plane, which was flying right side up. Rumanian captain Alex Papana finished his routine by picking a handkerchief off the ground with a hook on his left wing tip. Unfortunately, this first day would also see tragedy. Ralph Johnson, a World War I veteran of the Royal Canadian Air Force, was demonstrating loops for the crowd. The first one was flawless, but something went wrong on the second one and he plunged into the ground almost directly in front of the stands. He was killed instantly. Young Tony LeVier, only a year older than me and relatively new to the air racing circuit, won the first day's 75-mile feature race at almost 250 miles per hour.

Preliminaries for Sunday's 100-mile race included a pilot named Mike Murphy who took off from a platform atop a moving automobile. Then after flying around for a few minutes and giving the car time to get back into position, he came in and landed on the same moving platform. This was a great crowd pleaser, and he performed the stunt several times. Everything went smoothly until a gust of wind caught him as he was about to land once and flipped the plane off the car and into the field nose first. Tony LeVier won the feature race again, but this time the race itself was marred by the crash and death of Gus Gotch during the first lap.

The final feature race on Monday was also the longest, 150 miles, and was not limited to planes with engines smaller than 550 cubic inches of displacement as the first two had been. Seven planes started the race, and by the time it was over it had been one of the most exciting of all time. On the final lap the lead changed hands three times, with Earl Ortman nosing out Roscoe Turner by only about a hundred feet. Both men broke the existing closed course speed record, and Tony LeVier came in third at just over 260 miles per hour.[2]

Then the races were over and it was back to work. Captain Mangrum was to be my flight instructor, but he had to balance that assignment with his duties as commanding officer of the Marine

Reserve unit stationed at the Oakland airport. Because of all his other responsibilities he did not have a lot of time for me, so my initial flight training was on a rather erratic, catch-as-catch-can schedule. Luckily, I had learned the rudiments of flying during the handful of lessons I had been able to afford with Wally, so this benign neglect did not hinder me as much as it would have otherwise. Actual cockpit time at this stage of naval aviation training was limited to about ten hours. After that the instructor determined whether or not to trust the student alone in the airplane. By the time my ten hours were up, Captain Mangrum turned me loose in the bright yellow Navy N3N trainer for my first solo. I was nervous at first, but it was one of the most exciting times of my life. I have sometimes gone over that flight in my mind trying to determine how differently my life would have turned out if I had flubbed my chance.

After I brought the plane down, Captain Mangrum congratulated me and assured me that I had won a place in an upcoming flight class at the naval air station at Pensacola. I could not have been happier. My dream *would* come true. I walked on air for quite some time, and even my classmates' celebratory dunking of me in an estuary of San Francisco Bay failed to dampen my spirits. Not all of my classmates were as fortunate. Gordon Sherwood graduated with me. So did Frank Jones, Manuel Gonzales, and Ken NorthHammer, but the other four washed out of the program and returned to civilian life.

My successful completion of "E" Base training provided a welcome shot in the arm for my self-confidence, but I tried to retain a firm grip on reality. Even though I now felt certain that I would soon be a certified naval aviator there remained that one chance in a million that something might go wrong, something completely unforeseen and over which I had absolutely no control, that would keep me from this goal. If that happened I would not only finally have to give up my dream, but I would have to begin looking for employment. President Franklin Roosevelt's New Deal had suffered a setback the year before, and it seemed as if the Depression would last forever. So even though the navy had accepted me for further training I decided that it would be a good idea to request an extended leave of absence from Pan American. When I explained my situation to Chief Engineer John C. Leslie he gladly granted me the furlough, saying that he wished he were going to Pensacola, too. (My leave of absence was still in effect when I retired from the Marine Corps in 1959.)

I was now on my way to *real* flight training at Pensacola.

2

Flying at Last

Completion of "E" Base training guaranteed me a chance at further training, but it might be from several weeks to several months before enough spots opened up for all of the applicants from bases besides Oakland. In fact, Ken NorthHammer wound up flying for the Army Air Forces because he heard from them before the navy called him. I knew that it could be some time before my orders came, but I was too keyed up to go back to Pan American, so I packed my tools and other belongings into the Model A and headed back to my parents' farm in Endicott. To occupy my time, as well as to earn some money until my orders arrived, I went to work in the harvest for five dollars per day. It was a lot more money than I had been making at Pan Am, but it was certainly not a job I was willing to make my life's vocation. It was hard to think about anything else except my upcoming training. I even daydreamed about flying while I drove Ray Darden's Caterpillar tractor, pretending that the dual brakes and clutches were my rudder pedals.

The mailman finally brought my long-awaited orders to report to Pensacola Naval Air Station. The government would pay for my rail transportation to Pensacola, but from Oakland, not Endicott, since my place of residence when I entered the program *was* Oakland. That meant traveling back to California. My car was not quite as fully packed this time. I would not be needing my tool set, nor would I need very much in the way of extra clothing. I guess I could have taken the train to Oakland and left my car at home, or I could have driven to Oakland alone and sold my car when I got there. Instead my brother Clair went with me, sharing the driving and giving me some company along the way. Clair also had an interest in flying, and among the topics of discussion were two recent aviation-related news items. Howard Hughes and a four-man crew had just set a new around-the-world flight record of just under ninety-one and a half hours in July, and a couple of days later Douglas "Wrong Way" Corrigan surprised the world by leaving New York for California but instead flying to Ireland.

There were other topics, such as the ongoing war between Japan and China and the growing menace of Nazi Germany in Europe, that should have lent themselves to serious discussion since both of our lives would be much more directly affected by them than by anything "Wrong Way" Corrigan or Howard Hughes did.

Japanese forces had invaded Chinese Manchuria back in 1931 and established a puppet government to rule over what they now referred to as Manchukuo. Official government opinion in the United States was opposed to this blatant disregard for China's sovereignty and Japan was urged to evacuate. Since Japan had no intention of doing so, and since neither the United States nor any of the other Western powers with interests in China were ready to go to war over the issue, Manchuria remained under Japanese control.

Manchukuo was not enough to sate Japan's appetite for more territory, and in July 1937, Japanese troops invaded China itself. By the end of that year the cities of Peking, Tientsin, Shanghai, and Nanking had all fallen to Japanese forces that ruthlessly raped and murdered civilians in staggering numbers.

American public opinion seemed to be that even though what was happening in China was horrible it was not worth risking American lives to bring it to an end. This isolationist attitude did not change appreciably even when two dozen Japanese warplanes attacked American ships on the Yangtze River in late 1937. The navy gunboat U.S.S. *Panay*, prominently displaying large American flags, was escorting three American-owned oil tankers up the river away from the fighting at Nanking when the attack occurred. When it was all over three Americans lay dead, with eleven more wounded. The United States lodged official protests with the Japanese government, but the justification for the attack was that the pilots had thought the ships to be Chinese. When American spokesmen pointed out that it was absurd to think that Japanese pilots could have mistaken, on a bright sunny day, the American flags on these ships for anything else, the response from Tokyo was that the pilots had thought that the Chinese were using American flags on their ships as a ruse. Still, the Japanese government apologized for the loss of life, paid reparations, and the incident blew over.

Events in Europe were even more ominous for world peace, and the main culprit seemed to be a rejuvenated Germany. Terms of the treaty that had ended World War I had been very harsh with regard to Germany's ability to raise or maintain a military. The German army could contain no more than 100,000 men, and it would be allowed no tanks, heavy artillery, or airplanes. Naval manpower could not exceed 15,000, and the fleet could include no submarines. During the 1920s, Germany secretly circumvented these restrictions, and by 1935, under the leadership of Adolf Hitler, was openly rearming itself well in excess of treaty limitations.[1]

Hitler undoubtedly took heart at the ease with which Italian troops invaded Ethiopia in 1935, for he sent German troops into the demilitarized Rhineland in the following year. His justification was that the people living there were German and deserved to be reunited with the German government. He employed the same reasoning to explain the German takeover of Austria in March 1938, and was now eyeing the western end of Czechoslovakia, known as the Sudetenland, which had a rather vocal minority of Germans.

Like most Americans at that time, however, my brother and I did not concern ourselves very much with anything that took place outside our own national boundaries. I spent a couple of days in the Bay Area showing Clair the sights, but it was soon time for us to part company. After we said our good-byes I headed east on the train and he drove my car back to the farm.

I reported to Pensacola in August 1938, one of three hundred navy and Marine aviation cadets who would undergo flight training during that year's cycle of classes. The cadets came from all across the country and from all sorts of backgrounds. For a few of them this training was a godsend. It provided a steady paycheck and included regular, healthful food. An awful lot of people stayed hungry during the 1930s, and many of my classmates found the food at Pensacola to be "magnificent."

Personally, what followed was one of the most enjoyable years of my life. I was finally doing what I really wanted to do. Not only that but I was being paid seventy-five dollars a month, with uniforms and room and board thrown in for good measure. My home during my stay there, assuming I did not make some irredeemable blunder and wash out of the program, was an imposing two-story brick barracks building. Our personal accommodations included metal institutional bunk beds and wall lockers, and, for every seventy-five men, a half dozen showers, urinals, toilets, and shaving mirrors. Under these living conditions you soon learned the value of planning. For example, the cadet who waited until the last minute to shave or take his shower might find himself waiting in line behind ten or twelve others with the same idea.

The naval air station at Pensacola was a beautiful place. Nearby Mustin Beach and Santa Rosa Island were favorite off-duty spots for swimming or just for soaking up the warm Florida sunshine on the Gulf of Mexico. The base had its own library, bowling alley, and billiards parlor, and the officers' club served bottled beer for fifteen cents and mixed drinks for twenty cents. The city of Pensacola, just a few miles from the base, also offered a wide variety of diversions. Visiting cadets could enjoy a meal at one of the restaurants and then cap off the evening with drinks and dancing—to jukeboxes—at the San Carlos Hotel, the B & B Casino, or Carpenter's. If we really wanted to treat ourselves to a good meal, we could go to Bartell's, just across the state line in Alabama.

Even though I had received a limited amount of dual-control training, and had even soloed briefly at Oakland, I quickly found out that I was a long way from being an accomplished aviator. (Sometimes, when you are young, the realization of the patently obvious takes time.)

Most of my classmates had been civilians when they entered the aviation cadet program, so the first few weeks of training consisted of a basic indoctrination into military life. Once again, my prior experience as an Army Reserve officer stood me in good stead when we got to such things as military etiquette, the manual of arms, and close order drill. A considerable portion of this phase of training, however, was aimed at preparing *naval* officers and included study of the functions of different types of ships, the chain of command and the duties of different officers aboard ship, naval engineering and gunnery, and basic seamanship. Written examinations followed each step. Even though I was pretty sure I would never need to know how to man the helm of an aircraft carrier or how to keep a battleship's turbines functioning, it was all part of the training. If I did not pass this part, there would be no flying.

A few of the flight trainees were not cadets but regular officers in the navy or Marine Corps who had returned from fleet duty to learn to fly, and they breezed through these initial lessons. Their elevated rank also brought them other benefits. For instance, the cadet curfews did not apply to them, nor did they have to march like the rest of us did. This caused a slight twinge of jealousy among those of us of less exalted station, but we were soon too busy learning to fly to dwell on any such minor differences in our status. If we made it through the year at Pensacola, we would earn the title of naval aviator, which carried with it a fifty-dollar-per-month pay increase, plus lodging and thirty dollars more for food. That alone was a major incentive to apply ourselves to every phase of the training.

Our flight instruction was set up in squadron levels. As we mastered one level of training or one type of aircraft, we advanced to the next training squadron, where we either learned more advanced flying techniques or learned to fly different types of planes. We spent six weeks in Squadron 1 learning to fly two-seat, open-cockpit N3N biplanes fitted with floats so we could land them in the water. These planes, as well as some of the other trainers, were painted bright yellow so they were easy to see. This helped us see other cadets in the sky in plenty of time to avoid collisions with them. And, in the unfortunate case of a plane's going down, either in the water or in the woods, the bright color made it easier for the rescue parties to spot. Because of this color scheme generations of student pilots dubbed these planes the "Yellow Perils."

We had to master a lot of classroom instruction before we actually could begin to fly. The initial lessons covered basic aerodynamic principles so we would have some idea of just what it was that kept airplanes from falling out of the sky. After the opening lectures on aerodynamics, I received almost another two hundred hours of instruction on aircraft construction and maintenance, and engine systems and troubleshooting. My stint as a Pan Am mechanic helped out here because I was already familiar with the basics of engine design. Our training class was in two sections so that while half of us were in the classroom the others would be in the air. This system prevailed throughout my time at Pensacola.

When it came time to fly there was a set routine. The student carried two parachutes out to the waiting aircraft, his own and his instructor's, and if he needed a seat cushion to see over the edge of the cockpit he also brought one of those along. After the instructor pilot arrived and climbed aboard, the student went around to the front of the aircraft and wound up the engine's inertia starter. On some of the seaplanes this meant balancing on the pontoon while doing so. The student then scrambled into the front seat, strapped his parachute on, and buckled his safety belt while the instructor taxied forward.

One day one of my classmates, Bucky Buchanan, was a little slow getting himself arranged in the front cockpit. The instructor took off before Bucky had had time to buckle himself in, and then he almost immediately cut the throttle and pushed the stick forward. This was a common maneuver, intended to see how smoothly and how quickly the student could recover control of the plane and bring it down in an emergency landing. It was nothing Bucky had not experienced before, but in those earlier instances he had been securely strapped in place. This time the violence of the plane's movement nearly catapulted him completely free of the aircraft. He was barely able to grab hold of the sides of the cockpit in time to save himself. Needless to say, while he was thus occupied he was not able to control the airplane, so the instructor had to take over and Bucky earned a "down" on that flight. Too many "downs" and a pilot washed out of the program.

The instructor had to be able to talk to the student in flight, but the noisy open-cockpit airplanes of the late 1930s usually made such communication almost impossible. The leather flying helmets we all wore cut off some sound, even on the ground, but once in the air there were many other sources of noise. We sat right behind the big radial engine, and it produced a tremendous racket. At high speeds the guy wires between the upper and lower wings set up a resonant humming or singing, and the rush of wind past the cockpit also contributed to making it nearly impossible for one to hear his own voice, let alone the voice of someone else. The solution, such as it was, was called a "gosport." It was simply a very primitive speaking tube that connected the plane's two cockpits. At the instructor's end, the gosport resembled an oxygen mask covering the lower half of the face and had a flexible tube leading forward into the front cockpit. The student's half looked like a stethoscope, connecting itself to both ears. This setup left both men's hands free, and the close fit meant that the pilot's words would go directly toward the student without any chance for the wind to rip them away before they reached his ears. The configuration of this apparatus also meant, however, that there was no dialogue—no two-way conversation. The student was to listen! If he had any questions he could ask them later—on the ground.

My actual flight lessons began—as any instruction should—with the basics. I learned how to taxi the plane through the calm waters of Pensacola Bay. This *looks* very easy from the beach, no more difficult than learning to drive a car around on a well-paved parking lot. The perspective from inside the cockpit, however, is altogether different. Nevertheless, I soon mastered it and began to receive instruction in taking off, in simple straight-ahead flying, and in landing. One of the tricks our instructors taught us was to determine the wind direction by noting the direction of the streaks on the surface of the water below us. And since this was, after all, a *naval* air station, they also taught us enough basic seamanship to sail our floatplanes back to the beach, if we had to, using only the wind for motive power.

I got about fifty hours of flight time in Squadron 1, but I continued to have trouble making landings. Part of the problem was that my instructor was an "old lady." He seemed to regard the airplane as his own personal property and was very reluctant to turn complete control of it over to a mere student. Therefore, when I *was* flying it his hands hovered near his set of controls constantly, and at the first indication that I might not be making a perfect flight he took over again. His extreme caution did not allow me to get much "real" flying experience. In spite of that, after I had completed the number of flight hours specified in the training syllabus, it was time for me to try to solo. The fact that I had done it once, back in Oakland, was certainly no guarantee that I would be able to do it again, but it was an important check to see how much flying wisdom

I had absorbed. I survived, and a change of instructors soon followed. My new teacher was not an "old lady," and I quickly was able
to gain much more confidence in myself.

We flew Stearman NS-1s in Squadron 2, but these had wheels on
them instead of floats and offered some new challenges. While it is
true that there was very little difference between *flying* an N3N with
floats and *flying* an NS-1 on wheels, there is *considerable* difference
when it comes to getting into the air in the first place and safely getting down again. When taking off from water, the pilot, even if he is
flying from the rear compartment, has a fairly unobstructed view of
what is in front of the plane. The fuselage sits horizontally. Outfitted
with wheels, however, the same plane assumes an entirely different
attitude. The rear end is much closer to the ground, making it almost
impossible for the occupant of the rear cockpit to see what is ahead
while taxiing. This lack of vision can lead to catastrophic results in
situations where several planes are using the same flying field. One
way to overcome this is for the pilot to make a series of S-turns
while taxiing. He swings the tail around toward the left, getting a
glimpse of whatever is to the left front, and then alternately swings
the tail around to the right for a visual check in that direction.

Landing also presented interesting problems. Landing a float-
plane in the water is much simpler than landing on hard-packed
earth or rock-hard concrete. Of course that is why our Pensacola
training started with the floatplanes. The water is much more forgiv-
ing of minor errors. There is another difference, too. As naval aviators, we would be making lots of landings on aircraft carriers so we
had to be able to set our planes down in relatively limited spaces. An
eight-hundred- to nine-hundred-foot moving runway is a far cry
from a mile or two of calm harbor, especially when only the rearmost third of that runway is available for landings.

Because of the likelihood of having to land in a very limited space,
we learned to make full-stall landings. In other words, when the aircraft had approached to within a few feet of the ground, the pilot cut
the power and waited for gravity to take over. The plane's small rear
wheel touched down first, followed almost immediately by the two
wheels of the main landing gear. At least that was how it was *supposed* to work. Some of the trainees had a very difficult time getting
the feel of landing. Sometimes a student pilot cut the power too
soon, when he was still thirty or forty feet in the air, and did not
maintain gliding speed. The result was a bone-jarring landing at
best. Sometimes the force of these landings completely collapsed the
landing gear and led to serious embarrassment for the young man at
the controls.

Land planes also introduced us to the existence of ground loops—
also embarrassing. Any deviation from a planned straight course

while taking off, landing, or taxiing is called a ground loop. Among the many factors contributing to ground loops are bad brakes, a blown tire, or simply poor pilot technique or judgment. Sometimes pilots on the ground tried to turn their aircraft too sharply or at too great a speed. Since the landing gear wheels are so close together as compared to the wingspan, a sharp turn can easily throw the aircraft over on its wing tip and cause the plane to rotate in the opposite direction. For example, a plane making a sharp right turn would wind up on its left wing tip. Then, because the engine was still running, this wing tip would begin to act as a pivot, and the plane would tend to turn toward the left.

Even with all these new problems to confront, I soon mastered the NS-1 in its ground configuration and graduated to basic aerobatic maneuvers. This phase lasted eighteen weeks. We practiced the three-plane, vee-shaped formations that were standard at the time. We also began to conduct cross-country flights, which included forced landings at emergency sites and night-flying exercises. Having gained a certain amount of confidence in these areas, we also began to do more complicated aerial stunts, the kinds of aerobatics that might very well keep us alive during plane-to-plane combat. We flew loops, snap rolls, wingovers, Immelmans, and split S's.

The loop is the simplest of these maneuvers to master. After pushing the stick forward slightly to gain airspeed, the pilot simply pulls up into a great vertical circle, ending up flying in the same direction as before. Snap rolls are precision maneuvers in which the airplane rotates a full 360 degrees around its own longitudinal axis without changing overall direction. An Immelman combines the first half of a loop with the second half of a snap roll. In other words, once the plane has reached the top of the loop and is upside down, the pilot rolls it over into an upright attitude and continues flying in the opposite direction to that from which he entered the loop. A split S is just the reverse. It begins with the first half of a snap roll and ends with the last half of a loop. The pilot rolls the plane over on its back and then dives downward until he is going in the direction from which he came. Each of these latter two movements can prove extremely useful when engaged in aerial combat.

Another aspect of the training in Squadron 2 was power-off precision landings from different altitudes. From eight hundred feet, for example, I learned to land from a 180-degree turn. I then applied the same technique for landings from twelve hundred feet and a 360-degree turn. Another precision landing drill was to land within a designated hundred-foot circle, with power off, from an altitude of three hundred feet.

By the time I reached Squadron 3 I was gaining confidence daily. It was at this level of training that we learned more navigation, gunnery, and radio techniques. The gunnery targets were large fabric sleeves about the length of an airplane that were towed behind one of our planes by a long cable. It did not take me long to realize that shooting down an enemy plane was not something that could be learned overnight. To be successful you have to learn to gauge the distance to your target and the speed at which it is moving. Then you have to aim far enough ahead of the target so that by the time your bullets cover the intervening distance the enemy pilot has effectively flown into your stream of fire. In that sense, it is not unlike hunting birds with a shotgun or throwing a touchdown pass to a receiver running at full speed. You have to learn not to aim *at* the target but to aim at the point your target will reach when your bullets get there. Adding to the difficulty of aerial gunnery is the fact that in an airplane with fixed wing-mounted guns you have to aim the entire aircraft and not just the guns.

Our gunnery instructors had a very simple way of determining who was hitting the target and who was not. Prior to taking off the armorers saw to it that each student pilot's .30-caliber bullets were painted a different color. That way, when—or perhaps if—our bullets passed through the target they would leave enough of a paint smudge around the bullet holes to let our instructors know which of us had made the most "kills."

During this phase of our training the aerobatics we learned increased greatly in complexity, and we made the transition from the purely training-type airplanes to the O2U and O3U observation planes. They were similar in configuration to what we had already learned to fly, but they had about twice the horsepower. Since these planes, when fitted with pontoons, were the scout planes launched from catapults on, instead of actually flown off, battleships, we also had to master that particularly daunting maneuver.

The training facility had a catapult built along the seawall. Once the plane, with its pilot in the front seat and an observer in the back, was atop the catapult there was no way to get down but to fly down (if there had been another way I would have taken it). My first time up I was in the observer's seat. Launching from the catapult was definitely a "learn by doing" lesson. I had seen those before me survive the experience so I knew in my heart that I would, too, but there were more than a few butterflies in my stomach as I strapped myself into the observer's seat and braced my head against the pad at the back of the cockpit. The catapult fired with such force that within a distance of only two plane lengths the aircraft reached a speed of a mile per minute. At the end of the short flight the pilot landed in the water and taxied over to the starting point, where a large crane lifted the plane back up to the catapult for the next flight. On my *second* catapult launch, seasoned by the first, I was the pilot.

We continued to gain cross-country flight experience, during which we practiced our navigation and radio skills, and we also began to fly in nine-plane formations.

After surviving these nine weeks I advanced to Squadron 4, where I spent nine more weeks learning to fly big twin-engine flying boats such as the P2Y2 and the P3N. Not only did we have to master piloting these ungainly-looking things and learn to sail them on the water, each of us also had to be able to perform all of the functions of each of the other crew members. That meant more navigation training, learning how to launch torpedoes with a reasonable expectation of hitting our targets, functioning as bombardiers for horizontal bombing runs, and being familiar with the radio communications system on board.

I spent the final seven weeks in Squadron 5, in the cockpits of Boeing F4B-3 and F4B-4 fighters and folding-wing Douglas Devastator (TBD) torpedo bombers. Squadron 5 provided an interesting mix. The open-cockpit fighters we trained in had only recently given way to a similar, but faster, Grumman version aboard the navy's aircraft carriers, and even the Grummans' days were numbered. The TBD, on the other hand, seemed to represent the future in naval aviation. Its three-man crew was completely enclosed, and its nine-hundred-horsepower engine allowed it to reach speeds over two hundred miles per hour. We not only learned to fly the Devastator, but each of us got to drop three practice torpedoes.

It was also in Squadron 5 that we learned how to fly without any visual contact outside the cockpit. This would be important for those times when we would be flying at night or in thick overcast. Rather than risk its airplanes and our lives, the navy made use of a training aid that Edwin A. Link had invented several years before. These Link Trainers reminded me of the broomstick-and-ball-joint device I had built back in the basement of my parents' home outside Endicott. Unlike my contraption, however, the Link was completely enclosed and had a full set of working gauges, including an airspeed indicator, artificial horizon, bank-and-turn indicator, radio controls, and altimeter. Not only that, depending on what the student pilot did with the stick and rudder pedals, the Link actually moved in response. If I pushed the stick forward, the nose of the cockpit actually dipped down and the altimeter reading reflected the beginnings of a dive.

While the student pilot was in the Link Trainer an instructor pilot sat at a nearby desk and fed him information and instructions through the radio hookup. The Link also automatically plotted the pilot's actions so the instructor could compare how well he reacted to changing conditions and instructions. I sometimes spent several hours in the Link, realistically simulating a cross-country flight. At the conclusion of the "flight" the instructor showed me where I had made minor mistakes and how I could avoid them in the future. This was certainly much more inexpensive than sending us up in actual airplanes, especially since some of the students made errors in the Link Trainers that would have been fatal in actual aircraft.

Within a few years these Link Trainers had improved to the point of being frighteningly realistic. One student, who had not done very well in following his instructor's orders, soon found that according to his instruments he was hopelessly lost and almost out of fuel. Having gone through a mental checklist of all his options he did the only thing he could. He quickly pulled back the canopy and bailed out—only to break his ankle when he hit the floor, three feet below.[2]

When we had successfully "flown" the Link, we got to try instrument flying for real in SNJs, and it was quite a thrill when everything worked as it was supposed to. We took off, practicing level turns, climbs to specified altitudes, and other maneuvers all without being able to see anything but our instruments because of the sliding canvas hood that covered the windows. After several hours of instrument flight, it was particularly gratifying to get permission to slide the hood back and find that you were in a final approach for landing at an elevation of three hundred feet—just as was indicated by all the instruments.

In spite of all the training in carrier-based airplanes our instruction program included no actual landings on the decks of aircraft carriers. The closest we came was in an exercise we called "skipping rope." A rope was stretched across the end of the runway about ten feet off the ground to represent the edge of an aircraft carrier's flight deck, and we practiced coming in low and slow and landing in as short a distance as possible beyond that rope.

War clouds continued to gather in Europe through 1938 and 1939 while I was undergoing my flight training. Hitler continued to clamor for the western end of Czechoslovakia. British Prime Minister Neville Chamberlain and French Foreign Minister Edouard Daladier met with the German leader and decided that appeasing him was wiser than risking the possibility of going to war. In late September 1938, upon receiving Hitler's promise that he would seek no more territories in Europe, they agreed not to oppose Germany's takeover of the Sudetenland. Within six months, however, the rest of Czechoslovakia had been swallowed up by Germany, Poland, and Hungary.

These events probably should have had a rather profound effect on me. After all, I was not preparing myself to become a commercial airline pilot. I was training to fly combat airplanes—planes that were designed for little else than war. It is surprising, therefore, how little attention we all paid to world events. One of my classmates was the son of the newly appointed American ambassador to France, and he undoubtedly followed world events more closely than the rest of us, but I was too busy with my training to worry about how soon I might be called upon to put it to use.

We were all young men, after all, and proud to be doing what we were doing. What free time we did have we put to use in less cerebral pursuits. Classes were staggered to make optimum use of the aircraft on hand, and a cadet from one of the more advanced training squadrons and I pooled our money and bought a secondhand 1933 Ford V-8. This greatly increased our off-duty mobility. I do not know whether it was simply my bad luck with this car or something more sinister, but it seemed as if it always needed some minor tinkering when it was *my* turn to use it. Maybe one of the tires gave out and had to be replaced. Perhaps the battery had finally given up the ghost. One good part about the arrangement, however, was that my co-owner graduated a few months before I did, and I thus gained sole ownership. My good fortune did not last. One Saturday night, after having imbibed a little too freely while out on the town, I at least had the good sense to realize that I was in no shape to drive. One of my less inhibited classmates volunteered to drive us back to the base, and I complimented myself on allowing him to do so. My smugness was fleeting. While passing a slower car, my friend rolled the Ford over into a ditch. Nobody had any serious injuries—perhaps it is true that God looks after drunks and small children—but the car was a total wreck. When the tow truck arrived, the driver must have felt sorry for me; he offered me the grand sum of twenty-three dollars for the twisted pile of metal that had been my pride and joy. I gratefully accepted it.

The Marine Corps selected a few outstanding cadets from each class and offered them commissions as regular officers. Since otherwise all the graduates would retain cadet status for three more years, I decided to apply for one of the available commissions. The last stop in the interview process was Colonel Field Harris (who would go on to become a major general and head of all Marine aviation). One of the questions he asked me was what would I do if I were chosen as a regular officer and later found out that I could no longer fly in the Marine Corps? My answer was automatic; I didn't have to think about it at all: "I would resign from the Marine Corps because I want to keep flying," I told him. Of course, when my buddies found out what I had said they were unmerciful in their gibes. How could I have been so foolish, they wondered, as to answer that question the way I had? They assured me that I had blown any chance I might have had at a regular commission. We were all amazed a short time later to find that I *had* been selected, along with a navy flier named Bill Kellum.

The defense budgets in those days were rather meager, and the Marine Corps apparently had not allotted money to provide dress uniforms for its aviation cadets in time for the graduation pictures that were to be published in the annual *Flight Jacket*. Bob Fraser, who was due to graduate in the class immediately ahead of mine, did have the proper uniform and he was gracious enough to loan it out to those of us in need. There were a couple of problems, however. Bob was a little bit bigger than I was, so when I donned his uniform I did not exactly present a picture of the trim, well-turned-out Marine Corps aviator I now felt myself to be. I solved this little difficulty by putting a few sheets of newspaper across my shoulders so the coat did not appear so loose across my chest, and I used a similar newspaper padding in the hatband of Bob's cover. This solution was most satisfactory, but the second problem with the borrowed uniform was one that none of us discovered until the pictures came out. Bob had inadvertently put the eagle-globe-and-anchor Marine Corps emblems on the wrong sides of his collar. The anchors were supposed to point inward, and his faced out. It is easy, therefore, to look through that year's issue of the *Flight Jacket* and spot those wearing Bob Fraser's uniform. We all have the Marine Corps emblems on backward.

As the end of my training cycle drew near I was able to look back with a definite sense of accomplishment. Only a year earlier I had been an aircraft mechanic in California. Since that time I had learned to fly a variety of military aircraft and was about to embark upon an aviation career. There was little in my life to worry about— except for one thing. One of the last skills we had to master before we could pin on the golden wings of a pilot was Morse code. The test on the code was the final hurdle. To pass, the student had to be able to receive twenty-five words per minute without making a mistake, and he had to be able to send accurately a minimum of twenty words per minute. In many of the classes before mine the cadets viewed the code test as a mere formality. It was understood that one could achieve a passing score by finding out the favorite brand of whiskey of the navy chief administering the test and making sure that he was well supplied with same. Not too long before my class was to graduate, however, this changed. A cadet from an earlier class had written back to Pensacola from fleet duty and emphasized how important it was to have a firm grasp of this particular phase of training. Gone were the days when a quart of Scotch was all that was necessary. I passed—but that was about the last time I ever used the code for anything except to identify navigation stations.

I received my commission and brass second lieutenant's bars on July 1, 1939. I finished my flight training a couple of months later, and Rear Admiral Chester Nimitz signed my certification as brand-new naval aviator number 6051. I was now one of a rather select breed. There had been only 169 regular pilots in the Marine Corps, and I was number 170. I next reported to the Marine Barracks at Philadelphia Navy Yard on September 3 for a year's academic training at the Marine Basic School.

I reached Philadelphia just after the outbreak of World War II in Europe. Beside myself, the only other aviators among the 130 "brass bar cadets" in the 1939 Basic School Class were First Lieutenants George Graves and Pete Haines. They had each spent time with the fleet after completing flight training, and were now being rotated through Basic School. The three of us spent a lot of time together over the next year, both on duty and off, and became very close friends. Also among my classmates at Basic School were two Naval Academy graduates with whom I was to share a considerable adventure in 1945, Richard M. Huizenga and James D. McBrayer.

Those of us who were pilots also had assignments to the Naval Aircraft Laboratory in Philadelphia, and this gave us the opportunity to fly any time we were not supposed to be doing something else. This made the tedium of the classroom more bearable, because I spent part of every weekend in the air and often took classmates for short rides during our lunch hours. I became very familiar with the N3N, the O2U, the O3U, and the BM-1 Martin bomber (although it was on the verge of being phased out of service). I took advantage of this time to fly over to Pittsburgh and visit with Alvene Litzenberger. He was now the personal corporate pilot for the president of Mesta Machinery Company and also ran a flight school.

While at Basic School we three aviators got permission for a cross-country flight to Atlanta flying O3U observation planes. Each of us took a nonflying classmate along in the observer's seat. Everything went smoothly on the way down, but when we started back my engine suddenly failed. I could not stay in the air, so Lieutenantant Jim Anderson, my passenger, and I both began to look for a likely landing site. We did not have too many to choose from and very little time to make a decision, but I got us safely down thanks in large part to the power-off landing drills I had learned at Pensacola. Lieutenant Anderson was forced to continue the trip by railroad to get back to Philadelphia on time, while I had to wait for repairs to be made to my aircraft. (In spite of this rather inauspicious experience, Anderson later also became a pilot and a very good squadron commander during the Korean War.)

After graduation George Graves and I both received orders to the naval air station at San Diego, although we were to be in different squadrons. I had a little leave time before I had to report, so I planned to drive home from Philadelphia for a short visit with my family. (I had replaced my wrecked Ford with a 1936 Plymouth sedan before leaving Pensacola the year before.) The long cross-country road trip did not seem as endless as it might have because, just as he had on my drive from Endicott to Oakland almost two years earlier, my brother Clair accompanied me. He, too, was a pilot now, although the army had washed him out of its aviation training program, and he had come out to Pennsylvania to see about a job with Piper Aircraft. After the interview he decided not to accept the job after all, and he was ready to return to Washington State College and finish his degree. Now, with both of us pilots, our conversations during the trip were more aviation related than ever. It was good to reach the farm and see my folks again, but I was also anxious to report to my new assignment with VMB-2, a dive-bomber squadron flying the Great Lakes Dive Bombers (BG-2s).

I had a bit of difficulty flying the BG-2 at San Diego. Actually flying it was easy enough, but landing it properly required a great deal of practice. If I was not very careful my main landing gear, which was very stiff, would touch down before the tail wheel. Then, because the main gear was positioned forward of the center of lift of the wing, I inadvertently increased the angle of attack—the angle between the wing and the ground—and caused the plane to become airborne again. Since I had already reduced power by that time, however, the plane only hopped into the air before coming down hard again and repeating the whole cycle. I am sure that onlookers were reminded of some huge mechanical porpoise playing in the waves. Nor did I have much opportunity to improve because I soon received orders transferring me to VMF-2, the same fighter squadron as my friend Lieutenant Graves.

It did not take long to see that all of the pilots in my new squadron were good fliers and hard workers. Second Lieutenant David Kliewer had become a military pilot in spite of his family's pacifist leanings, but what he really wanted to do was to earn enough money in the service to help put himself through medical school when he got out. Another pilot in the squadron with civilian aspirations was Second Lieutenant Henry "Spider" Webb, who had similar plans for financing a law school education. One of the most aggressive pilots was Captain Henry Elrod, who would win the Medal of Honor posthumously for his gallant actions at Wake during the opening weeks of American involvement in World War II. When it was Elrod's turn to practice aerial gunnery he was so determined not to miss that he held his fire until he was about to fly right into the tow target. One time he decided that the squadron could get airborne much more quickly if we took off in pairs. The idea was fine, but the execution left something to be desired. He selected Lieutenant Kliewer to be his wingman, and as the two pilots applied full throttle the tremendous torque exerted by Elrod's engine caused him to begin moving toward the other plane. Lieutenant Kliewer jammed on his brakes to avoid a collision, and his plane piled up on its nose and then went over onto its back while Elrod, apparently unaware that anything was amiss, took off into the sky.[3]

In addition to Henry Elrod, the squadron's roster in late 1940 contained the names of several other future Medal of Honor heroes. Greg Boyington, after temporarily resigning from the Marine Corps and flying with Claire Chennault's American Volunteer Group in China, would return to command a Marine fighter squadron in which he would win the medal for shooting down twenty-six enemy planes in a little less than four months. Harold W. Bauer, commanding another squadron in the fall of 1942, shot down nine Japanese fighters and bombers (and possibly a tenth). Bob Galer, with whom I flew several cross-country flights in training as his wingman, won the medal for shooting down eleven planes in a period of less than a month over the Solomon Islands.[4]

It was also while I was at San Diego that I finally got the chance to land on an aircraft carrier, and I immediately discovered that there was a world of difference between "skipping rope," as I had done at Pensacola, and the real thing. Actually, we still did a lot more dry-land practice at an area of the naval air station at San Diego that had been laid out to look like the flight deck of an aircraft carrier. Bob Galer was our landing signal officer (LSO) and positioned himself with a paddle in each hand where we could see him, at the left rear of the "deck," as we made our final approaches at about sixty to seventy knots—just above stall speed. He had to be able to tell very quickly if we were lined up correctly and whether we were coming in too fast or too slow, too high or too low. If, from almost straight ahead, the LSO could see the plane's rear stabilizer above the wing it meant the pilot was coming in too fast and he signaled that information to him. Likewise, a plane coming in too slow showed the rear stabilizer below the wing. After several landings each, Galer met with all the pilots and offered constructive criticisms on our landing techniques. A good LSO can save the reputations—and lives—of a lot of pilots.

After days and days and what seemed like an endless number of practice landings, we were finally deemed ready for the real thing. On the appointed day we boarded the aircraft carrier at the dock and got under way. We would first observe from the carrier's rear gun turret as more experienced pilots landed our planes, and then it would be our turn. It was very exciting, and I have to admit to a certain amount of butterflies in my stomach the first few times I came around on final approach. It is amazing how small something as large as an aircraft carrier can seem when you are trying to land an airplane on it. The straight 888-foot flight decks of the early carriers such as the U.S.S. *Saratoga* and the U.S.S. *Lexington* looked like postage stamps from the cockpit of my F3F-2, nor did I even have the entire length in which to land.

The front third of the flight deck was where planes were parked prior to takeoff. The center third was where the elevators for moving planes between the flight deck and the hangar deck below were located. We had only the rearmost section—perhaps three hundred feet—on which to land. This section had several cables strung across it that were to engage the tail hook on the aircraft and bring it to a sudden stop. In the unfortunate event that the pilot missed all of the cables, there was a movable crash barrier to prevent him from entering the middle section of the deck. When it was finally my turn, I kept my eyes on the LSO all the way in and the jerk of the arresting cables was a *very* welcome sensation.

By the summer of 1940, although most of America still preferred to remain out of the war in Europe, there began to be stirrings in favor of military preparedness. The Military Training Camp Association, a private, nongovernment body, sought to introduce in Congress a bill that would set up a system of compulsory military service for America's young men that would enlarge our army substantially. Opponents pointed out that the Atlantic Ocean insulated the United States from the European war and that our navy could defend our shores quite adequately. Association spokesmen then raised the question of what would happen if Nazi Germany succeeded in overrunning all of Europe and thereby had the combined navies of Germany, Italy, France, and England with which to launch an invasion into the Western Hemisphere. While the public debate continued in this country, France surrendered to Germany. Not long after that, Congress passed the Selective Training and Service Act of 1940, our first peacetime draft.

Other legislation increased the authorized strength of all the regular branches of the service, and this led to several Marine Corps Reserve officers being brought into the regular Marine Corps. Among them was my first flight instructor, Captain Mangrum, who joined VMB-2; another was a reserve captain I had met at Oakland, Herbert Freuler, who came into VMF-2.

The entire group at San Diego received orders for temporary duty in Hawaii in January 1941, and I looked forward to spending some time in that beautiful tropical paradise. Because this was not to be a permanent change of station for us, the amount of baggage we were allowed to bring was severely restricted. Since there would be no extra space aboard ship for a lowly lieutenant to transport his personal automobile to the islands, I sold my car to a Plymouth dealer in San Diego for $150 and a promised $350 discount on a new car when I got back. We realized, particularly those of us who were unmarried, that we would be in a much better position to enjoy Hawaiian social life if we had some way to get around when not on duty, so we all chipped in and bought a used 1936 Buick for a squadron car. Because this was not the private property of any one member of the squadron but was intended to be shared by all, room was found aboard ship to send it along with us.

As soon as the large shipyard cranes hoisted our planes onto the forward portion of the aircraft carrier's flight deck, we were almost ready to depart. We were all excited about the trip, and when the ship—I think it was the *Saratoga*—stopped for a day at Long Beach, several of us took advantage of the sunny weather to spend the time at the beach getting suntans. It certainly would not do for us to show up in Hawaii looking as pale as ghosts. I would have been better off pale. I overdid it and spent the entire voyage nursing a bad case of sunburn.

Sunburn was not the only affliction that troubled me on this, my very first ocean voyage. I became violently seasick. It was a miserable trip. I spent most of it either walking on the crowded flight deck among our airplanes or in my bunk praying for the journey to end.

Our arrival in Hawaiian waters finally brought an end to my ordeal when we flew our fighters off the ship and landed at the navy airfield on Ford Island, right in the middle of Pearl Harbor. It was good to be back on solid ground again, and I was eager to explore my new surroundings, but my sight-seeing would have to wait. There were no permanent housing facilities available for us, so while we temporarily parked our planes on Ford Island we formed working parties and set about clearing a Marine landing strip at the site of the old mooring mast at Ewa. It had been set up originally in the 1930s to receive the airships *Akron* and *Los Angeles*, but they were never deployed there. Our planes needed a lot more takeoff and landing room than had the airships, so we had to clear a great deal of the area assigned to us. Captain Freuler was in charge of cutting the cane fields that covered our new home, and it was a backbreaking task. Wielding a machete in the tropical sun is a job that needs to be experienced only once to make you fully appreciate less physical pursuits. We finally got the cane cut to the point that heavy equipment was able to come in and finish grading and paving the area for our runways, and we flew our planes in from Ford Island.

Our living conditions at Ewa were certainly not what I had envisioned. We lived in tents, and our sanitation facilities were quite primitive. Our latrine consisted of a hole in the ground with a platform of two-by-fours over it upon which to sit. The only concession to modesty was a surrounding wooden framework over which were stretched some burlap privacy shields. After several days of operation this facility became pretty offensive to tender olfactories, so once a week someone would pour kerosene into the hole and burn the waste. Of course, the resulting soot left a residue on our seating platform that was very hard to get off and imparted itself to everyone who sat there. In one instance, some Marines from Ewa got into a minor disturbance in one of the many houses of ill repute over in Waikiki, and the madam had no trouble verifying to the Shore Patrol that they were Marines from Ewa and not soldiers or sailors. It was simple, she said; they all had black squares on their backsides.

Hawaii was a very important place in 1941. Terms of the 1922 Washington Naval Treaty had placed severe restrictions on strengthening any of our possessions farther west—such as Guam, Wake, or the Philippines—and the growing threat of a militant Japan meant that War Department planners devoted more and more time to Hawaii. Pearl Harbor was now home to the navy's Pacific Fleet, Schofield Barracks was headquarters for army ground forces in Hawaii, and the Army Air Corps had a bomber base at Hickam Field and fighters stationed at Wheeler Field. This combination of army and navy power convinced many American military leaders—probably *most* American military leaders—that Oahu was impregnable to enemy attack. Official memos referred to the island as the strongest fortress in the world. There was even a piece in *Collier's* magazine to further this idea of invincibility. According to this article, American planes regularly patrolled far out to sea looking for evidence of any enemy fleets. (Not true. There were never enough planes to do that.) Bomber pilots routinely hit lifeboat-size targets from thirty thousand feet up. (Also untrue. That level of precision bombing was impossible.) Oahu, according to such accounts, was invincible![5]

The command situation on Oahu seemed tailor-made for confusion, since there were both army and navy forces there. Nevertheless, the different branches of the service soon worked out an agreeable compromise. It was to be the army's responsibility to protect the island itself, and that included any ships of the fleet that were in port. It would be up to the navy to provide long-range reconnaissance and to carry out any action at sea. Under this arrangement any aircraft deployed at sea came under navy command, while those in action in the immediate vicinity of the island answered to the army. For example, if navy patrol planes spotted a hostile fleet steaming toward the islands, they would sound the alarm. The naval commander, Rear Admiral Husband E. Kimmel, might very well order my squadron to participate in aerial attacks on the enemy ships under these circumstances. On the other hand, if an enemy landing force were to try to come ashore, the army commander, Lieutenant General Walter Short, might order Marine or navy aircraft to strafe the beaches in support of his effort to defend the island. Because of the various possibilities facing us, we took part in exercises involving both army and navy aviators.

While those of us in the military tried to hone our skills, many of Oahu's civilians also sought to prepare for what many now saw as an inevitable war with Japan. Because of the island's intricate ties with the military, some of this planning was of a joint nature. For example, in March the army published its "Plan for Protective Measures for the Civilian Population of Oahu in Case of Bombardment." By that same month, the Red Cross had turned out two classes of women motor corps volunteers. Not only had these women undergone traditional first aid training, they had also learned how to keep their automobiles mechanically ready for emergency use, how to drive at night during blackout conditions, and what to do in case an enemy launched a poison gas attack against the island. General Short provided further impetus when he addressed a Chamber of Commerce luncheon on Army Day, April 7. In addition to praising the preparedness work already begun, the general urged his audience to begin stockpiling food supplies and advocated the organization of a police auxiliary that could be alert against sabotage and guard utilities installations.

The citizens of Honolulu organized the Major Disaster Council in June and almost overnight enrolled several thousand volunteers. The various subcommittees of the council put these people to work right away. Since transportation of all kinds would be necessary in the event of war, one of the subcommittees began compiling an inventory of all the vehicles on the island—automobiles, trucks, fishing boats—as well as who the responsible person was for each of them. In case the need arose to commandeer someone's pickup truck to carry emergency supplies, for example, the authorities would know exactly whom to contact. Service stations and repair facilities of all sorts were also included on the list. Yet another subcommittee kept track of the availability of sandbags and found that there were over two million of them within reach should the need arise.[6]

When Japanese troops invaded southern Indochina in July, President Roosevelt imposed a freeze on all Japanese assets in America, including Hawaii. This order created quite a stir among the thousands of Hawaiians of Japanese ancestry, and General Short became more anxious than ever over the possibility of some sort of fifth column movement that would seek to sabotage our strength. After late July, army guards maintained around-the-clock vigilance at highway bridges, utilities, and similar essential locations.

In spite of the growing threat of war in both Europe and the Far East, Hawaii was a good place to be for a young American male. There were a lot of ways to fill spare time. Sometimes, after we had knocked off for the day, Lieutenant Webb and I headed for the golf course at Wheeler Field. Neither of us was ready to take on the likes of Ben Hogan or Jimmy Demaret, but it was good exercise and a lot of fun. But golf was not our only social diversion. Tourism, which had slowed to a trickle during the 1930s due to the effects of the Depression, had begun to revive as American industries geared up to provide all sorts of goods for the warring nations of England, France, and China. And among the growing numbers of tourists who arrived in the Hawaiian Islands aboard the Matson liners were fair numbers of unattached American women on vacation. My squadron mates and I had foreseen just such a circumstance before we even left the States. That was why we had chipped in on the Buick. Unfortunately, our squadron commander virtually took over the car after we got to Hawaii, and we were again afoot. I located a rather decrepit 1929 Ford touring car for sale for $125. That would have been a rather high price for a car of that age on the mainland, but it was the best deal I could find on the island. And I would have passed it up, too, if I had not had a considerable amount of mechanical aptitude. I had learned a lot about repairing farm machinery from my father and from Ray Darden. This basic knowledge was constantly put to the test as I tried to keep that old Model A on the road. Of course its age was also something of a blessing in disguise because there were enough others like it in the local junkyards that reasonably priced spare parts were not difficult to find (although I did wind up using a doorbell button to activate the car's horn).

With my personal transportation situation at least temporarily solved, the next step was to locate suitable bachelor living quarters. Frank Tharin, Herb Freuler, and several of the other married officers in the squadron lived with their wives at Pearl City, while some others lived about forty miles west of the base at Haleiwa. Bob Galer, who was also single, decided to share an apartment with me near the beach at Waikiki. This meant that we had about an hour's drive each way from the airfield to our apartment, but we decided it was worth the time and trouble since Waikiki was where most of the tourists spent their time.

The location of our apartment made it only natural that we spend a lot of our free time on the beach trying to meet girls. We sometimes had to compete with the local boys, whose athletic skills on their surfboards were hard to top. The surfboards they used were very different from those today. Some were shaped from redwood planks over three inches thick and sixteen feet long, and they often tipped the scales at over 120 pounds! Since I had never learned to swim very well as a youth, I was not very tempted to try my luck at this ancient sport. Another way to experience the thrill of riding the waves, and only slightly less intimidating than the surfboards, were the native canoes. These were simply hollowed-out koa logs with outriggers on one side for added stability. I still felt more comfortable on dry land, but I did venture into the boats a few times.[7]

When the sun went down our entertainment pursuits returned to dry land. There were not as many nightspots then as there are now. The hotels usually had clubs where a man might satisfy his desire for something stronger to drink than coffee. The Royal Hawaiian at Waikiki was the best known, and it catered to the more well heeled clientele. Unfortunately, this meant that its prices put it out of reach of a young military officer like myself. The Moana was next door to the Royal Hawaiian, and I found its prices much more in line with my salary. Bob and I sometimes patronized the roof garden of the Alexander Young in downtown Honolulu and listened to Ray Kinney's (no relation) orchestra play the latest tunes as we scouted around for willing dance partners.

For those with lower paychecks, or perhaps lower expectations, there were cheaper places of entertainment. The Black Cat, on Hotel Street, and Moose Taussig's Pantheon, on Nuuanu, were among the favored watering holes among the enlisted men. Nor was drinking the only way a man could spend his money. There were tatoo parlors, shooting galleries, barbershops, peep shows, and souvenir stands of all kinds. Honolulu, like all cities near large military bases, also had its share of whorehouses. Most of these were located along River Street and had names like the Anchor, the Ritz, and the New Senator. On weekends when the Pacific Fleet was in port, the sidewalks in these areas teemed with military personnel looking for a good time.[8]

Being pilots, my squadron mates and I had a lot more sight-seeing opportunities than the sailors and soldiers. It was not unusual, for example, for a couple of us to fly over to the big island of Hawaii or over to Kauai. Of course, we then had to arrange some sort of ground transportation, but it was a rather simple thing to rent a car and act just like civilian tourists, driving up the beautiful Waimea Canyon or visiting one of the volcanoes.

Of course, we did not spend *all* of our time in such pleasant diversions. We soon settled into our training routine at Ewa, and in addition to my flying chores—which I loved—I also served as the squadron's communications officer. I was lucky to have Technical Sergeant William Hamilton, one of our enlisted pilots, to help keep our transmitters working during the many fleet problems. (Sergeant Hamilton would also prove very valuable to the squadron on Wake.) Our workdays began at seven A.M. to allow us to get a jump on the heat. By the middle of the afternoon it had usually become too hot to continue working so we knocked off for the rest of the day.

We sometimes made twenty-four-plane takeoffs from nearby Wheeler Field and also participated in mock dogfights with the army P-40s stationed there. It was very exhilarating, and because of our planes' better maneuverability we were able to outclass them in camera gunnery. We could not, however, outrun them.

In mid-May, the army received twenty-one of the big Boeing B-17 bombers. These heavy, four-engine machines were but the first installment of possibly as many as two hundred that would be based on Oahu by mid-1942. This reinforcement was short-lived. Nine of these planes flew on to the Philippines, and all of those that arrived later were similarly destined for points farther west.[9]

A few weeks later the British light cruiser H.M.S. *Liverpool* pulled into Pearl Harbor. It had been damaged in fighting in the Mediterranean and was then on its way to the Mare Island Naval Yard in California for repairs. The World War I–vintage H.M.S. *Warspite* made a similar stopover in August. Both of these visits served to remind us that even though the United States was still not at war, we very soon could be. These reminders were healthy. They helped to keep our minds on why we were where we were.[10]

In July, the Marine Corps redesignated our squadron VMF-211, in keeping with a new numbering system, and told us we were on the list to receive new planes—Grumman F4F Wildcats—as soon as the navy squadrons got theirs. They would be a decided improvement over our F3F-2 biplanes.

By October, the situation with regard to Japan's intentions in the Far East had deteriorated even further. It seemed almost certain now that war was imminent. Admiral Harold Stark, Chief of Naval Operations, notified Pacific Fleet commander Admiral Kimmel to implement plans to protect the airfields then under construction on Midway and Wake islands. Kimmel immediately dispatched a dozen navy reconnaissance planes to Midway and began planning to send six more to Wake.

As part of this preparedness effort the U.S.S. *Wright*, a seaplane tender, left Pearl on November 20, 1941, heading west. It was on its way to Wake Island, a tiny coral atoll some two thousand miles closer to Japan, and Midway. One of the Marines on board was Major Walter J. Bayler, whose job was to install up-to-date equipment for air-to-ground communication on each island. Other passengers included forty-nine enlisted men from Marine Air Group 21, under the command of one of my fellow pilots, Second Lieutenant Robert J. Conderman. The *Wright* was transporting supplies and making other preparations for the eventual deployment of aircraft to the islands. The top brass had not yet decided which type of planes to send to the island. They might be Marine fighters, in which case there was a strong likelihood that VMF-211 would get the assignment, or they might be Marine dive-bombers (SBDs or SB2U3s). They might not even be Marine aircraft at all, but some of the army's new P-40 fighters. Whatever decision was made with regard to the type of aircraft to send, I was pretty sure that my Hawaiian stay was at an end. If we did not go to Wake, we would probably go to Midway or some other island base to guard against possible Japanese aggression.

3

War Clouds

None of us had any way of knowing how long we would remain at peace with Japan, but just in case that time was short we hastened to familiarize ourselves with our newly acquired airplanes. The F4F-3 Wildcats were the latest single-wing fighters from the Grumman Corporation, and we were anxious to gain cockpit experience. We took advantage of the fact that both the U.S.S. *Yorktown* and the U.S.S. *Enterprise* were in Hawaiian waters to qualify in carrier landings with our new fighters. Such landings are perhaps the single most important skill that a navy or Marine Corps pilot must have, so that was our first order of business. I had landed on aircraft carriers a few times before, but I quickly discovered that my new airplane would take some getting used to. It did not seem to have enough rudder surface, for example, to make decent landings within the short distances allowed aboard ship. Some of this difficulty was probably due to the four gaping four-inch-diameter holes in the leading edges of the wings where the fairings for the .50-caliber machine guns were yet to be installed. We had received some of our planes without these weapons, and until they arrived and our armorers could install them we would continue to experience difficult landings. There were also other deficiencies that would become painfully obvious within a few short weeks.

After Lieutenant Conderman and the advance party left Oahu, the rest of us got in some exhaustive around-the-clock flying. The army had installed a few radar stations on Oahu, some at fixed locations and others in trucks, and we worked in conjunction with them. The radar technicians trained by scanning their oscilloscopes for evidence of any approaching planes—in this case navy PBY flying boats acting as the enemy—and VMF-211 and other fighter squadrons scrambled to intercept the intruders. If nothing else, these alerts prepared us for the hectic pace we were soon to face when our targets were not U.S. Navy planes but Japanese bombers.

On November 27, Admiral Kimmel held a meeting with top navy and army brass to discuss defense measures in preparation for what was now an inevitable war with Japan. Time was running out, and Kimmel had difficult decisions to make regarding the defense of those islands west of the Hawaiian chain. Guam, because of its proximity to Japanese bases in the Marianas, would probably be impossible to protect. The defensibility of Wake and Midway was open to some question. Neither of these islands as yet was prepared to receive a Japanese attack, but work was progressing rapidly to correct that defect.

One of the specific points of discussion at this high-level meeting was what kind of air support to dispatch to these two island outposts. One proposal was to send some of the army's new P-40s along with a contingent of ground troops. This might lead to some command complications, since these army troops would be sharing the islands with navy personnel already there. The deciding factor, however, seemed to be the potential for a Japanese attack in the near future. While everyone at the meeting believed that the Japanese would strike somewhere soon, they all seemed to agree that they were much more likely to hit Wake and Midway before risking an attack on Oahu. In fact, about the only people anywhere in the world who believed that the Japanese would attack Hawaii first were aboard the six aircraft carriers, nine destroyers, and four battleships of the Japanese task force already plowing eastward through the swells of the northern Pacific. American planners believed that the Japanese would logically hit the outlying islands first and that the most they could expect from these outposts was that their garrisons would delay the attackers as they bore down on Hawaii. It therefore seemed counterproductive to risk the army's modern P-40s to almost certain destruction, so Kimmel decided to send a task force under Vice Admiral William F. Halsey with a contingent of F4Fs.[1]

The whole question took on an added sense of urgency when, after the meeting had broken up, Kimmel received a message from Washington: "This dispatch is to be considered a war warning. Negotiations with Japan looking toward stabilization of conditions in the Pacific have ceased and an aggressive move by Japan is expected within the next few days."[2]

Later that afternoon, Admiral Kimmel summoned Major Paul Putnam, our new squadron commander, and told him to select twelve of his eighteen pilots for deployment to Wake on board the *Enterprise*. He stressed secrecy. There were thousands of Japanese living in Hawaii, and there was little doubt that at least some of them were passing information on American war preparations back to Tokyo.

Kimmel wanted to be sure that no word of this movement leaked out. The admiral did not want the Japanese to be able to claim that this transfer of planes to Wake was a violation of the 1922 Washington Naval Treaty and, therefore, a threat to their security. If they thought it was, they might use it to justify a preemptive strike that would bring on war immediately. Of course, what no one realized was that the Japanese strike force had already left its home waters on its way to attack the American Pacific Fleet at Pearl Harbor.

When Major Putnam returned to Ewa he simply told twelve of us that we were to fly to the island of Maui the next day for a routine overnight exercise. There was nothing unusual about that, and since we all would be back at Ewa the next day most of us packed nothing more than our razors and toothbrushes. We would probably be too busy practicing night flying to need much else. The next morning Major Putnam briefed the assembled group of pilots. Besides myself, the other pilots were Captains Henry Elrod, Herbert Freuler, and Frank Tharin; First Lieutenant George Graves; Second Lieutenants Carl Davidson, Frank Holden, David Kliewer, and Henry Webb; Technical Sergeant William Hamilton; and Staff Sergeant Robert Arthur. Putnam really did not have too much information to pass on to us other than that we would fly over to Ford Island, in the middle of Pearl Harbor, where he would receive further instructions.

We made the short hop over to Ford in a matter of minutes and then waited around for more orders. When Major Putnam joined us he simply told us that we were going to rendezvous with the U.S.S. *Enterprise* and observe two army P-40s try to take off from the deck. If they could do it, it would greatly speed up delivery of these planes to the Philippines and other island bases, because the carriers would not have to dock and wait for cranes to lift the planes ashore. They could launch them while still out to sea and then begin their return voyages. The rest of the *Enterprise* planes were parked next to our F4Fs, and Putnam told us that if anyone had trouble starting his air-craft, he was to go over and ride with one of the *Enterprise*'s torpedo planes (TBDs). "We want all of you on this exercise," he said. "Are there any questions?" None of us spoke up, but I for one was curi-ous. Why was it so important to have all the pilots on board even if not all of the planes made it? Oh, well, I would soon find out.

As luck would have it, Lieutenant Holden's plane, number 7, would not start, so he hopped aboard a waiting navy TBD and we all headed for the *Enterprise*, already at sea. The exercise was not very complicated and did not last very long. As we circled the carrier the P-40s took off without a hitch and headed back to Oahu, and I began to wonder what else was in store for us before we headed on to Maui. A signal from the carrier snapped me out of my brief reverie. We were to come aboard.

The *Enterprise*'s planes—fighters, torpedo bombers, and dive-bombers—had also flown out from Ford Island, and we followed them on board. As soon as we landed, the *Enterprise*'s crewmen whisked our planes below to the hangar deck. It looked like we might be there for a while, and while I tried to figure out what was going on the boatswain's whistle shrilled through the ship's public address system. "Now hear this. The last mail plane has departed. Stand by for further orders." We did not have to stand by for long. Almost immediately we heard: "Now hear this. This is War Order Number One! The U.S.S. *Enterprise* is now under way for Wake Island to deliver VMF-211. Our scouting aircraft will cover our advance. They will be fully armed and prepared to shoot on sight any enemy aircraft; they will sink any enemy surface vessels we meet! More details later in Battle Order Number One." There was little doubt in anyone's mind who the "enemy" was.

The captain of the *Enterprise* soon issued the slightly more formal Battle Order Number One:

1.   The *Enterprise* is now operating under war conditions.

2.   At any time, day or night, we must be ready for instant action.

3.   Hostile submarines may be encountered.

4.   The importance of every officer and man being specially alert and vigilant while on watch at his battle station must be fully realized by all hands.

5.   The failure of one man to carry out his assigned task promptly, particularly the lookouts, those manning batteries, and all those on watch on deck might result in great loss of life or even loss of the ship.

6.   The Captain is confident all hands will prove equal to any emergency that may develop.

7.   It is part of the tradition of our Navy that, when put to the test, all hands keep cool, keep their heads, and *fight*.

8.   Steady nerves and stout hearts are needed now.

For the rest of the trip the *Enterprise* kept planes in the air throughout the daylight hours.[3]

Although all of us had realized that war was imminent, Battle Order Number One was still something of a shock. Admiral Halsey later remarked that this order had had the same effect on the task force as a bursting thousand-pound bomb.[4] There was, of course, considerable discussion following the order, but I noticed no uneasiness among those on board. It was reassuring to know that our training prevented any outward show of fear in the face of this news. Of course, we were not at war yet, but with the diplomatic negotiations in Washington at an impasse, it was probably only a matter of weeks—perhaps days—until war began. I inwardly applauded Battle Order Number One because it meant that our leaders, both civilian and military, were determined not to be caught off guard.

Admiral Halsey's Task Force 8, of which the *Enterprise* and the eighty-three planes aboard her were an integral part, also included the heavy cruisers *Northampton*, *Chester*, and *Salt Lake City*, and nine destroyers. The battleships *Arizona*, *Nevada*, and *Oklahoma* had been part of the operation when we left Pearl Harbor, but Halsey detached them so they would not slow down delivery of VMF-211 to Wake. They proceeded to their regular maneuver area and ultimately—and tragically, as it turned out—returned to their berths alongside Ford Island by December 7.

Before leaving Oahu, Halsey had verified that there should be no American ships or planes anywhere on our route to Wake, so he issued "shoot on sight" orders to his command. This led to an immediate hum of activity as the ship's armorers got to work making sure that all the planes had full supplies of belted machine-gun ammunition, that each of the TBDs had its torpedo in place, that five-hundred-pound bombs were attached under the wings of the dive-bombers, and that all of the five-inch guns and antiaircraft guns on the ship itself were fully supplied. For the rest of the trip the *Enterprise* sent planes into the air every morning and evening to patrol a three-hundred-mile radius and look for any sign of a Japanese fleet. The ship's guns were manned continuously, and antisubmarine patrols were up all day long.[5]

The fact that we were at last on our way to Wake presented us with some immediate problems, both personal and mechanical. Personally, neither I nor most of the other Marine Corps pilots had bothered to bring a change of clothes along. After all, we were expecting to be back on Oahu by the next day. I resolved my own clothing shortage, at least in part, by purchasing an extra khaki shirt and trousers from the Marine detachment on board. I figured that it might take as long as a couple of weeks before the rest of my clothes caught up with me, and this way I would at least be able to have something to wear while I laundered the clothes I had come aboard in. I was still stuck with only a pair of dress oxfords for footwear. Perhaps I could find more suitable shoes after I got to Wake.

I spent a little time familiarizing myself with what was to be my home for the next several days and discovered several friends among the navy fliers. Ensign James G. Daniels and Lieutenant (j.g.) Wilmer E. "Swede" Rawie had both been at Pensacola when I was, and Manuel Gonzales had survived "E" Base training with me at Oakland. My informal reconnaissance also revealed that the *Enterprise* lacked sufficient spare officers' quarters to accommodate the extra Marine fliers on board. I did not fancy sleeping in a broom closet or some other such quarters, but Ensign Daniels came to my rescue by insisting that I take over his bunk while I was aboard; he slept on the floor.

The mechanical difficulties facing VMF-211 were not so quickly remedied. Only six of our eleven aircraft had their machine guns in place, and even these planes were less than 100 percent effective because their guns did not have sights. Our previous F3Fs had used telescopes with speed rings for estimating how far to lead our targets. Our new planes did not even have these. Marines are nothing if not willing to improvise, however, and we soon came up with a stop-gap measure for the sights. We would simply mount a bolt in the top of the engine cowling as an aiming point. Then we would paint an oval on the sloping windshield to give us some method by which to lead enemy airplanes into our line of fire.

Of greater concern than the missing sights was the fact that our Wildcats had no navigation equipment, no automatic direction finders, and, in fact, no way to help us find our way back to an island base except by eyesight. Not only would this severely limit our patrol radius, it meant that we could not fly at all at night or in bad weather. The Pan American Airways facilities on Wake had the conventional radio range that sent out homing signals, but our receivers could not be changed to Pan Am's frequency. Even if we could change them, it would only help us in the quadrants oriented toward Midway and Guam. Perhaps by the time we got to Wake, Major Bayler would have completed installation of the proper radio equipment because there was nothing else there in the way of direction-finding apparatus that could give us a friendly "steer" back home.

One thing in our favor was that Admiral Halsey was himself an aviator and therefore very sympathetic to our problems. He ordered one of the *Enterprise*'s F4Fs turned over to us to replace Lieutenant Holden's airplane, and a navy paint crew quickly went to work painting it to match the others in our squadron. It was hoped that the light gray undersides of our planes would make them hard to spot by enemy antiaircraft crews, and, since most of our flying would likely be over the ocean, the blue paint on the tops of our planes was intended to make us blend in with the sea in case there were enemy planes overhead. While this was going on I was able to get some wire and a three-by-one-foot sheet of nonmetallic insulating material with which to rig up a homing device for my plane. I rolled the sheet into a tube, coiled the wire around it, and installed it behind the headrest of my plane where there was no metal structure to block out the signal. The admiral also ordered his mechanics to go over every inch of our Wildcats to get them in tip-top shape. They installed machine guns and fairings in the planes that had been lacking them, and we got gun sights from the navy squadron on board. We would at least not have to rely on the oval-and-bolt expedient for sighting our targets. While it was certainly nice to be on the receiving end of all this attention, Major Putnam probably echoed the feelings of all the pilots of VMF-211 when he wrote that he felt "like the fatted calf being groomed for whatever it is that happens to fatted calves."[6] But at least we would start into the unknown with planes in the best possible condition.

While the ship's mechanics and armorers fine-tuned our planes, navy intelligence officers briefed us on the types of Japanese aircraft we were most likely to encounter when the war finally began. The pictures they showed of what we all assumed were the best planes in Japan's arsenal were of some antiquated seaplanes and old four-engine flying boats. If these were the aircraft with which the Japanese hoped to conquer all of Asia, then we would not have much trouble knocking them down. After all, how could any nation with such outdated equipment expect to fight a successful war against the United States of America? This situation only reinforced the stereotype most Americans held of the Japanese people as short, bandy-legged men with prominent front teeth and very thick eyeglasses. We were convinced that even if the Japanese planes were mechanically adequate it would be all the pilots could do to fly them in straight lines. They would be no match for American aerobatic maneuvers. I found out much later how amazingly uninformed our briefing officers were with regard to the Japanese planes. In spite of the fact that Japanese pilots had been active in China for several years already, our briefing included absolutely no information on the twin-engine Mitsubishi G3M bombers that would come to be known as "Nells." These were the planes that we would see in the sky over Wake. We would also learn that the men in the cockpits were skilled aviators.

By the early morning hours of December 4, we had steamed to within two hundred miles northeast of Wake and were ready to fly the rest of the way. A navy PBY flew out from the island to guide us in, and planes from the ship's bombing squadron, VB-6, also accompanied us part of the way. We departed the carrier at about dawn, but before we left "Swede" Rawie presented me with a bottle of Scotch whiskey, saying, "You will need this more than we will." Of course, none of us realized at the time how prophetic those words were. Nevertheless, I was grateful for this gift and resolved to save it for some special occasion. The traditional celebration of the Marine Corps' birthday had taken place in the previous month, but perhaps there would be something else to drink to.

The two-hour flight to Wake was uneventful, and we used it to gain a little more familiarity with our planes. When we arrived over the island we set down one by one on the narrow coral runway. I hoped that there would be enough time before hostilities began to improve the condition of the airfield. It was long enough for our needs, but only about fifty or sixty feet in the middle of the three-hundred-foot-wide clearing was compacted enough to use for landings and takeoffs. If there ever came a time when we had to get all of our planes into the air in a hurry we would need a much wider usable area from which to launch planes simultaneously. That was not yet possible at Wake. The coral in the rest of the area allotted to us was too soft to take the weight of the Wildcats, and as yet the work crews had not completed any other runways. Nor were there any protective revetments ready for our planes.

I knew very little about Wake before arriving there. About all I knew was that it was a small, very low lying island in the Pacific with little vegetation. Over the next few weeks I would come to know it very well. From the air I was able to see that it was actually three islands, the remains of some ancient undersea volcano. Wake itself was the largest of the three and was shaped somewhat like a large wishbone with the arms pointing west and northwest. Separated from the western end by a small inlet was Wilkes Island, while Peale Island lay similarly off the northwestern tip of the main island. A reef enclosed the whole group at a distance varying from thirty to eleven hundred yards from shore.

I learned much later that the first known European visitor to the island was the sixteenth-century Spanish explorer Alvaro Mendaña de Neyra, who called it San Francisco. Since there is no naturally occurring fresh water on Wake, except what rainwater can be collected, and no food, it was not a very inviting spot for humans, and so it remained uninhabited for a long time. The atoll took its current name from a British ship captain who stopped there briefly in 1796, and when U.S. Navy Commander Charles Wilkes visited in 1840 he named one of the smaller islands for himself and the other for the naturalist Titian Peale, who was along on the expedition. Wake remained unoccupied until Pan American Airways established a way station there in 1935 for its newly inaugurated transpacific route.[7] (The Clippers I worked on at Alameda from 1936 to 1938 all stopped here.)

As Japanese troops continued to ravage China in the 1930s, it became more and more likely that the United States would become embroiled in a Pacific war. The navy, therefore, decided to establish naval air stations on Wake and some other islands as forward warning posts. Civilian construction crews began arriving in January 1941, and by early December there were almost twelve hundred men hard at work building airstrips, underground ammunition storage bunkers, seaplane facilities, water purification plants, and everything else necessary.

Major Putnam reported for orders to Navy Commander W. Scott Cunningham, who was in command of all American forces on Wake, and he also conferred with Marine Major J.P.S. Devereux, commanding the 1st Defense Battalion, and Commander Campbell Keene, who was slated to command the navy patrol squadron as soon as construction on the naval air station was completed. When he returned to the airstrip, Putnam told us that beginning the next morning our twelve planes would be on a rotating schedule with four-plane combat air patrols sent out three times per day—dawn, noon, and dusk. While the patrols were up, four other planes would be on standby, ready to scramble in case those aloft spotted anything suspicious. The remaining planes would be in the engineering area, where our mechanics would keep them in a condition of constant readiness, or they would be engaged in bombing or gunnery practice.

In the meantime, we spent the rest of our first day on the island sorting out supplies and finishing the erection of our tents. It did not take long to discover that we needed a lot of time to adequately prepare the tiny atoll for a proper defense. There were shortages everywhere. Not only did the dozen Wildcats on the island represent less than a full squadron—VMF-211 left six planes in Hawaii—but spare parts were almost nonexistent and there was an extreme shortage of mechanics who had any experience working on Wildcats. Even if there had been replacement parts and trained technicians, however, no one had remembered to send along repair manuals for our planes.

In spite of the shortages the patrol flights began as scheduled on the morning of December 5, and even though we were not yet at war they still had an element of danger to them. With the lack of up-to-date radio equipment in the Wildcats, I found myself constantly plotting my speed, bearing, and time on course so that I could find my way back to the island again. I could not relax my vigilance for a minute during these flights because scattered clouds cast shadows on the ocean that, from the air, looked just like so many islands. I could only imagine what it would be like to be lost and low on fuel and to try to land on one of these "islands." By this time, however, Major Bayler had set up new radio facilities on the island so we could receive a homing signal, and when I tried out my homemade radio loop it was so successful that I decided to recommend that we make them for all of our planes.

Everybody on Wake had too many things to do and not enough time to do them, but Major Putnam convinced Commander Cunningham to divert some of the construction workers over to the airfield to begin building revetments for our planes. He emphasized that we were not after any architectural awards with these structures so there was no need for precise engineering calculations or detailed designs. Time was of the essence. Nevertheless, a survey crew arrived that afternoon and began carefully laying out the proposed work. Major Putnam could not believe his eyes. He spent the next hour using the most explicit language at his command getting a couple of bulldozer crews to work and sending the survey party back to the contractor's camp.[8] In the meantime we tried to disperse the Wildcats as much as possible beside the airstrip until the revetments were completed. We did not want them all grouped together because in case of a surprise air raid one lucky bombardier might be able to destroy several planes at once.

While we pilots averaged at least one patrol per day, we certainly did not spend the rest of the time in idleness. There were a million things to do to make our planes and our ground facilities combat-ready. For example, we had to remove the hard tail wheels from all of our planes and replace them with pneumatic tires. The hard wheels were ideal for carrier operations, where their small size increased the plane's angle of attack and made it easier to take off from the relatively short flight decks. In the soft coral sand of Wake, where we had a five-thousand-foot runway anyway, they were worse than useless. Another general problem that had to be worked out concerned our ability to drop bombs from beneath the wings of the fighters. The bombs that had been delivered to the island for our use were of a type used by the Army Air Corps, but they would not fit our bomb racks. Captain Freuler solved this problem by scrounging around and adapting metal bands from our water-filled practice bombs to our racks. This modification would allow us to use the army bombs—we hoped. There was a very real danger, however, that if for some reason a bomb got hung up on one of these jury-rigged bomb racks after the pilot had attempted to drop it, he could very easily blow himself to pieces while attempting to land with the bomb dangling beneath his wing. Freuler successfully tested his "Wake Model Band" a couple of days later by releasing a few practice bombs into the ocean east of the island.

While the ground crews were making these general modifications to all the planes in the squadron, individual planes soon required specific attention. In spite of the care taken by the navy mechanics on board the *Enterprise* the mechanics of VMF-211 stayed busy. They had to replace the fuel pump on Wildcat number 11, my plane. Luckily our meager supply of spare parts included an extra pump. A couple of days after our arrival, Lieutenant Holden's new plane refused to start and we traced the problem to water in the fuel. This was probably due to the fact that we had to use barreled gas. If the barrels were not filled just right, a small air pocket remained inside the top of the barrel, and this allowed condensation to form and to mix with the gasoline.

We also spent a lot of time working on the facilities surrounding the airstrip. We quickly discovered that when warming up a Wildcat in the tie-down area the loose coral often blew up into the propellers, causing serious damage. We solved that problem by getting some lumber and building platforms for each plane to warm up on. Another problem was the tie-down stakes for the planes. They tended to vibrate out of the soft coral very quickly, so the civilian workmen fabricated some for us that looked like corkscrews, and they worked like a charm.

On Saturday, December 6, Major Devereux gave the defense battalion half a day off, and they deserved it. Some of them had been on the island since August, and they had all been working feverishly to emplace their three-inch antiaircraft guns, their five-inch seacoast guns (salvaged from some World War I–vintage warships), and their water-cooled .50- and .30-caliber machine guns. We did not begrudge them their swimming, loafing, and relaxing, but we had too much work to do to join them. Two huge gasoline tanks were hooked up adjacent to the airfield and we began to fill them from the barreled fuel supplies on the island. At the time I remember thinking what juicy targets these would make to any enemy bombers.

On Sunday, while VMF-211's pilots flew their scheduled patrols, the rest of the squadron joined the island's other occupants in a day off. It gave me an opportunity to see what else was on the atoll besides the airstrip and its immediate surroundings. Marines of Major Devereux's defense battalion had erected a battery of two five-inch guns at Kuku Point, near the outer tip of Wilkes Island. Nearby were four three-inch antiaircraft guns, and various .30- and .50-caliber machine gun emplacements dotted the beach on the seaward side. Another pair of big naval guns occupied a position at Toki Point, on Peale, and they were also kept company by an ack-ack battery and several machine guns. The remaining two five-inch guns looked out to sea from Peacock Point, near the airfield on Wake proper, with the last three-inch battery not far away and machine guns wherever else they would do the most good.

The other Marines on the island were just as shorthanded as VMF-211. Major Devereux's command had all of its heavy weapons but only about half of the men required to man them. A full-strength defense battalion called for almost a thousand officers and men; Devereux had fewer than four hundred. Six of the three-inch guns had no crews at all. And the manpower shortage was not the only problem. The only antiaircraft battery that had the necessary height finder and fire control equipment was on Peale. It then had to relay the necessary targeting information to the battery at Peacock Point by telephone. There was a desperate shortage of proper lubrication fittings for these guns, too. Whereas the standard allowance for the number of guns on Wake was fifteen spares, only two were available. The men of the defense battalion had been so busy trying to get their guns into place that they had not even had time to get in any live-fire target practice with them. They did not know it yet, but they would get on-the-job training against the Japanese beginning the very next day.[9]

Other than the gun emplacements on Wilkes, there was not much else to see there except for an unfinished boat channel slowly being blasted through from the lagoon side. Passage between Wilkes and Wake was by small boats manned by sailors. Near the western tip of Wake was Camp 1, the tent city that was home to the Marine defense battalion. Pan American Airways had established its seaplane base over on Peale and had erected a small hotel there for the convenience of Clipper passengers. The construction workers' living quarters, Camp 2, were on Wake near the bridge between the main island and Peale.

I also went over to Peale Island to see the Pan American *Philippine Clipper* make its scheduled stop on the way from the States to the Philippines. Among the Pan Am crew was Flight Engineer Ed Barnett, whom I had met a few years earlier when I worked for Pan Am. As we chatted and caught up on old times I noticed that one of the modifications I had made on this very plane back at Alameda was still functioning perfectly. Before he left, Ed reported that Pan Am was evacuating all of its women dependents from Manila as a precaution so they would not be caught there when the war finally began.

As I headed back to my quarters I thought about what Ed had said. I sure hoped that the war would wait a little longer before it got to Wake. None of us in VMF-211 had ever even fired the machine guns in the Wildcats yet. This was about to change. Our tow targets were ready, and we were scheduled to begin aerial gunnery practice the next day. With a war coming on we would surely need the practice.

On Monday morning, December 8 (Sunday, December 7, in Hawaii), I took off on schedule with the dawn patrol, and the Clipper lifted off from the lagoon to begin its fifteen-hundred-mile flight to Guam. In addition to the usual load of mail and passengers, it also carried two hundred airplane tires for Claire Chennault's American Volunteer Group (the Flying Tigers), fighting the Japanese in China. The big plane had barely gotten out of sight to the west when Commander Cunningham received a message that the Japanese had attacked the U.S. fleet at Pearl Harbor. If a Japanese force had gotten to Hawaii there was no way of knowing where other enemy fleets might be, so Cunningham immediately ordered the Pan Am station manager to recall the Clipper before it ran into a Japanese attack. The Pan Am pilot, John Hamilton, was almost out of range of the radio transceiver on Wake when he got the message to turn back.[10]

A few minutes later Hamilton set his craft down in the lagoon and taxied up to the pier. The passengers returned to the Pan Am hotel, the freight and mail were unloaded, and the fuel tanks were topped off. After consulting with Cunningham, Hamilton agreed to conduct a long-range reconnaissance around the island, looking for any sign of the Japanese. Lieutenants Conderman and Graves would fly along as an armed escort in case the Clipper ran into trouble or uncovered a likely target.

Meanwhile, I arrived back from the early patrol at about seven-thirty. In light of the news from Pearl Harbor, Major Putnam and Commander Cunningham decided to keep planes in the air through-out the daylight hours. So rather than wait until noon for the second scheduled patrol, four planes again took to the air at about eight o'clock. Captain Elrod and Lieutenant Davidson comprised one sec-tion of the patrol, relieving Major Putnam and Lieutenant Webb, and Sergeant Hamilton and I went back up in the other two planes. We still had not received confirmation of the Japanese attack at Oahu, and nerves were on edge. It seemed to Major Putnam that the near-est bases from which the Japanese could hope to launch planes against Wake were in the Marshall Islands, some six hundred miles to the southwest of Wake. Sergeant Hamilton and I therefore took a heading of 200 degrees, keeping our eyes peeled for anything that might look like a formation of hostile planes. Elrod and Davidson swept north of the island just in case the Japanese swung around and came from that direction. The weather did not do much to calm my uncertainty over whether or not the reports from Pearl were authentic. It was not a very good day for flying. As we headed away from Wake at an elevation of thirteen thousand feet, above the over-cast, I observed several rain squalls below us.

I decided not to conduct our patrol beyond sixty miles out from Wake. Without homing devices in our planes and with a none-too-efficient transmitter back on the island, I wanted to make sure we could find our way back home. Sergeant Hamilton and I maintained visual contact with one another and for the most part stayed off the radio. If there *were* any enemy ships or planes in the area we did not want them to learn anything by eavesdropping on our idle chatter.

After several hours in the air without spotting anything of signifi-cance, we headed back to Wake. A few minutes after noon Sergeant Hamilton and I came down through broken clouds within a few miles of the island and I saw two bomber formations flying toward the southwest far beneath us. They were, I later learned, Mitsubishi navy attack bombers—a type that the intelligence officers on the *Enterprise* had not told us about. The sight of these planes was certainly disquieting, but I had as yet received no confirmation that war had actually begun. While I pondered for a few seconds about what my course of action should be I saw several columns of smoke rising above Wake. That was all the confirmation I needed. Hamilton and I cleared our guns and wheeled around to try to catch up with the rapidly retiring Japanese planes. Unfortunately, we were unable to catch them before they disappeared into a cloud bank. To have pursued them any farther with our low fuel reserves would have been asking for trouble, so we turned back. We stayed in the air for another thirty minutes or so just in case there were more bombers in the area, and to make sure that the ground crews had time to remove any debris from the landing strip. We would now have the opportunity to put all of our combat training to the test. We were at war!

4

Battle for Wake

The destruction that greeted me when I landed was more than I was prepared for. The enemy bombers had come in low, the constant roar of the surf masking the noise of their engines, and caught most of the men on the atoll by surprise. Our total lack of radar further prevented their detection until they were already over the island and beginning to release their bombs. None of our aircraft revetments were complete. Our planes on the ground were like targets in a carnival shooting gallery, stationary targets that could not shoot back. The Japanese pilots began that day to disprove the stereotypes we had of them as being only mediocre aviators and so nearsighted that they could not hit their targets. Japanese machine-gun fire and bomb fragments hit every one of our planes still on the ground. Seven of them were so badly burned as to be completely unsalvageable. The eighth one (number 8) looked like it might be able to fly again, although it had received hits in both wings, the tail fin, stabilizer, fuselage, elevators, hood, fuse box, radio cables, left flap, and auxiliary gas tank. (The seven wrecks certainly provided a likely source for spare parts over the next two weeks.) To make matters worse, Captain Elrod's number 9 had hit some debris on the airstrip that bent the prop on his plane when he came in from his patrol. Thick black smoke boiled skyward from the two above-ground fuel tanks as 25,000 gallons of gasoline burned fiercely, and many of the individual drums of gas stored at various points were also hit. Our tents were shredded or burned, some of our oxygen bottles were destroyed, and our air compressor and virtually all of our meager supply of spare parts were gone. Major Bayler's ground-to-air radio gear was reduced to so much scrap metal.

The area around the airfield seemed to have received the brunt of the attack, but there was also considerable damage elsewhere. On

Peale, the Pan American Airways hotel suffered extensive damage, as did the airline's radio facility and machine shop. The Clipper, moored in the lagoon, was a sitting duck and was repeatedly hit by Japanese machine-gun fire. Almost miraculously, however, none of the bullets hit anything vital. It could still fly.

Worse than the material losses, of course, were the loss of life and the injuries. My decision to remain aloft as long as I did after the raiders departed saved me from actually witnessing all the human carnage on this first day of the war. By the time I landed, the military and civilian medical staffs had begun to treat the wounded at the hospital at Camp 2, and able-bodied survivors had taken all the dead to the refrigerated storage facility until proper burials could be arranged.

Hardest hit on this first day were the men of VMF-211. Out of the fifty-five personnel on the ground when the attack struck we lost twenty-three killed and eleven wounded—a casualty rate of almost 62 percent—in the course of about ten or fifteen minutes! Three of my fellow pilots—Major Putnam, Captain Tharin, and Sergeant Arthur—suffered minor wounds but continued to perform their duties. Lieutenant Webb, my golfing partner from Ewa, was in much more serious condition. Japanese bullets had taken three toes off his left foot and another bullet had lodged in his abdomen. Three other pilots died. When the enemy bombers first appeared, Lieutenants Graves, Conderman, and Holden were together discussing the upcoming escort mission for the Pan Am Clipper. Frank Holden scrambled for the relative safety of some nearby trees but was killed before he reached them. George Graves and redheaded "Strawberry" Conderman both sprinted for their Wildcats, hoping to get into the air where they would have a chance to inflict some damage on the attackers. Graves made it into the cockpit, but before he could get under way a Japanese bomb scored a direct hit on his plane. Machine-gun fire cut Conderman down before he could get to his plane, the bullets tearing into his neck and both legs. Corporal Robert Page did not wait for the attack to subside but immediately tried to help Conderman and other wounded Marines nearby. Conderman may have realized that his wounds were so serious that there would be little Page could do for him, because he told the corporal to attend to the other wounded first. He really had guts. He remained conscious all day but died that night in our little hospital.

Major Devereux's artillerists made it through without a single man being killed or wounded, but two sailors were killed near the channel between Wilkes and Wake, and ten Pan Am employees died from the effects of a single bomb blast.

Batteries D and E—at Peacock Point and on Peale, respectively— both opened fire with their three-inch antiaircraft guns, and the

Marines in the machine-gun batteries joined in, but there was no evidence that any of their shots had any effect on the attackers.

Among the many topics of conversation in the aftermath of this raid was: Where did they come from? When will they hit us again? We knew, of course, that they were from a different strike force than the one that started the war at Pearl Harbor. We were much too far away from Hawaii for them to have been the same planes. The planes that attacked us were medium bombers, the kind that required fairly long runways from which to take off. They were too big to take off from carriers—Colonel Jimmy Doolittle would prove this thesis wrong by April 1942—so they must have come from another island base somewhere. We knew that the Japanese controlled the Marshall Islands, six hundred miles south of Wake, and determined that the bombers must have come from there.

Knowing where the Japanese were coming from did not solve any of our immediate concerns. More important was to know when we might expect them to show up again. We did not think the Japanese pilots relished night flying over the ocean any more than we did, so we calculated that they would probably not leave their bases until first light. Then, figuring in the distance they had to travel along with their estimated speed, we guessed that we probably would not see them again until about noon the next day.

Meanwhile, VMF-211 had to find some way to carry on in spite of its tremendous human and material losses. Sergeant Earl Hannum, our only mechanic with any experience at all on our new planes, was in the hospital with dysentery, so Major Putnam approached me. "Kinney," he said, "you are now the squadron engineering officer—we have four planes left. If you can keep them flying, I'll see that you get a medal as big as a pie." I replied, "Okay, sir, if it is delivered in San Francisco." I selected Sergeant Hamilton as my assistant, and I could not have made a better choice. He worked untiringly for the rest of the siege, helping me mend and patch our few fighter aircraft.

Under different circumstances I might not have accepted my new responsibility so cheerfully. We had absolutely no repair manuals for the F4Fs and virtually no spare parts (except what we could scavenge from the wrecks). But we were at war. My life and the lives of others on the island might very well depend on how well we kept our planes performing, so we started in on our task right away.

Some of the contractor's work crews continued bulldozing revetments for our few remaining planes, so in future attacks no single bomb would destroy more than one of them. The civilians were needed at many other locations, too, so Marines continued to pitch in right alongside them to get the work done as quickly as possible. We were somewhat hampered because the raid had destroyed most of the tools we had brought with us, so the contractor, even when he could not afford to send any more workers over to the airfield, was very generous in providing us with tools.

Sergeant Hamilton and I started in on number 8 because, even though the damage to it was more extensive than the damage to Elrod's plane, it was over all easier to fix. We patched up bullet holes with scraps of sheet metal and self-tapping screws, spliced in new radio wires, and made what other repairs we could. The auxiliary gas tank was beyond hope and the hood would have to serve without all its Plexiglas intact, but by the next morning that plane was ready to fly.

While Hamilton and I did what we could with the planes, everyone else got busy preparing the island's defenses for what we all knew would be another attack. While men used picks and shovels to dig individual foxholes, bulldozer operators scraped out large bunkers in a few quick passes. With the mechanical excavation complete, groups of men wrestled huge twelve-by-twelve-inch timbers into place to form the roofs and then piled four or five feet of loose coral on top for further blast protection. Marines at the gun emplacements filled sandbags and erected whatever camouflage screens they could. A number of civilians realized that Japanese bombs and bullets had no way of differentiating between the military personnel at Wake and the noncombatants and volunteered to help out in whatever capacity was most needed. Some of them were soon at work distributing artillery and machine-gun ammunition to the various fighting positions. If a Japanese bomb had hit our centralized ammunition storage shed we would soon have been defenseless.[1] Although there was plenty of food on the island, a protracted siege might find us short of drinking water, especially if enemy bombers put our distillation plant out of order, so other men began cleaning out empty gasoline drums, filling them with fresh water, and stashing them at various points around the island. Over at the Wilkes channel, sailors filled one of their lighters with concrete blocks and dynamite so they could anchor it—and, if necessary, sink it—in the middle of the inlet to keep Japanese landing forces out of the lagoon.

In spite of all the damage around the airstrip, the runway itself had come through the aerial pounding unscathed, and it seemed possible that the Japanese had purposely spared it for their own later use. Maybe they meant to land on it and bring in ground troops. To counteract this possibility Marines set to work implanting explosives every fifty yards or so along the runway. If necessary, we would destroy our own airstrip rather than allow the Japanese to use it. Someone brought up the possibility of a nighttime landing, one for which there might not be enough advance warning to detonate the charges, so every night various pieces of heavy equipment—road graders, bulldozers, and such—were parked at intervals across the strip.

Japanese bombers again appeared over the island at about midday on December 9. This time, however, we were a little better prepared, as all four of our planes were in the air to greet them. They came in higher this time, probably hoping to fly above our antiaircraft fire, but they could not escape the Wildcats. Sergeant Hamilton sent one of the bombers into the sea, Lieutenant Kliewer got another, and the antiaircraft batteries sent several of them homeward trailing smoke. One of the planes exploded when still within sight of the island and gave the gun crews reason to cheer. Captain Freuler was also in the air, in the newly rejuvenated number 8, but he did not have the good fortune to shoot down an enemy plane. It was reassuring nonetheless to know that the repairs we had made on this plane held up during his flight, which included a 350-mile-per-hour dive.

After the bombers departed and I was able to survey the damage around the airfield I breathed a little sigh of relief because the landing strip itself was still intact, and it did not look as if there were any significant new losses in the immediate area. Most of the bomb damage seemed to be north of the strip, along the edge of the lagoon. Other parts of the atoll, I quickly learned, had not been as lucky. One of the antiaircraft guns at Peacock Point was disabled, and fragments from exploding bombs and shattered coral perforated the range finder tube for the five-inch battery there and shattered one of its lenses. With no spare parts available for repair, this would be a serious loss.

Most of this day's damage was on Peale and the adjacent area on Wake. The bombers had hit the unfinished naval air station on Peale hard, with perhaps the greatest damage being the destruction of the navy radio equipment. With the loss of Major Bayler's radio and the Pan Am radio in the previous day's raid we were now almost without communication with the outside world. Luckily, there was a five-man team of army communications specialists on the island, there to assist B-17s on their long flights from the United States to the Philippines, and their mobile radio truck was as yet unscathed.

The destruction in the vicinity of Camp 2 was devastating. Barracks buildings, both civilian and navy, were riddled, machine shops and warehouses flattened. The most devastating aspect of that day's raid, however, was the damage done to the civilian hospital at Camp 2. All of the wounded from the first day's attack were there when the bombs started falling again. The hospital took at least one direct hit, probably several, and quickly burst into flames. Some sick patients were wounded, some wounded patients were hit again, and many were killed. A quick tally showed that only four Marines were among the day's fatalities, but fifty-five civilian construction workers died.[2]

That afternoon, Sergeant Hamilton and I continued to work on the bent propeller on Elrod's plane. Again the lack of maintenance manuals and proper tools made this more of a job than it should have been. We replaced the prop motor, one blade, and the relay with items from one of the burned-out hulks, and the next day it was ready for a test flight. I climbed in and headed east down the runway, gathering more and more speed but unable to get airborne. I pushed it harder and harder until, with the tachometer needle brushing 3,600 rpm and the plane still on the ground, I knew that I did not have the correct low pitch setting, so I shut it down. I was sure glad that I had five thousand feet of runway while taking this unsettling ride. After adjusting the prop setting and making a successful takeoff, number 9 was able to rejoin our small air force.

By this time, of course, everyone on the island knew that we were down to only a handful of our original airplanes, and they had also begun to hear that Sergeant Hamilton and I were "wiring them together." As a result, we soon received a large roll of electric wire from the construction camp to aid our efforts. Actually it came in quite handy, as we used some of it to fashion homemade radio antenna loops so the remaining Wildcats could more easily home in on the island's sole remaining transmitter. The wire also came in handy for connecting detonators to the explosive charges that had been set on the runway.

Some of the civilian workers began volunteering to take a more active part in the defense of the island. A few of them had prior military service, some in World War I, and were ready to reenlist on the spot. There were no extra weapons with which to arm them, however, and there was some question as to how the Japanese would treat armed civilians in case they were captured. Instead, we found other tasks, equally necessary but less overtly military, for all those who offered to help. Our planes were consuming large amounts of machine-gun ammunition, so some of the volunteers went to work linking armor-piercing and tracer rounds together for us. Others went to the antiaircraft batteries to serve as ammunition passers. Most stayed hidden in the brush, and some of us talked of knocking off flying and driving some of this potential—and urgently needed—labor out of hiding by force to finish the revetments. Major Putnam twice sought permission from Commander Cunningham to do this, but was twice refused.

During the latest air raid Marine Gunner Clarence McKinstry noticed that one of the attackers did not join wholeheartedly in the bombing but seemed to be merely observing the action from a safe

distance. McKinstry suspected that this pilot might be taking reconnaissance photographs for the next day's raid, and if that was the
case the bombers almost certainly would target the battery of antiaircraft guns at Peacock Point. He relayed his suspicions to Major
Devereux as soon as the raiders departed, and Devereux ordered
Battery E's guns to be moved to a different location as soon as it got
dark and dummy wooden guns to be erected in their original location. Marines and contractors worked virtually all night moving this
ordnance to its new site about six hundred yards away and erecting
suitable camouflage around it.[3]

The dawn patrol on Wednesday, December 10, returned to Wake
without having seen anything suspicious, but after refueling, the
same four planes were back in the air again by ten A.M. to prepare
for the expected noon raid. They did not have long to wait. Eighteen
bombers attacked at ten-twenty. Captain Elrod shot down two of
them and the defense battalion scored hits on two more with their
three-inch guns. The newly relocated guns of Battery E came
through unscathed, but their previous position was plastered.

This time most of the destruction was on Wilkes. Most of the vital
targeting apparatus for both of the five-inch guns there was damaged beyond repair. One of the Japanese bombs found the storage
shed where the construction crews kept the dynamite they had been
using to cut the new channel into the lagoon, and the entire supply—
125 tons—went up in an ear-splitting roar. This blast was so powerful that it knocked out one of the unmanned three-inch guns nearby,
wrecked a searchlight truck over half a mile away, uprooted small
trees and brush, and detonated all of the ready ammunition (both
three-inch and five-inch) on Wilkes. Surprisingly only one or two
Marines died and another handful were wounded. I say "only" one
or two died, but these were men for whom there were no ready
replacements. The Japanese could continue to inflict half a dozen
casualties per day on the military personnel at Wake, and we would
very quickly become too weak to repel an actual invasion.[4]

As the gravity of our situation intensified, more and more of the
contractor's men began pitching in to help. The cooks over in Camp
2, for example, prepared meals for everyone and sent a truck around
to various points with the hot food. Since Sergeant Hamilton and I
were too busy to go for our own food, this mobile delivery service
was quite welcome, although it occasionally passed us by. We also
stockpiled some canned food, just in case the Japanese knocked out
all the cooking facilities on their next raid.

A little before three A.M. on December 11, Commander
Cunningham's headquarters began to receive reports of dim shapes
out at sea south of Wake. As the lookouts peered intently into the
dark the shapes came closer. Soon there was no doubt that they

were ships. The only question then remaining was whose. After three days of heavy pounding by Japanese bombers some of us dared to hope that these might be the ships of an American relief expedition bringing us reinforcements and more planes. A few civilians even grabbed up hastily packed suitcases and began moving toward the beach for evacuation. By five o'clock, however, the ships opened fire on us and removed all doubt as to their nationality.

Our new visitors belonged to Rear Admiral Sadamichi Kajioka's task force and had left Kwajalein two days earlier. With two submarines scouting far ahead, the rest of the small fleet was made up of three light cruisers, six destroyers, two older destroyers converted to transports for the landing force, and two other transports. Everyone on the island was tensely aware of the approach of this new threat, but we also all had orders to hold our fire. The range of the ships' guns was probably greater than that of our five-inch guns, so we wanted to draw the ships as close in as possible before firing. We also were not sure if the Japanese knew the locations of our seacoast guns from the earlier air raids. If not, there was no sense in giving away their positions too soon.

For two hours, lookouts kept the fleet under observation. Finally, at about five o'clock, Admiral Kajioka, in the lead cruiser, the new *Yubari*, opened fire from about four miles away. We were all dug in as much as we could be so the big naval shells were not causing any personnel casualties yet, but some oil tanks near Camp 1 that had so far escaped destruction now took some hits and began to burn brightly.[5]

Bill Hamilton and I had been up most of the night working on Wildcat number 8, which regularly refused to start. We were huddled together in our little dugout about two feet deep and covered only by a thin sheet of plywood and some coral. We were reasonably safe from the shrapnel of near misses, but of course a direct hit would have wiped us out. We had not heard any reply from our own guns, and as we listened to the whistling of the large enemy shells overhead I decided that this was certainly as good a time as any for some prayer.

I asked Bill if he was worried. "Sure, aren't you?" he answered. And I was. "It is not like making a run on a bomber formation," I reminded him, "where you can see the tracers streaming toward you and you can return some of the same medicine. Here, you can't see them. We don't even know how many there are."

Our guns finally responded when the Japanese fleet had pulled into close range, and it was like music to our ears. First Lieutenant Clarence A. Barninger's Battery A, at Peacock Point, took on Kajioka's flagship. The first shot from one of his guns was too high and sailed harmlessly over the *Yubari*. But it was not entirely wasted. The artillerists on shore did not realize that the *Yubari* was screening a destroyer from their view. The seemingly errant shell slammed into this latter, unlucky ship. Barninger quickly adjusted the range and put two shells into the *Yubari* near the waterline. The wounded cruiser immediately tried to pull away, but two more rounds from Battery A crashed into it. This was pretty good shooting considering that a Japanese air raid had previously destroyed this battery's range finder and Barninger was having to guess at all of the distances. In fact, this "seat of the pants" shooting contributed to even greater losses among the Japanese ships.

Over on Wilkes, Second Lieutenant John A. McAlister's Battery L, also without a range finder since the dynamite blast the day before, opened up on the enemy destroyers. Focusing on the *Hayate*, leading two others, the gunners poured half a dozen rounds into it in quick succession and it broke apart and sank in a matter of minutes. The cheering artillerymen then turned on other targets in their area. They hit the destroyer *Oite* and one of the transports before the remaining destroyers began laying down smoke screens and heading out to sea.[6]

The third five-inch battery, First Lieutenant Woodrow M. Kessler's Battery B, over on Peale, also entered the fray as soon as targets presented themselves. The targets, in this case, were more of the Japanese destroyers. Almost as soon as this battery went into action one of its guns suffered a mechanical breakdown and was rendered useless. The other gun continued to fire and soon scored hits on the *Yayoi*, starting fires aboard. Before this one-gun battery could register hits on any of the other enemy ships they had steamed out of range and begun their return trip to Kwajalein.[7]

The mere fact that the defense battalion's artillery could no longer reach the fleet did not mean, however, that the battle was finished, because this was not to be entirely a duel between enemy ships and land batteries. Major Putnam and Captains Elrod, Freuler, and Tharin took to the air as soon as it was light. Even parked in their revetments our planes would not have been completely safe from the big Japanese naval guns, and we did not want them on the ground in case enemy planes had accompanied the fleet. After convincing themselves that the invasion attempt was not supported by enemy aircraft, and after waiting for the defense battalion's five-inch guns to open up, the Wildcats attacked the ships. Again and again they dove through fierce defensive fire to try to land their hundred-pound bombs where they would do the most good. Then it was back again to the landing strip for more bombs and more .50-caliber machine-gun ammunition.

As the planes continued ferrying back and forth between the fleet and the island they began to show increasing amounts of battle damage. Captain Freuler, flying number 11, took two heavy-caliber slugs in his engine and just barely made it back to the airfield. Captain Elrod's plane had so many holes in its oil system that his engine froze up due to lack of lubrication. He barely made it back to the island, but he could not quite make it to the landing strip and crash-landed on the beach.

In the meantime, Sergeant Hamilton and I relieved Putnam and Tharin and continued to attack the ships, many of which showed the effects of the earlier sorties. This would be my first chance to practice dropping bombs from our new planes. As Hamilton and I hurried to overtake the retiring enemy fleet I spotted the wounded destroyer *Kisaragi* limping along beneath me. It was on fire, the result of someone else's earlier bomb run, and I was anxious to finish it off. The flames aboard must have reached an ordnance storage area just as I began my attack, because a huge explosion engulfed the ship and she rapidly began to sink. From a purely detached point of view this was a welcome sight, but on a personal level I had a brief feeling of having been cheated out of a chance to sink this ship myself. The feeling soon passed, and I looked around for another target upon which to practice my bombing skills before returning to the island.

Flying west, I soon located another destroyer trying to escape. I regretted the fact that there had been no opportunity for us to practice our bombing skills with the Wildcats before the war began, but there was no point fretting over that. I lined up for my bomb run, hoping that my on-the-job training would suffice. I released both bombs at what I calculated to be the most opportune moment, but instead of seeing another Japanese ship go up in smoke and flames I saw two near misses. With no more bombs aboard, I headed back to the island.

After Hamilton and I landed following our final sortie, I began to hear the battle reports from the other parts of the atoll. The defense battalion's five-inch guns, useless against airplanes, had done great work against the Japanese ships. Damage due to enemy gunfire had been negligible. We had lost more of our diesel fuel, but human casualties were limited to four wounded, and none of them were serious. Japanese losses, on the other hand, were staggering. We sank two ships, damaged seven others, and probably caused the loss of between five hundred and seven hundred lives.[8] We all felt justifiably proud of our performance. This was to be the first instance in the war of a defender successfully turning back an invasion!

The Japanese had been so sure that they would be camped on Wake that night that they had already issued press releases announcing their success. People in Japan cheered their brave troops who had defeated the Americans on December 11! Saving face is such an important facet of many Asian cultures that the Japanese authorities never did admit the truth to their people.

We knew that it would be unwise, if not downright foolish, to rest on our laurels, so by about nine-fifteen, Lieutenant Davidson and I took off again with full loads of fuel and ammunition. I had my flight goggles pushed back on top of my head to increase my peripheral vision. I did not want even the frames of the goggles to prevent me from seeing any enemy planes that might appear at the edges of my field of sight. We had to be alert to another air raid, and the fact that we had repelled the surface fleet did not mean that the bombers would not visit us that day.

Sure enough, we had not been in the air more than about fifteen minutes when we picked up seventeen enemy planes approaching from the east. They split into two groups as they neared Wake, and Davidson took after the nine planes headed toward the southwest. I stayed high above the other eight and waited for them to pass over our antiaircraft guns. I certainly did not want to engage these planes only to be shot down by our own defensive fire.

When I attacked it was head-on from out of the sun. The bomber crews had evidently not seen me—they were still strafing ground targets—and I was able to get in very close before they discovered me. I flashed through the formation with all my guns going but was apparently unsuccessful. As I turned back for another pass I saw them circle north of the island and head back toward the east. I made a second attack from down sun, and this time I saw a stream of gasoline pouring from the bomber I had been concentrating on. There was no time to congratulate myself on this because at about this time a Japanese bullet crashed through the Plexiglas in front of me and burrowed through the left lens of my flight goggles.

After taking stock of the situation and finding that *I* was still not hit, I began to prepare for my third run. I forced myself to get well ahead of the bombers before climbing above them and turning back. A quick count showed only seven planes still in the air, so I guess the one that was leaking fuel had had to ditch. After this third pass through the enemy formation I flew on back to the airfield. I don't know if I did any more damage or not, but I learned when I got back that Lieutenant Davidson had also shot down a bomber and that the antiaircraft crews had knocked one down and damaged three others. The bombers inflicted no American casualties.

On Friday there was a break in the pattern of midday bombing raids; only two Japanese four-engine flying boats attacked at about dawn. Their bombing accuracy was not very good, perhaps hampered by the defense battalion's antiaircraft fire. Captains Tharin and Freuler both got into the air, and Tharin chased one of the intruders out to sea, where he shot it down. This early-morning attack was the only one we had that day.

About four o'clock in the afternoon, Dave Kliewer was patrolling about twenty-five miles southwest of Wake when something on the surface of the ocean caught his eye. There, ten thousand feet beneath him, was a dull gray submarine seemingly unaware that there could be any hostile aircraft in the area. Kliewer knew that the American submarines *Triton* and *Tambor* were operating in the waters around Wake and certainly did not want to fire on one of them by mistake. Still, this was the type of target that presented itself only on rare occasions. If it *was* a Japanese sub and the crew learned of his presence they would take the boat down as quickly as they could.

As all of these thoughts raced through his mind he flew to a position west of his target and started his approach directly out of the sun. As he dove closer he looked for any markings that would identify the nationality of the boat, but the only thing he saw was an unfamiliar mark on the conning tower that he decided must be Japanese. He might only have enough time for one pass, so it had to be a good one. As soon as he was close enough to be sure of his aim he began firing his wing-mounted .50-caliber machine guns, but he waited until the last possible moment to release his bombs. When he did, both bombs exploded almost on top of the sub—and, in fact, the blast damaged the underside of his plane as he pulled out of his dive. By the time he gained altitude and came around again the sub had disappeared, leaving only an oil slick to indicate that it had ever been in the area at all.[9]

When Kliewer landed and told the rest of us about his most recent victory we all shared in his elation. Major Putnam put a little bit of a damper on our small celebration by reminding us of the two friendly submarines in the neighborhood and he cautioned us to be sure of our targets before opening fire on them. He also decided to fly out to the area in question to see what he could see. What he found was *another* submarine on the surface. This one was painted a dark olive green with white identification numbers. It was operating in an area far from where our own subs were patrolling, but Putnam thought perhaps it was a Dutch boat and, since he was not sure of his target, did not engage it.[10]

By this time Sergeant Hamilton and I had been reinforced by a navy enlisted man, Aircraft Machinist Mate First Class James F. Hesson, and a couple of civilians from the construction camp who had experience working on tractors. Of more importance, perhaps, than the extra hands was the fact that work also began on this day on a couple of makeshift aircraft hangars that would be usable for repair work twenty-four hours a day. Some of the contractor's men deepened one of the new revetments with bulldozers and then made roof frames of steel beams, over which they draped large tarpaulins. We would soon have a place into which we could push an F4F and work on it all night, if we had to, without giving away our position to any Japanese scouting planes that might visit the area.

It was good that the enemy spared us a heavy attack that day, because we needed all the time we could get to repair our planes. My small crew and I next turned our attention to the crippled plane (number 8) that Captain Freuler had nursed home after the battle with the Japanese fleet. Luckily, the engines on most of the planes that had been destroyed on the first day were still in good shape, so we were able to pull two cylinders from number 5 for use in number 8. Dark overtook us before we finished, however, and before our new hangar was ready.

Maintenance was a constant headache. Even though we had gotten number 9 back in the air, it now was reported to be running rough on the morning patrol. I changed two of the magneto leads to see if that would cure the problem, but it still ran rough on the noon patrol. I decided to fly it myself at dusk to try to isolate the problem. I discovered that not only was the engine still running rough but its two-stage supercharger would barely run in the low-speed setting. It did not run at all in the high-speed setting, which is so important for takeoff. After landing I did some more tests and found that I could not get more than 1,500 rpms out of the engine. Something was seriously wrong, but any solution would have to wait until daylight.

We received fairly regular radio reports from the United States that discussed our plight. One commentator went to great lengths to praise our small garrison in the face of erroneous Japanese reports that Wake was the most strongly held American post in the Pacific. But that wasn't enough. He then had to go on and say, "There was no indication of the size of the force on Wake Island, but it necessarily must be small, and it would be assumed that the Japanese would send preponderantly heavier forces against it." Nothing like letting the enemy know our status.

But this was not the worst of it. At about the same time we heard another radio report full of praise and bravado. That part we didn't mind, but the report continued by saying, "When asked if they needed anything the Marines had said, 'Send us more Japs!'" This, of course, was ridiculous—we had more than enough already. More Japanese were absolutely the *last* thing we needed.[11]

On Sunday morning, December 14, the Japanese treated us to another predawn raid by patrol bombers, but they did not do much damage. We only had three planes—numbers 8, 10, and 12—that were in good working order, but we continued to work on balky number 9. This was the plane we had received from the navy squadron on board the *Enterprise* when Lieutenant Holden's Wildcat refused to start back at Pearl Harbor. As such it had a different maintenance history than the rest of the planes we started with, so I decided to quit wasting any more time trying to diagnose its elusive malady and simply replace the entire engine. No single one of the wrecked planes had a completely usable engine, so I decided to cannibalize a couple of them. We would use the nose section of number 5 and the main section of number 2. We would make one complete engine from these two and then put it into number 9.

A little before noon, as Sergeant Hamilton, Corporal John S. Painter, a couple of civilian volunteer mechanics, and I were pulling the engine from number 5 in the tie-down area, someone said he thought he heard approaching aircraft. Painter reproved him with, "Oh, don't be so damned scared. Those are our own aircraft on patrol!" Still, no one was sure, and we all stopped to listen. Within seconds bombs began exploding in Camp 1, and we all began to run for an open dugout about a hundred yards away. The bombs walked right down the runway until one fell so close that it covered us all with dirt and coral. Two other members of VMF-211's ground crew were killed not far from us, and Machinist Mate Hesson took a bomb fragment in the hip.

One of the forty-one Japanese bombers in this raid scored a direct hit on Wildcat number 10 in its revetment. This left us with only two planes. Upon closer inspection of number 10 I found that the bomb had hit near the tail section and had not damaged the engine at all. The oil tank and intercoolers were gone, and the plane was on fire, but this craft had our best engine. If we could get it out of the burning plane we could put it into number 9 and not have to cobble an engine together from two other wrecks as we had intended.

A couple of us set to work unbolting the engine while someone else went and got one of the contractor's rubber-tired hoists to lift it out. The engine was almost too heavy for the hoist. We were only able to get it out of the plane by putting six men on the back end of the hoist to keep its rear wheels on the ground. We then hooked the hoist up to a tractor and pulled it over to number 9, where Sergeant Hamilton and two other men had already removed its engine.

While we worked we were delighted to discover that the Grumman factory had apparently foreseen the possibility of such a transplant becoming necessary. It had attached the entire group of pressure lines, except for gasoline and oil, to two blocks of aluminum, held together by two bolts and provided with a gasket in between to prevent leakage. This enabled us to disconnect all the lines by merely removing these two bolts. Then all we had to do was reconnect these bolts to the plate of the new engine and all the lines were properly connected.

The civilians had still not completed our aircraft hangar as nightfall approached so we had to stop work to observe the blackout. Major Putnam put more pressure on the contractor's superinten- dent, N. Dan Teeters, for help in finishing the hangar, and Teeters's response was to round up three hundred workers and a heavy-duty crane. Unfortunately, the job could only reasonably employ about fifty of these men, and the extra personnel just got in the way. In fact, they contributed in a way to a further reduction in our air defenses.

As the evening patrol prepared to take off, this crowd edged out onto the airstrip to watch. Some of them came so far onto the run- way that Captain Freuler, in number 12, had to veer to the left to keep from running into them. The F4F was not the easiest plane to control on the ground, and Freuler soon found himself starting a ground loop that had to be continued to miss the crane. He avoided the people and the crane, but was unable to keep from crashing into the brush. The plane was a total loss. We towed it back to the edge of the runway the next day to act as a decoy, and the amount of additional damage it suffered over the next eight or nine days attests to its efficiency in this regard.

At eight P.M., Bill Hamilton and I turned in for some much needed rest. We were exhausted. An hour and a half later, I was awakened and told that the hangar was ready for use. Two more hours elapsed, however, before it was *really* lightproof and usable. I let Sergeant Hamilton sleep and aroused three of the civilians who had been helping out. By then it was almost midnight, but by three-thirty the following morning number 9 was ready to fly again. It had taken us only nine hours to perform the engine swap, a very commendable time even under ideal conditions.

Our planes had now become so patched together that it was diffi- cult to tell one from the other. One day Major Putnam's main fuel tank ran dry at eighteen thousand feet. Thinking he was in number 8, whose auxiliary tank had been destroyed on the first day, he made a perfect dead-stick landing only to find out that he was in a plane that *did* have a reserve tank and still had sixty gallons of fuel left.

And even with only two planes left in flying condition, various shortages were beginning to plague us. We had already replaced the destroyed cleaning rods for our planes' machine guns with welding rods. Captain Freuler had devised a makeshift—and potentially explosive—system of transferring oxygen from a large welding tank to the small oxygen bottles we needed in our planes. This oxygen was pressurized at only about half the pressure our bottles normally had, but it was better than nothing, and it was absolutely essential for high-altitude flight. And now we were afraid of running out of starter shells for the planes. These devices—looking a lot like shot- gun shells but without the pellets—were used to explosively crank the engine on the F4F. Unfortunately, they were good for only about one revolution each, so if the plane did not start right away, and ours seldom did anymore, we had to use more and more of our precious supply of shells. To overcome this problem I built a sort of giant slingshot like those we had used in Hawaii to start our planes. At Ewa these devices were made from two bungee cords connected by rope to a leather "boot" that fit over the tip of one propeller blade. Groups of men then took hold of the ropes at the other ends of the cords and pulled to start the prop turning. Of course, on Wake I did not have access to anything quite as exotic as bungee cords, so I improvised by cutting up a couple of truck tire inner tubes. When it was time to use this mechanism, a couple of men took hold of each rope and positioned themselves in a V so that after they pulled and the boot came clear it would pass between them rather than hitting them and causing injuries. This starter system was very effective. We usually got at least three good revolutions per attempt and were thereby able to keep our planes in the air.

We were now well into the second week of the war, and the days all began to run together. There was always too much work to be done and too little time in which to do it. Wildcat number 8 was getting more and more temperamental, often refusing to start at all. I checked the valves, but they seemed to be alright. We achieved some improvement when we changed the magnetos, but the carburetor would not stop flooding. We replaced it, but the flooding abated only somewhat. Running out of ideas, we just decided that whoever was flying number 8 should simply shut off the fuel after he landed and let it run itself dry until the engine stopped.

Battle damage and the lack of spare parts were also making themselves felt during combat, but sometimes we were able to compensate. For example, early in the afternoon of December 16, Lieutenant Kliewer and I were both in the air when our daily visit from Japanese bombers occurred. Just before we began our attacks we radioed back our own altimeter readings to the antiaircraft crews. This meant that the antiaircraft crews, even without functioning height finders of their own, were able to set their fuses accurately. Kliewer and I each made two passes through the bomber formation, but the wear and tear on our planes meant that we could not be as effective as we hoped. Only one of my four machine guns worked at all. One jammed, another lost a side plate, and the ammunition belt links feeding the other one broke.

By December 20, we were reduced to only one serviceable plane, since number 8 just would not cooperate, but we received some good news that afternoon when a navy PBY arrived from Pearl Harbor with word of a relief force headed our way. We all hoped that we could hold out until it got to us, because by then, in addition to suffering from exhaustion, wounds, and the anxiety that afflicted almost everybody, we were also beginning to fall prey to dysentery due to our poor eating habits since the beginning of the siege.

The relief expedition had come into existence quickly. Within two days of the opening of hostilities, Admiral Kimmel and his staff, in addition to sifting through the physical and emotional wreckage left behind at Pearl Harbor, began to put together plans to reinforce the defenses of Wake. Aircraft losses in VMF-211 on the first day meant that we urgently needed more fighters. The rapidly evolving relief plan called for the Brewster Buffaloes (F2A-3s) of VMF-221 to fill that gap. This squadron had embarked from San Diego en route for Honolulu on board the U.S.S. *Saratoga* within twenty-four hours of the attack on Pearl.

Of equal importance to those of us on Wake was the dispatch of some radar sets, spare parts for our antiaircraft guns, ammunition, and enough Marines to provide full gun crews for the artillery already on Wake. Detachments of the Fourth Marine Defense Battalion were earmarked for this role. This force had only arrived at Pearl Harbor from its previous duty station at Guantanamo, Cuba, on December 1, but had managed to get three antiaircraft guns and several machine guns into action on the seventh. They would travel to Wake aboard the seaplane tender U.S.S. *Tangier*.

Kimmel's staff planned for Task Force 14 to accompany the air squadron and defense battalion. In addition to the *Saratoga* and the *Tangier*, three heavy cruisers and nine destroyers were to provide escort protection. Of course, sending such a force out alone would surely entice the Japanese into attacking it, so two similar forces also fitted out for other islands. Task Force 11, which included the aircraft carrier U.S.S. *Lexington*, was to head for a suspected enemy base at Jaluit, eighteen hundred miles south of Wake. Admiral Halsey, on the *Enterprise*, would lead Task Force 8 and patrol an area west of Johnston Island.

At Pearl Harbor on the night of December 10 (December 11 on Wake) stevedores began loading the *Tangier* with necessary supplies for Wake. Included in this cargo were desperately needed replacements for fire-control instruments, height finders, and data transmission systems for the three-inch and five-inch guns that had been destroyed. We had shot a lot of ammunition at the Japanese planes and ships so far, so the *Tangier* was bringing us three million rounds of belted .30- and .50-caliber machine-gun ammunition and 21,000 rounds of three-inch and five-inch shells. The artillery shells were equipped with a more modern time fuse than the World War I–vintage fuses then available on Wake, and would give our antiaircraft guns the ability to hit the bombers at greater altitudes. One element of cargo aboard the *Tangier* was not a replacement for

something we already had on the island. It was something new—
radar! If we had had a reliable radar set on December 8, we might
not have been caught with eight airplanes on the ground. With all
twelve of our Wildcats in the air, we could have given the enemy
bombers a much hotter welcome than they actually received.[12]

By now, Japanese military planners had apparently become quite
uncomfortable with the fact that they had been unable to conquer
the small force on Wake. The fleet that had attacked Pearl Harbor,
now passing to the northwest of Wake on its return to Japan,
received orders to detach two of its six aircraft carriers and a covering force of destroyers for operations against Wake. Planes from the
Soryu and the *Hiryu* arrived over Wake shortly after the PBY left on
the twenty-first. We were pretty sure that their arrival meant there
was another invasion force approaching, and the Japanese were
probably not going to be so easily put off as they had been on the
eleventh. Major Putnam got into the air in our only flyable plane as
soon as the bombers left and attempted to locate the Japanese aircraft carrier but without success. About noon we got our usual visit
from the land-based bombers.

The carrier bombers were back again the next day, and this time
they were accompanied by a new type of fighter that we had not
seen before—the Zero. We had coaxed one more flight out of one of
the balky Wildcats, and Captain Freuler and Lieutenant Davidson
were on patrol when the Japanese arrived. They immediately ripped
into them. Freuler quickly shot down two of the enemy planes, ironically exacting a little Pearl Harbor revenge in the process. The pilot
of one of these planes was Petty Officer Noboru Kanai, whose bomb
release over the *Arizona* two weeks earlier had sealed the fate of that
ship.[13] Of course, Freuler had no idea *who* he shot down, nor would
he have had time to care at the time. Bullets from his machine guns
ripped into another enemy plane, and it exploded so close under him
that the blast damaged the control surfaces of his own plane and
made it exceedingly difficult to fly. With a Zero on his tail and tracers whizzing past, Freuler dove for the ocean, hoping the enemy
pilot would not follow him very far. The Japanese pilot broke off his
pursuit, but not before putting bullets into Freuler's shoulder and
back. In spite of the injuries to both himself and his plane, Freuler
was able to get back to Wake. His injuries made it difficult to land,
but he was able to get his landing gear down and bring the plane in
safely before losing consciousness. The damage to his plane was
extensive, but Sergeant Hamilton began immediate repairs.
Lieutenant Davidson did not return. The last that was seen of him
was when Freuler looked back and saw him attacking one Zero with
another one right behind him.

With no more planes to fly, Major Putnam volunteered the personnel of VMF-211 to help Major Devereux's defense battalion in any way they could.

By this time, many of the men on the island were sick. The steady, exhausting labor of repairing damage from Japanese bombings and strengthening defenses against future attacks was wearing us all down. Coupled with the constant workload was the fact that our diets were also suffering. Food arrived at irregular intervals and we were often left to our own devices to scrounge around for something to eat. Like a lot of the men, I began to suffer from recurring, almost constant, bouts of diarrhea. None of us wanted to give in and go to the hospital when so much work remained to be done, but I finally got to the point that I was hardly able to do anything productive. I had flown eleven missions and had worked endlessly to keep our few Wildcats airworthy. I was exhausted, I was sick, and I finally checked myself into the hospital on December 22 for whatever treatment might be available.

That night, just after midnight, Marine lookouts observed lights far out to sea north of Wake. It was a rainy night, but these did not appear to be lightning flashes. It looked as if a sea battle was taking place, but whatever the cause it was too far away to be heard over the surf around our island. Perhaps this was the American relief expedition on its way to Wake, pausing to pummel a Japanese fleet that got in its way.

Unfortunately, the offshore light show did not indicate the near presence of American reinforcements. There were ships out there, but they were Admiral Kajioka's Japanese ships again. He had replaced the two destroyers we had sunk on the eleventh, repaired the *Yubari* and the other ships we had damaged, and further bolstered his force with another destroyer, another transport, and a seaplane tender with about two thousand Special Naval Landing Force troops—Japan's version of our Marines.[14] Another screening force of cruisers and destroyers under Rear Admiral A. Goto steamed northward east of Wake. And, finally, the detachment of carriers and other ships from the Pearl Harbor Strike Force still remained in the area northwest of us.

Admiral Kajioka had learned some important lessons from his earlier assault on Wake. This time he came at night, when it would be harder for our gunners to make accurate range estimates. Hedging his bets even further, he kept most of his ships far out of the range of our five-inch guns and hoped that his landing parties could get safely ashore along the south coast of Wake and Wilkes before daylight.

Everyone on the island who was physically able was at a battle station straining his eyes seaward in the dark, knowing that it was just a matter of time before the enemy would be making the landing attempt. The overcast skies masked the approach of the Japanese boats so that they were almost ashore before the defenders saw them.

Two converted destroyers carrying about a thousand Japanese troops beached along the south shore of Wake not far from where Second Lieutenant Robert M. Hanna had gathered up a scratch crew of Marines and civilians to man one of the three-inch antiaircraft guns for use against surface targets. The first shot from this gun hit the Japanese patrol craft, and in the next few minutes Hanna's gunners hit it fourteen more times, turning it into a pile of flaming rubble. In spite of this rather spectacular success, most of the troops had already gotten ashore, so Hanna switched his fire farther up the beach to the other patrol craft, now brightly illuminated by the fiery hulk of the first.[15]

Major Putnam, Captain Elrod, and other members of VMF-211, with no more planes to fly, filled in for the rest of the night as riflemen protecting this battery against Japanese assaults. Lieutenant Kliewer and three other members of the squadron took up a position near the airfield where they manned the generator attached to the explosives planted all along the runway. The last thing we needed would be for the enemy to bring in planeloads of fresh troops while our attention was occupied in trying to repel the attack along the beaches.

Two landing barges, similar to our LCMs, tried repeatedly to crash over the reef near the channel between Wake and Wilkes but had trouble finding a weak point in the barrier. The light from the burning hulk of the beached destroyer revealed their presence to Second Lieutenant Arthur A. Poindexter, commanding a mobile machine-gun force of four .30-caliber guns. He immediately had his men begin laying fire into the landing boats, but with little effect. He realized, after watching the tracer rounds apparently bouncing off the steel sides of these craft, that he was just wasting ammunition, so he had his gunners stop firing. Then Poindexter, along with a navy boatswain's mate, a Marine cook, and a civilian volunteer, waded into the surf tossing hand grenades toward the enemy craft. At least one of the grenades landed squarely within one of the boats, killing and wounding most of the men inside.[16]

Within about a half hour of the Japanese landings—that is, by about three o'clock—Major Devereux's command post had lost communication with many other sections of the atoll. There was absolutely no word from Captain Wesley Platt over on Wilkes, so Devereux assumed that the enemy had overwhelmed his position. Devereux continued to direct the defense, but by five o'clock there were probably a thousand Japanese on the island, and Commander Cunningham sent a tersely worded message to Pearl Harbor that simply said: "Enemy on island. Issue in doubt." He then broadcast a message, in the clear, that he hoped the American submarines in the area would pick up. It asked them to attack the Japanese ships off Wake. There was no answer from either sub, but a reply was forthcoming instead from Pearl Harbor. It simply said that the subs were not there anymore and that, in fact, there were no friendly ships within twenty-four hours' steaming time of Wake. The relief force had been recalled!

While all of this was going on, those of us in the hospital bunker had no idea of what was happening outside, only that the Japanese had again attempted a landing and seemed to be enjoying more success than the last time. I could not see how valiantly the men of VMF-211, with Captain Elrod encouraging them all the way, had turned to as infantrymen to help defend one of the defense battalion's gun positions. (Elrod would be killed at his post this night and posthumously awarded our nation's highest military honor.) Nor could I see Lieutenant Kliewer's frustration when battle damage to the electrical wires meant that he was not able to blow the charges that lined the airstrip. Perhaps I was better off without this knowledge, and throughout the night my weakened body gave in to its most pressing need at the time—sleep.

Sometime later I was awakened by the *crack* of rifle fire. Then the *brrrp . . . trrt . . . brrp* of automatic weapons . . . the *zing zing brrp* of more firing and bullets ricocheting around the ventilator shaft above me. There was no mistake now as to what was happening. Japanese forces were on the island, and I was stuck in the hospital without so much as a sidearm to defend myself.

The field phone rang and Dr. Gustave Kahn, the navy surgeon on Wake, picked it up. Whoever was on the other end of the line made the message short, and when Dr. Kahn hung up he announced, "The Japs have landed! Many parts of the island have been overrun! Many strong points are out of communication." The overall mood that greeted this announcement was one of quiet gloom, although some men seemed on the verge of panic. Then someone thought of the red cross painted on the roof of our hospital bunker. Would the Japanese see it in the predawn dark? Would they respect it if they did see it? We could only lie there and wait and hope.

Dr. Kahn went back to tending those who most needed his help, and then finally he ordered all of those who could do so to get dressed and crawl under their bunks. I did as he ordered, but I wasn't really too sure just how much protection my hospital mattress would provide. Meanwhile, the sounds of battle ebbed and flowed outside the hospital. Sometimes I could have sworn that the shooting was just on the other side of the bunker's steel door, while at other times it seemed several hundred yards away.

At about eight o'clock the phone rang again. This time the message left no doubt as to the progress of the battle. Dr. Kahn relayed the message to all of us. Commander Cunningham had recognized the futility of further resistance. He had ordered the island to be surrendered. We were dumbfounded. What would be our fate? Many of us had seen the newsreels of Japanese treatment of the Chinese. Would they even bother to take us prisoner, or would they just kill us all where we were?

5

Captured

As we waited to see what would happen next, someone—I don't remember who—got the idea that we had better eat a last meal of whatever was at hand in the hospital, because even if the Japanese didn't kill us outright they might not go to any great lengths to keep us from starving to death either. Eating was an excellent idea except that there was not very much food available. The last regular food delivery from the contractor's kitchens had been the night before.

About an hour and a half after we learned of the surrender order Japanese soldiers finally arrived at our part of the island and began banging on the steel door of our hospital bunker with their rifle butts. Dr. Kahn opened the door, and all of us who were able to do so raised our hands above our heads. We were unarmed and completely at their mercy, and we did not want them to think that they had stumbled into a fighting bunker and come in shooting. It did not matter. They fired a few random shots from just inside the doorway anyway. As bullets ricocheted around the room several patients were hit. Two men near my bed were killed, and a few others were so badly rewounded that they died soon after. Apparently satisfied with thus establishing their authority over us, the Japanese made it known, through a combination of gestures, grunts, and sign language, that we were to move out onto a nearby road where prisoners from other parts of the island were assembling. They did show at least a small shred of humanity by allowing Dr. Kahn to remain with those hospital patients unable to move.

When I got out of the bunker I still heard the sounds of gunfire. The lack of operable wire communications, along with battle damage to some that was working, meant that not everyone had gotten the word about the surrender yet. Japanese carrier-based planes circled overhead, diving on any likely targets. They met rifle and machine-gun fire from those Marines who had not yet surrendered, and we inwardly gave a small cheer when one of the planes began smoking ominously as it passed over one of the few remaining pockets of resistance. We tried not to display any outward elation for fear that our guards might take that as a sign of an uprising and finish us off right there.

There was communication between Major Devereux's command post and two of the defense battalion's batteries on Wake itself, and Devereux told the men there that the island had been surrendered. While those Marines waited for the Japanese to physically take them prisoner, they occupied themselves by making sure that the enemy would not be able to use the American guns against other Americans. The men at Battery E were quite inventive when it came to disabling their three-inch guns. They stuffed blankets into the barrels and then fired the guns, hoping that the obstructions would cause the barrels to split. They were not entirely successful, so next they rolled grenades down the barrels to blow them up. Then they stripped the essential firing mechanisms from the guns and buried them. First Lieutenant William Lewis administered the coup de grace with his .45-caliber pistol by firing three magazines' worth of bullets into the height finder and other delicate mechanisms. At Battery A, Lieutenant Barninger used similar measures to disable his five-inch guns.[1]

Meanwhile, our captors tried to tell us something, but of course we had no idea what they were saying. Frustrated by our mutual inability to communicate, their voices got louder and shriller and their gesticulating more animated until finally they began pulling at our clothing. It finally sank in that they wanted us to undress, which we did. When we had stripped down to our shorts they prodded us onto the road with the points of their bayonets. While some of the Japanese kept their rifles trained on us, others rummaged around near the road and came back with several pieces of our own communication wire with which to truss us up. A guard came up to me and roughly motioned for me to cross my wrists behind my back. When I did so he tied them tightly together, severely restricting the flow of blood into my hands. Then he took another piece of wire, looped it around my neck, and tied it to my wrists. This arrangement made any degree of comfort nearly impossible, because if I relaxed my arms enough to let my wrists fall a little bit and relieve the growing discomfort in my shoulders it would pull down against the wire around my neck and I would strangle myself.

After they tied us all up the guards ordered us onto our knees, and we spent the next several hours in that uncomfortable position. In spite of the coral sand digging into my bare knees and the pain beginning to throb through my arms and shoulders, I had time to ponder the possible outcome of the Japanese victory on Wake. I sought to recall the instructions I had received in the Marine Basic School covering the rules of land warfare and the Geneva Convention for Prisoners of War. Nothing I could remember, however, seemed to reflect my current treatment. Instead, my mind kept coming back to a conversation that Captains Tharin and Elrod had had with me on the evening of the twenty-first. At that time we had all seemed to agree with Elrod when he reminded us, "The Japs don't take prisoners." As the day wore on nothing in my situation seemed to dispel this belief. In fact, the only reason I could think of to explain why we were still alive at all was that the Japanese were trying to think of a way to dispose of all of us with the least expenditure of resources. One scenario that kept running through my mind was that they were going to line us all up in nice straight lines so they could kill at least three or four of us with a single bullet. If that happened I was determined to break and run. I knew that I could not survive, but at least I would force them to use more of their precious bullets.

Finally, we were ordered to our feet, and we began to march along the road toward the beach. The hot coral burned my bare feet, but other thoughts quickly crowded the pain out of my mind. They were going to kill us without using *any* bullets, the bastards. They were going to march us into the surf, and with our hands tied as they were there would be no chance to save ourselves. We would all drown. But then the column stopped, and we again knelt down.

Our guards were still waiting for the final resistance to end. When that happened, in the early afternoon, they herded all of the Americans on the island together onto the airstrip. In the meantime, they had decided that there was nowhere for any of us to run so they untied us and allowed us to pick up a few pieces of discarded clothing from where other prisoners had stripped. Our own clothes likewise wound up on the backs of others. When we were all assembled, the enemy naval commander, resplendent in a white uniform, prepared to address us through a Japanese interpreter. It was at this time that we began a practice we were to continue throughout our imprisonment, and that was to nickname the guards. We were usually unaware of their actual names, and even when we did know them they were not the sort of names that fell lightly off our tongues. We instead picked some physical characteristic, much as a cartoonist might do when preparing a caricature, and assigned nicknames accordingly. In the case of this interpreter we focused on his mode of dress. His uniform included white shorts, and he wore garters to hold his socks up. We immediately referred to him as "Garters."

Garters let us know that the "Great Empire of Japan" had laid claim to Wake, a claim of which we were only too aware. He went on to say, in slightly less than fluent English: "The Great Empire of Japan who loves peace and respects justice has been oblidged [*sic*] to take arms against the challange [*sic*] of P resident [*sic*] Roosevelt. Therefore, in accordance with the peace-loving spirit of the Great Empire of Japan, Japanese Imperial Navy will not inflict harms to those people though they have been our enemy—who do not hold hostility against us in any respect. So, they be in peace! But whoever violates our spirit or whoever are not obedient shall be severely punished by our Martial law."[2]

As we then listened to the next rattle of orders in Japanese, I breathed an inward sigh of relief. At least we were not going to be summarily executed. My relief, however, was short-lived; Garters began speaking again. "Certain individuals will be shot for military reasons—Major Putnam, Captain Tharin, Captain Freuler, Lieutenant Kinney, Lieutenant Kliewer." They had obviously obtained a roster of those pilots still alive who had flown against them, although there were a few omissions. Lieutenant Webb's name was not on the list, probably because he was still in the hospital suffering from the serious wounds he had received during the initial Japanese attack. Our two enlisted pilots, Sergeants Hamilton and Arthur, also escaped this special honorary mention. If our captors had wanted to punish those who had done them the most damage they should also have singled out the commanders and crews of the antiaircraft guns and the five-inch batteries, but for some reason they chose not to.

As I was mulling over my apparent fate there was a slight rustling among the prisoners and my summer flight jacket mysteriously appeared from the midst of the crowd. Whoever had picked it up from some pile of discarded clothing had now decided to return it to me for my final hours. Or perhaps the fact that my name and flight wings were conspicuously sewn to the front of the garment meant that whoever was wearing it did not want the Japanese to mistake *him* for this Lieutenant Kinney whom they had singled out for execution. Whatever the motive, I was glad to have it back since I had no shirt, and the jacket would help protect me from the hot daytime sun and the cold nighttime rain.

We spent the rest of the day on the airstrip waiting for whatever was to come next. That night our guards must have decided that we would be easier to keep an eye on if they put us into the big unfinished maintenance hangar nearby. It was empty now, since there had not yet been time to move our one remaining Wildcat—Captain Freuler's—into it. The inside measured about forty feet on a side, which gave each of the approximately fifteen hundred men about one square foot of area. The guards tried to push us back until we were all inside, and then they wanted us to sit down. Even standing was almost impossible, and when the guards lowered the tarp (our planned blackout shield) across the entrance, the air inside quickly became stifling. Fortunately, they allowed us to move back out into the open air that evening to sleep. I was exhausted and was still fighting off the effects of dysentery. I should have been able to sleep anywhere, but a tiny voice in the back of my head kept repeating what Garters had said about certain officers being executed.

The next morning the Japanese rounded up some of the civilian workers and took them over to Camp 2 to get the water distillation plant back into operation. No matter what they did with us the Japanese would have to have fresh water if they were going to stay on the island. Water was also becoming a major concern for us, and about noon a truck arrived from Camp 2 with a load of barreled water. There were still significant traces of gasoline in the water, but most of us were too thirsty by this time to complain and eagerly pushed and shoved forward to get at least a mouthful or two.

Although Commander Cunningham and several of the higher ranking officers were being held someplace else on the island, I and the other officers present were alarmed by the reaction to the distribution of water. If we allowed ourselves to descend to the status of a howling mob every time food or water was delivered (assuming there would be food and more water), the Japanese might mistake our actions for the beginnings of a revolt. The result might well be a complete cutting off of all food and water, or worse. We had to reestablish discipline. This should not be too difficult for the Marines, sailors, and soldiers because they were trained to accept the discipline imposed by their officers. Most of the prisoners, however, were members of the civilian work force, and they might not be as easy to control. We officers held a hushed conference on the matter and decided to separate the military prisoners from the civilians, and to try to get the construction foremen and supervisors to continue to assume leadership roles over their crews. This arrangement met with no dissension, and when another truck arrived with more water and some food there was much less pandemonium, even though the food ran out before each prisoner got his allotted half slice of bread.

Later that day the Japanese began assembling work crews from among the prisoners. One group left on the food-and-water truck to try to set up the kitchens in Camp 2 again so we would have better food. Other details were sent out to bury the dead (Japanese and Americans), dig latrines, and bring back clothing and eating utensils. The language barrier contributed to the fact that not all of these work details ran smoothly. For example, in the galley in Camp 2 one of the newly constituted work crews was busy preparing a stew when, due to some sort of misunderstanding, a guard got angry and destroyed the entire batch. That ended our hope for food for the day.

My own hopes took a turn for the worst in the afternoon when, after calling us all to attention, Garters called out the names of Major Putnam, Captain Tharin, Lieutenant Kliewer and myself and loaded us onto a truck. Well, this was it, I figured. They were going to take us off somewhere and execute us. Instead, however, the truck delivered us to Camp 2, where we met a Japanese naval officer and a Japanese pilot. The pilot, who spoke some English, did most of the talking. They were curious about various aspects of our defense of Wake. I think they found it hard to accept that a force as small as ours had been able to inflict so much damage on theirs.

The session was very informal, and they treated us with respect. They did not ask us any questions that would have required us to give away any military secrets. But they did want to know what had happened to one of their four-engine flying boats that had been sent to bomb us but had not returned. Captain Tharin informed them that he had shot it down. They next wanted to know what had happened to a certain submarine of theirs that appeared to have disappeared from nearby waters. Major Putnam told them that Lieutenant Kliewer had sunk it. About the only other question they asked was, "Where are the women?" There weren't any. The few that had been on the island, the Pan Am station manager's wife, the wife of the general superintendent of construction, and a few others, had long since been evacuated. Our answer to this question seemed to puzzle the Japanese more than the other replies. They found it hard to believe that there would be no women on the island.

After this brief question-and-answer session the Japanese officers told us that they were going to move all the prisoners from the airstrip to Camp 2, where they would find temporary quarters in what was left of the barracks there. Earlier in the day, work crews had surrounded the buildings with barbed wire, and by nightfall the transfer was complete.

Christmas of 1941 arrived on schedule, of course, but it was certainly not the happy occasion of earlier years. Within the last couple of days we had lost our island, most of us had suffered a long period when we were tied up so that circulation was cut off to our hands, we had been without much in the way of clothes or shelter, and we had spent forty-eight hours without food and twenty-four hours without water. In spite of this litany of complaints, there were some bright spots. We were able to count noses and account for most of our casualties, and, most important to me, there had as yet been none of the promised executions. After our removal to the civilian barracks in Camp 2 we at least had roofs over our heads, and in some of the barracks the toilets and the saltwater showers still worked.

The Japanese, of course, had searched all the buildings very carefully before allowing any of us to enter them. They did not want us to find anything that might contribute to our morale. Nevertheless, I found a broken portable radio that the guards must have figured was worthless because of the broken case and the punctured speaker diaphragm. When I surreptitiously plugged it in and turned it on I was able to get a loud hum out of it, and I hoped that under ideal atmospheric conditions we might be able to get some news from the outside world.

I knew that I could get into serious trouble if the Japanese caught me listening to this radio, so I tried to be very careful. Shortly, however, when I was trying to tune in a station I inadvertently tuned into some loud music. The noise immediately attracted the attention of the guard stationed just outside the barbed-wire fence that enclosed our barracks. He burst into the room searching for the source of this sound, but my alert fellow prisoners began to hum the same tune and to sing, convincing the searcher that the source of the noise had been completely innocent. This was a close call, and Major Putnam then advised me to stop using the radio lest I bring down punishment on the whole barracks.

He was right, of course, but I just couldn't bring myself to discard any chance of getting war news, so I decided to keep the operations from my brother officers. I took one of the few mattresses in the barracks and folded it over me and my precious radio while I tuned in to a speech by Secretary of Labor Frances Perkins. In it she quoted a promise by President Roosevelt that American industry would build fifty thousand airplanes in 1942 with which to conduct the war. This was a heartening bit of news, and it served to stimulate the morale of many of us for months to come. This revelation also proved the value of my clandestine radio operations despite the possible consequences of discovery.

Unfortunately, my days of gathering radio news were limited. Apparently, tuning my little radio created a regenerative signal that caused interference in a radio being used by the Japanese to listen in on the same frequency. They conducted a search of the barracks area, discovered the makeshift antenna I had rigged up, and confiscated my battered little link to the outside world. They did not, however, punish me for having it.

As things settled down into somewhat of a routine, I began to think of escape. True, I was over two thousand miles from Hawaii, but I believed it to be my duty to escape so I could again make an active contribution to the war effort. Planning an escape is just like planning any other type of military operation. There are several general aspects to consider. I had to have a clearly defined objective. I must evaluate the enemy situation and learn intimately the disposition of all their troops in the immediate area. I had to try to find out if there were any friendly forces any closer than Hawaii. Maybe the aborted relief expedition had stayed at sea and was only a few hundred miles away. I had to weigh the pluses and minuses of every possible escape plan and settle on the most likely one, but without closing my mind to other alternatives that might occur. I then had to work out the timing for each plan considered and constantly be on the alert for any change in the routine of the enemy. I had to try to stay as healthy as I could, because strength and stamina are vital to any escape.

Since I would have to have help to make a successful escape I took Frank Tharin into my confidence. I had known him since Marine Basic School, and over the course of the last couple of months he had become one of my closest friends. He was as anxious as I was to somehow get out of the scrape we were in, and we separately worked out different versions of the problems facing us and their possible solutions. Then we got together for brief brainstorming sessions. Our first plan called for us to somehow get hold of a small boat and begin to row toward Hawaii. With any luck, American scouting planes or ships would spot us and pick us up long before we reached it. We had thus established our objective. Next we had to evaluate the enemy situation and locate a boat. None of the officers in our barracks remembered seeing any boats on the island; perhaps the Japanese had brought some in. We could look out onto the lagoon from our barracks, but we could see no signs of a boat there. So we decided this plan would have to be put on hold—not abandoned—until we could find out whether or not there was any chance of getting a boat at all.

Another possibility involved a faster method than rowing across two thousand miles of ocean. We could see big four-engine Japanese seaplanes in the lagoon every day. Maybe we could steal one of them and fly it to Hawaii. At first blush it seemed too fantastic an idea for success, but by then I was consumed with the idea of escaping. I felt as if I had to get back to my country. Escape planning almost became an obsession for me, but we could not rush into it and risk overlooking any possible obstacles. Tharin and I decided to give ourselves thirty days in which to complete the planning and make the attempt.

The first part of the escape would be relatively easy. We figured that we could get out of our barracks and through the surrounding barbed wire without too much difficulty just after dark. We could then slip into the lagoon and paddle noiselessly out to one of the planes on two surfboards that we had spotted about 150 yards from our barracks. Once aboard one of the planes, we would have the rest of the night to figure out how to fly it away at first light.

Captain Tharin had recently flown twin-engine land planes, and both of us had qualified in twin-engine seaplanes at Pensacola during our flight training. My experience as a civilian mechanic on Pan Am's big four-engine flying boats should also come in handy. I was completely familiar with the electrical, mechanical, fuel, and oil systems on Pan Am's planes, and I was also fairly well acquainted with the pilot's and flight engineer's controls. I knew that American designs had a way of being used by other countries, especially Japan, so there seemed to be a good chance that the Japanese planes would exhibit many similarities.

My co-conspirator and I became keen observers of the Japanese flying boats. We watched their pattern of operation on the lagoon, where they were each moored to a separate buoy. We were disappointed to see that the crews went back and forth in rubber rafts and that they apparently slept on board the planes. This would make stealing a plane more difficult. Perhaps the crew's routine would change after the Japanese got more comfortable on the island. Otherwise how could we overpower the crew without killing them? We did not want to kill anyone if we could avoid it because that might lead to disastrous results for us if our escape failed. Even if we succeeded, the Japanese might avenge any deaths that we caused along the way by murdering some of the remaining Americans. We wanted to escape, but not if it meant the deaths of some of our fellow prisoners.

Our continued observation revealed other problems that were just as difficult to overcome. The aircraft starting procedure, for example, required one of the crewmen to walk out on the wing, let down a step, insert a crank at the engine, and wind up an inertia starter that he would then engage when it reached the desired speed and the pilot was ready to start that engine. The crewman had to repeat the same steps for each of the other three engines before the pilot could taxi to the western end of the lagoon, where there was sufficient room for takeoff. The first thing we would have to do would be to locate the cranks. Where on the aircraft were they stored? Would we have time, once we reached the plane, to rummage around until we found them? Would we have time to crank all four engines into life before the Japanese discovered what we were up to and began shooting at us?

The more we thought about this plan the greater the number of obstacles we uncovered. Playing devil's advocate, however, is an important part of any such plan. At least if we could identify as many difficulties as possible ahead of time we would be less likely to be defeated by some unforeseen problem. What did the control system for the fuel flow look like? Where were the fuel booster pumps? Were they marked only in Japanese? Were they similar to those on

U.S. models? How much fuel was aboard? How far could we fly before running out? Could we predict which of the four aircraft was due to be flown on a particular day so we could steal it and perhaps avoid early detection?

Tharin and I, since we were both pilots, just naturally assumed that if we could get a plane into the air we could fly it successfully to friendly territory. Even if we got that far, however, there was yet another danger—American antiaircraft fire. We knew that the U.S.S. *Enterprise* was just returning to Pearl Harbor on the afternoon of December 7 from having delivered VMF-211 to Wake. We also knew that as the *Enterprise*'s planes flew off the carrier toward Ford Island jittery American gun crews in the area mistook them for returning Japanese planes and shot many of them down. In fact, my friend James Daniels was one of the few who landed safely. My "E" Base classmate from Oakland, Manuel Gonzales, was not so lucky and was a victim of this "friendly" fire. These were our own planes, in communication with our own airfield! What chance did a Japanese flying boat being flown in unannounced by a couple of Americans have? We decided to deal with that problem later. We estimated that our overall chances for a successful escape in this manner were probably in the range of one in ten thousand, but we decided that even if we failed we might at least be able to destroy one of the enemy's planes in the process. Besides, escape planning was good for our morale and gave us a way in which to pass the time.

Very early in our escape planning I learned, to my surprise, that Frank Tharin and I seemed to be the only ones in our barracks interested in escaping. (I later found out that Lieutenants John A. McAlister and Woodrow M. Kessler of the defense battalion were trying to find a boat to use to sail away toward Hawaii.) Most of the others, if they gave any thought to escape at all, let almost any obstacle stop them from planning further. Some thought that the war would end quickly and we would all be repatriated. Therefore, since we were all at least still alive, why rock the boat? Others just thought that the odds against a successful escape were astronomical, and that to even attempt such a thing was tantamount to suicide. Since no one else seemed interested in getting off the island we decided to keep our escape plans to ourselves and not openly discuss them with anyone else.[3]

Time ran out on all of our escape plans on January 12, 1942, when we learned that we were to embark on a Japanese troopship that had arrived on the south side of the island. Not everyone was going. Those prisoners who were seriously ill and those, like Lieutenant Henry Webb, who were recovering from wounds would remain on the island until they recovered, and a large number of civilian workmen were to stay on as slave labor for the Japanese. Herb Freuler, although numbered among the wounded, refused to be left behind. He insisted that his injuries were not serious enough to keep him from going along and sharing the fate, whatever it might turn out to be, of the rest of us.

As we prepared to board the ship a Japanese officer warned us that we were not to take any valuables with us, but this advice was rather superfluous. None of us had any rings, watches, or anything else of value because the enemy soldiers had already taken everything like that from us. Few of us even had a sufficient amount of clothing. We had only what we had been able to find where we had been held on the airfield or in the ransacked barracks. I did not even have a decent pair of shoes. The abrasive coral of the atoll had nearly worn away the soles of the pair I bought from the contractor's store upon my arrival. My only footgear was a pair of hip boots designed to be worn over work shoes. I had cut these down to about ten inches in height, but I soon found that walking in them was probably worse than going barefoot. They were heavy and had deep depressions to accommodate the heels of shoes. Since I had no shoes, the ridges in front of these depressions hit the bottoms of my feet just in front of my heels and raised very painful blisters within a few hundred yards.

Our captors gave each of us a copy of very explicit regulations concerning our behavior as prisoners of war.

1.   The prisoners disobeying the following orders will be punished with immediate death.

a)   Those disobeying orders and instructions.

b)   Those showing a motion of antagonism and raising a sign [of] opposition.

C)   Those disordering the the regulations by individualism, egoism, thinking only about yourself, rushing for your own goods.

d)   Those talking without permission and raising loud voices.

e)   Those walking and moving with out order.

f)   Those carrying unnecessary baggage in embarking.

g)   Those resisting mutually.

h)   Those touching the boat's materials, wires, electric lights, switches, etc.

i)   Those climbing ladders withou order.

j)   Those showing action of running away from the room or boat.

k)   Those trying to take more meal than given to them.

l)   Those using more than two blankets.

2.   Since the boat is not well equiped and inside being narrow,

food being scarce and poor you'll feel uncomfortable during the short time on the boat. Those losing patience and disord[er]ing the regulation will be heavily punished for the reason of not being able to escort.

3.   Be sure to finish your "Nature's Call," evacuate the bowels and urine, before embarking.

4.   Meal will be given twice a day. One plate only to one prisoner. The prisoners called by the guard will give out the meal quick as possible and honestly. The remaining prisoners will stay in their places quietly and wait for your plate. Those moving from their [places] reaching for your plate without order will be heavily punished. Same orders will be applied in handling plates after meal.

5.   Toilet will be fixed at the four conors of the room. The buckets and cans will be placed. When filled up a guard will appoint a prisoner. The prisoner called will take the buckets to the center of the room. The buckets will be pulled up by the derrick and be thrown away. Toilet papers will be given. Everyone must cooperate to make the room sanitary. Those being careless will be punished.

6.   Navy of the Great Japanese Empire will not try to punish you all with death. Those obeying all the rules and regulations, and believing the action and purpose of the Japanese Navy, cooperating with Japan in constructing the "New Order of the Greater Asia" which lead to the world's peace will be well treated.[4]

The grammar would have made an English teacher wince, but the message came through loud and clear. The Japanese could kill any one of us at almost any time for almost any reason, and it would be covered by these regulations.

When we reached the south shore of Wake we saw the *Nitta Maru* sending troops and supplies ashore in lighters. As each of these boats disgorged its cargo on the beach, it took a load of prisoners aboard for the trip through the surf back to the ship. When the boat I was in came alongside the ship the Japanese ordered us into cargo nets to be hauled aboard. Once on deck we were greeted by less than friendly crewmen who formed us into a single file between two lines of them. The purpose of the formation was so that a ship's medic could spray us with some sort of decontaminant, although since we remained clothed during the entire procedure I doubt if it could have been very effective. Unfortunately, this medical stop created a bottleneck in our progress and gave the crewmen more time to beat on us with everything from rifle butts and sword scabbards to their bare fists. I felt like a character in one of James Fenimore Cooper's novels running the gauntlet in some American Indian village during colonial times.

Prisoner accommodations aboard the *Nitta Maru*, formerly a fancy, high-speed civilian liner, were abysmal. Guards roughly ushered the enlisted men and civilians into cargo holds where there was no ventilation except for a partially opened hatch. Other Japanese shoved thirty of us officers into what had once been the ship's mail room, where we were not quite as crowded as those below. The only opening into the room was the door through which we had entered, and an armed guard stood watch there around the clock. Elevated racks lined two of the walls, and they were wide enough to accommodate some of the men. All in all we had enough room, barely, to lie down, but anyone moving around had to be careful not to step on the outstretched bodies of his companions.

A cabin boy brought us our food twice each day, and it usually consisted of water with a few grains of rice. Occasionally our captors supplemented this meager ration with small fish, a couple of olives, or perhaps a Japanese radish. When we got fish I soon learned to eat head and all in an effort to extract every bit of nutrition I could. At other times we got pieces of pickled seaweed, which was not very tasty but helped to combat scurvy. One morning, in an effort to be friendly, our cabin boy told us, "Tonight, hotsie." None of us were exactly sure what he was trying to say, but to me this meant that we were going to receive some sort of hot beverage. I had my hopes up for the rest of the day, thinking that we would get hot chocolate. It turned out to be warm water.

Another facet of our routine was a daily inspection by a guard officer who was quick to slap us hard across the face when we did not react speedily enough to his orders. Of course, since none of us understood Japanese these slappings were not infrequent. I cannot say that I was surprised by these events because I was expecting still worse treatment before I got home. The guards also used these occasions to steal any of our valuables that their counterparts on the island had somehow overlooked. Commander Cunningham, for example, now lost his Naval Academy graduation ring. The guard who took it assured him that it was for the Japanese war effort, that it would be melted down for the good of the empire. None of us believed his story.

One day the cabin boy brought in a set of photographs of Pearl Harbor taken by the Japanese aircraft during their final attack. As he gloated over them the effect on our morale was most disheartening. We had heard that the damage at Pearl had been considerable, but the destruction revealed in the pictures was numbing. The capsized and burning battleships alongside Ford Island seemed to dash any hopes we might have had for a short war. We wanted desperately to believe that what we had seen were actually Japanese propaganda photographs of scale models and not the pride of the U.S. Pacific Fleet.

It was against the rules for us to talk among ourselves, Rule 1(d), I guess, but we did converse in hushed whispers when the guard was not paying close attention to us. This usually worked pretty well, but one day the guards caught Captain Platt of the defense battalion talking and decided to make an example of him. They came into the room and dragged him into the hallway outside, where they proceeded to beat him severely with a wooden club about the size of a baseball bat. He was determined not to cry out or show any pain, but this only seemed to make the guards redouble their efforts. The manner in which Captain Platt withstood this punishment set an excellent example of resistance for the rest of us to follow during our period of captivity. We must never give in. We must always show our enemies that we were stronger—at least in spirit—than they were.

Other than Platt, the man in our room whose health was the most precarious during our voyage was Herb Freuler. He had assured all of us that his bullet wounds were not serious enough for him to remain on Wake with the other sick and wounded, but now they began to cause him considerable discomfort. Dr. Kahn was with us, but the Japanese had not allowed him to bring anything along in the way of medicines, so infection soon set into Freuler's wounds. Luckily, our guards finally allowed one of their doctors to treat him before the infections got too serious. The rest of us were also glad for the treatment because the wounds had started to reek of decaying flesh.

There was little to occupy the tedious passage of time during our voyage. Someone had managed to smuggle aboard a Bible and a couple of paperback books, and we all took turns reading these by the light of the single light bulb that burned continuously in the center of the room. Everyone read and reread *The Yearling* and Dorothy Parker's *After Such Pleasures*. I found that I could not read for very long at one time in the dim light, so I devised other methods of occupying my time. I decided to count all the rivets I could see in our steel room. Then I would count them again. I do not remember how many times I did this, but I could never get the latest number to agree with any previous total. It didn't matter. It was a way to pass the time. Another time-consuming measure I adopted was to mentally count all the beds that I had slept in since the age of four. It was surprising how much detail I recalled. I think perhaps the reason I chose to count beds was because our own sleeping arrangements were such a far cry from even the least comfortable bed I had known up until then.

Our chief form of exercise was going to the square five-gallon tin can just outside our room that served as our latrine. Our group came aboard in a pretty well evacuated condition since we had been eating very little. Our diet was such that about all we passed was water, and we became concerned about the effect on our health of the lack of bowel movements. Dr. Kahn reassured us that as soon as we started eating solid foods again our digestive systems would return to normal. As an indication of our poor diets, the average time between bowel movements was eighteen days, although one man went twenty-six days.

I used my own trips to the latrine to do a little blind navigation. The Japanese had taken all of our watches from us, so the only way we had of knowing whether it was day or night was that we got our food during the daytime. During the day, therefore, and knowing that our room was on the port side of the ship, I would feel the steel side of the ship and determine from the differences in temperature between one visit and the next whether we were traveling west or north. If we were sailing west the steel would be about the same temperature all day. If we were moving north, however, the port side of the ship would be away from the sun in the morning, and would be perceptibly warmer in the afternoon. I also knew that this very ship had set a transpacific travel record of twenty-one days from Japan to the United States before the war had begun, so I figured we were probably heading for Japan and would reach there after about six days at sea.

On at least three occasions submarine scares broke the tedium of our voyage. I greeted these events with mixed emotions. On the one hand, they encouraged me to think that American submarines might well be in the area. On the other hand, there was the fear that one of our boats might torpedo the *Nitta Maru* under the impression that it was crowded with Japanese troops instead of American prisoners. And since our guards locked our door during these alarms, if an American submarine should sink the *Nitta Maru* there would be no chance for any of us to escape drowning.

We finally reached Yokohama on January 18, 1942. The next morning the Japanese came and got some of the officers and some of the enlisted men and took them up to the main deck. The rest of the officers and some of the men then went up on deck for some propaganda pictures for a magazine called *Freedom*, a Japanese version of *Life*. We were a motley-looking crew, dirty, unshaven, and wearing a hodgepodge of nondescript clothing. I had hopes that the pictures might find their way to the United States, perhaps by way of Switzerland, so that our families might at least know we were still alive.

At the same time as the picture session the Japanese allowed some of us to record messages home. I had some misgivings about this, but I decided that I should try to get word to my girlfriend and my family that I was still alive in case the photographs did not get that far. Some of these messages actually were broadcast and picked up by ham operators in the States. In my case, my recorded message provided the only indication for nearly a year that I had survived the final battle for Wake. (An official Red Cross message some months later advised my parents that my name *was not* on a list of those held prisoner by the Japanese.)

The *Nitta Maru* stayed in Japan for only a short time before lifting anchor and steaming southwest toward the Japanese-occupied Chinese port of Shanghai. I did not know it yet, but I would spend the next forty months of my life in China.

6

Woosung Prison

When the *Nitta Maru* nudged against the dock at Shanghai the weather, cold and rainy, seemed to match our mood. Shanghai had been a very cosmopolitan city before the arrival of the Japanese in the 1930s, and it still contained a large number of international residents. In spite of the nasty weather there were a few curious civilians and a smattering of Japanese and Chinese newsmen on hand to record our arrival. We found out later that the Japanese had planned for us to be the centerpiece of a great propaganda display. They were going to march us through the streets of the city to our nearby prison camp so the civilians—the Chinese as well as those of other nationalities—could witness not only the humiliation of the American prisoners of war but also the superiority of our Japanese conquerors. When the Japanese decided that the severe cold weather would probably keep the attendance at our little "parade" down, they canceled it. That was probably the only time of my entire captivity that bad weather turned out to be a blessing in disguise. We all felt bad enough about being prisoners in the first place without the added disgrace of being put on exhibit like circus animals. Instead of leaving us off in Shanghai for the planned public humiliation, the *Nitta Maru* moved down the river to the nearby port of Woosung, where we disembarked.

The prison compound, a former Chinese or Japanese army cavalry camp, was three or four miles away from the docks, and we were to make our way there on foot, but even this relatively short march proved to be very difficult for us. It had been a month since our capture, and during that time we had never had enough to eat. We were weak. Many of us were sick. What clothing we had was of tropical weight, unsuited to the brutal Chinese winter. In my case, my footwear was still limited to the ill-fitting hip boots that I had adapted on Wake, and every step I took on that hike was painful.

The sun had long since set by the time we finally arrived at our new quarters. There was no snow on the ground, but it looked as if that could change at any time. The temperature was at or below freezing, and the humidity made it seem considerably colder. Upon our arrival, Colonel Yuse, the camp commandant, climbed up onto a chair and addressed us at great length. A very small man, even by Japanese standards, he spoke no English, so we had no idea what he was saying. We could tell by his gesticulations, however, that he was in deadly earnest about whatever it was he was telling us. Every so often he would stop to get a second wind and allow his interpreter a few words. The gist of the colonel's "welcome," as translated, was "You must obey."

Following Yuse's speech the guards issued each man a pair of thin blankets, a cup, a bowl, and a spoon. I had already become so conditioned to privation that even this minimal gesture of humanity took me by surprise. They then showed sixteen of us officers into a room in a barracks. The word *barracks* should perhaps be defined as it applied to this situation. About the only resemblance to an American military barracks was its general outside appearance. Inside there was no furniture. Instead, our room had six-foot-wide platforms along each side and about two feet off the floor. These would be our sleeping platforms.

After we had gotten settled somewhat we received our first food issue in our new home. In my bowl of watery soup I found what appeared to be a small piece of meat. I was overjoyed at my good fortune until I bit into it and found that it was only gristle. Nevertheless, I worked on it for a half hour, determined to extract any juices or nutrients it might still contain. Finally, my jaws tiring from the unaccustomed exercise, I returned it to my now-empty bowl. Another prisoner spied it and asked almost incredulously, "Aren't you going to eat that?" I shook my head and started to explain why, but he snatched it up and was already chewing on it before I could even begin to speak. He seemed so happy to have it that I didn't have the heart to tell him that I had been eating on it, too. I only mention this as an example of how poorly fed we were. There was virtually never any leftover food or garbage in the prison camp. Someone would always eat whatever was left by anyone else and be glad to get it.

In spite of our recently issued blankets it was almost impossible to get warm enough to sleep that first night. (The Japanese later issued us cotton bags that we filled with rice straw for sleeping pallets, but for the first couple of weeks we slept directly on the hard wooden platforms.) Those of us in my room decided to pool our blankets and conserve our body heat. We split into two groups on opposite sleeping platforms. There were nine of us in my group, and we tried to sleep spoon fashion. That is, each of us lay on one side snug up against another man facing the same direction. This only works, of course, as long as everyone is content to sleep on the same side as everyone else in the group. If one man wants to turn over onto his other side, all must do so. We soon found that it was a miserable way to try to keep warm. Our diet of watery rice soup did not stay with us very long in the cold so each of us had to get up several times during the night to walk outside to the latrine. The constant disruption of the rest of the group each time someone got up did not permit much sleep.

The first few weeks in prison were particularly difficult for all of us. In this new, alien environment, where we were without basic necessities and were plagued by the cold and hunger, we could not even think clearly. We knew it was up to us, both individually and collectively, to try to improve our situation, but we didn't know where to start. Instead we spent many days feeling sorry for ourselves and complaining to anyone who would listen. This only made our depression worse. Everyone was in the same boat. No one wanted to listen to another man's woes because they were the same as his own. Like many others, I withdrew into myself and began to spend most of my time quietly alone. It was in this self-imposed solitude that I began to recall some of my earlier attempts at improvisation. Perhaps some of these experiences would transfer to my present predicament.

I remembered that as an eighth grader back in Endicott I had taken the magnet from an old telephone and some miscellaneous scraps of wood, tin, and wire, and put together a primitive electric motor. Another time Ray Darden's obsolete harvester broke a sprocket, and he and I went to his junk pile and cobbled together a replacement by using a few different-size sprockets (since we could not find the correct size) and changing several drive gears until we made it all work. The more I pursued this line of thought the more I realized that there were other examples within the last couple of months of our making do with whatever was on hand. Hadn't we planned to jury-rig gun sights on the F4Fs until the navy mechanics on the *Enterprise* installed the proper items? Hadn't the lack of adequate direction finders in our planes prompted me to make my own by winding wire in a coil around a cylinder and installing it in my plane? Hadn't Herb Freuler solved our bomb rack problem by applying a little common sense? And hadn't he also found a way to use welder's oxygen in our planes when our supply was exhausted?

What did these problems and their solutions tell me about my present dilemma? The first thing I had to do was define the problem. It might be something as simple as: "How can I stay warm?" Another problem for which I sought a solution was: "How can I find out what is going on in the rest of the world? Is the United States winning the war or losing it?" Having identified individual problems, I next had to list all the possible solutions, no matter how far-fetched they might seem at first. The third step was to determine what equipment or materials each of these possible solutions required for implementation. Fourth, I must determine how much of this material was obtainable. Finally, I would choose the best solution for the problem that I could accomplish with the material at hand. With such an analytical approach, I felt sure that many of our day-to-day problems could be solved, or at least alleviated to a great degree.

We had a lot to learn about survival in this new and hostile environment, and our indoctrination began early on the morning of our first full day at the Woosung prison camp. A Japanese bugler rousted us from our chilly bunks with what I guess was the Japanese version of Reveille. Then we had a few minutes to police the barracks and make it presentable for inspection. Because of our spartan furnishings and almost complete lack of any personal possessions the cleanup did not take very long. We folded our blankets on our sleeping platforms and used a couple of homemade mops to wet down the floor. When we finished we stood in front of our beds and waited for the inspection party to arrive. This group included the officer of the day, his guards, and an interpreter. We were to bow as the party approached, and the officer would acknowledge this with a salute. The ranking American officer in each room then made a short, memorized recitation in Japanese that the room was ready for inspection, and then, still speaking Japanese, he called us to attention and ordered us to count off. We were all required to respond, even the sick: *"Ichi"* (one), *"Ni"* (two), *"San"* (three), *"Shi"* (four), *"Go"* (five), *"Roku"* (six), *"Shichi"* (seven), *"Hachi"* (eight), and so on.[1]

After the completion of our first morning inspection we were free to leave the barracks and get a look at our surroundings. I didn't see too much to encourage me. In addition to our barracks there were six other equally ramshackle structures housing the rest of the captives. Each seemed to be about a hundred feet long and twenty-two feet wide. A few feet from one end of each barracks were wash racks, and a short way beyond them were latrines. A dirt road encircled all of this, and across the road from the latrines were a storage facility, the prison galley, a bathhouse, and one or two other nondescript buildings. An electrified wire fence with only one gate enclosed the entire compound. The Japanese living quarters and camp offices were just outside the fence.

We Wake Islanders were not the only inhabitants of the camp. Other prisoners had also just arrived. They included British embassy personnel from Shanghai and the crews of two gunboats captured or sunk on the opening day of the war, the H.M.S. *Peterel* and, ironically, the U.S.S. *Wake*. There were also a handful of U.S. Marines who had been in Shanghai waiting to ship out for Manila when the war started, and the civilian crews of a few merchant ships unlucky enough to have been caught up by hostilities.

The freedom of movement within the camp gave us a chance to determine with a fair degree of accuracy what our casualties had been on Wake. But we were unable to account for three navy enlisted men and two Marines from VMF-211. Men in the camp remembered seeing them as recently as January 19, when we were in Yokohama. They had been on a detail to empty the five-gallon latrine cans from the enlisted men's area. The one thing that we *did* know was that they were *not* in camp. Maybe they had somehow managed to escape, we mused. None of us knew until after the war what their true fate had been.

Sometime during the trip from Yokohama to Shanghai, Captain Toshio Saito, a guard officer on the *Nitta Maru*, selected five prisoners' names, apparently at random, for execution. At Saito's direction guards went down into the hold of the ship and took Sergeant Earl R. Hannum and Technical Sergeant William Bailey, both of VMF-211; Seaman First Class John W. Lambert; and Seamen Second Class Roy J. Gonzales and Theodore D. Franklin topside. Shortly, the guards led the men, blindfolded and with their hands tied behind them, onto an area of the main deck where most of the rest of the guards were drawn up in formation.

Saito climbed up onto a wooden platform and harangued the Americans for having killed Japanese troops during the fighting at Wake. As he neared the end of his little speech he announced that they, as representatives of the American armed forces, would pay for this "crime" with their lives. "It will do no good to the world to let you live," he continued. Then, displaying a common Oriental belief in reincarnation, he wished them happiness the next time around. "When you are born again," he concluded, "I hope you will become peace-loving citizens."

Sadly, the prisoners did not have long to ponder their fates. The execution ritual seemed to have been well rehearsed. Saito issued no more orders to his men, but they knew just what to do. One at a time the prisoners were ordered to kneel and bend their heads forward. One at a time a different executioner swung his sword through the air and decapitated an American. After the first such murder, the remaining Americans probably pieced together what had happened just from the sounds they heard. Their last seconds of life must have been filled with an awful, awful fear.

After the fifth murder the guards occupied themselves for some little time mutilating the corpses with bayoneted rifles. This final indignity was a standard form of behavior for many Japanese troops. Luckily these five Americans were past the point of suffering any more pain, and when the Japs finally tired of their sadistic "sport" they pushed the remains unceremoniously over the side and into the sea.[2]

About a week after our arrival at Woosung another group of prisoners joined us. These were some two hundred U.S. Marines who had been part of the embassy guard details in Peiping and Tientsin in northern China. The Japanese had arrested them on the first day of the war, but they seemed to be in much better spirits than the rest of us. They knew that their status as embassy personnel entitled them not only to diplomatic immunity during peacetime but would also get them repatriated back to the United States within a few weeks. From all outward appearances they also had every reason to believe that their treatment during their temporary confinement would be good. They came marching into camp dressed in warm woolen uniforms and still in possession of duffel bags and footlockers full of blankets, clothing, personal gear, and even alcohol. We stared in disbelief as they entered the compound. Some of the Wake Island civilians thought, from their well-clad appearance, that they must be Russians, although Russia and Japan were not at war with one another. The North China Marines were just as shocked by our destitution as we were by their relative opulence, and they shared their clothes and blankets as much as they could.

In 1941 the Marine Corps was the smallest of the services, so small that most of the Wake Island Marine officers and a fair number of the enlisted men recognized friends among the new arrivals. I had been a Marine for only a few years, but I soon saw a couple of my Basic School classmates, Lieutenants McBrayer and Huizenga. I will be forever grateful to James McBrayer for giving me a spare overcoat and other items from his personal wardrobe. The Japanese also alleviated our clothing shortage somewhat when they issued us Japanese army uniforms and shoes, and in spite of the generally poor fit of these items they helped us a great deal during that first winter. Even with a little more clothing, our first few weeks were bitterly cold. We wore all the clothes we owned all the time and even wrapped our meager blankets around us during the day in our efforts to try to stay warm. Some of the prisoners then lay down on their sleeping platforms and spent hours and hours hardly moving at all, afraid that the slightest shift in position might so disarray their carefully arranged clothing as to admit an icy blast of cold air. Others spent equally long periods pacing back and forth, hoping to generate enough body heat through exercise to make up for the lack of adequate clothing. Getting warm occupied almost every waking moment.

One day a couple of men out exploring the compound discovered a piece of tin about two feet square. They brought it inside and placed it on the floor of the barracks beneath one of the vents leading to the attic. Then they scrounged around some more until they had enough wood scraps and dried weeds to start a small, smoky fire on the tin. For a short time there was blessed heat in one section of the barracks, but the buildup of smoke in the attic soon started to billow out of the gable louvers at the ends of the building. This attracted the attention of a guard, who came rushing in thinking that the barracks was on fire. Prisoner lookouts gave the alarm when they saw the guard coming, and their comrades grabbed up the tin hearth and tossed it and the fire out the window before the suspicious sentry reached their room. Smoke was still evident in the room when he got there, but they were able to convince him that the smoke he saw was from cigarettes they had all been smoking. He seemed to buy that explanation, and the Americans thanked their lucky stars that they had not drawn a severe punishment down upon themselves. We all knew that even if there was no specific camp regulation against such a fire, the Japs would find some rule that had been broken.

Even though this attempt at fighting the cold had been cut short, it had been successful enough during its brief life to make us determined to improve upon it. We started thinking that we should build a regular fireplace. In the officer area of Barracks 2 there was an unoccupied room that the Japanese had sealed shut by nailing a couple of boards across it and posting a KEEP OUT notice in Japanese. It did not contain the sleeping platforms the other rooms held and was larger than any of the other places we could congregate. It was the ideal location for some sort of fireplace heating device. We had already dubbed this room our "wardroom," and we surreptitiously used it whenever we wanted—except at inspection time, when we resealed the door.

Construction of the fireplace proceeded smoothly. One of the men located a wooden box about four feet square and fourteen inches high. We brought in enough clay from the prison yard to fill it up so it could serve as a fireproof base. Then we reinforced the sides with pieces of brick and rock mortared together with mud. We even appropriated a length of stovepipe to lead the smoke out a window.

We were about ready to begin using our new luxury when Major Devereux decided it would probably be a good idea to get approval from Colonel Yuse. After all, this project was on a much larger scale than the earlier throwaway fire, and there would really be no way to hide its existence once we began to use it. He took a written request to the camp commander, whose interpreter translated it for him. Colonel Yuse then made a quick notation in Japanese on the note and handed it back to Devereux. When the major returned, we posted this approval in a conspicuous location, sort of like a building permit at a stateside construction site, so that any inquisitive guards would be mollified. Then we settled in to enjoy our warm fires.

We searched everywhere for something to burn. We even went up into the attic and removed every other roof brace to use for fuel. The fireplace was wonderful. It gave us a chance to wash and dry some of our clothes without risking a serious chill in the process. We also learned that we could each heat a brick in the fire by day and then put it in one of our blankets at night so its absorbed heat could warm us as we slept.

Each night, just before roll call, we carefully resealed the room and returned to our respective places for the head count. With that formality over, we would return to our snug little den and soak up a little more heat before lights-out. One night about midnight one of our officers, Navy Lieutenant Robert C. Walish, thought he smelled smoke. We had had a particularly hot fire going all day, so he went into the wardroom to investigate. He found that the clay fireplace base had become so overheated that the fire had spread to the surrounding floorboards. The entire fireplace had burned right through the floor of the barracks and settled to the ground some eighteen inches below. Luckily, we were able to extinguish the still-smoldering mess without alerting the guard who was patrolling outside the barbed-wire fence.

We had some serious repairs to make, and the situation took a more urgent turn when someone reminded us that the Japanese had scheduled a big inspection for the next morning—an inspection that would include this room. None of us slept that night. We took up boards from the sleeping platforms, wherever we thought we could get away with it, to use for replacement floorboards. Of course, even if no one noticed the occasional missing planks from the sleeping platforms, the rebuilt floor stood out like a sore thumb because the replacement boards were not as worn and dirty as the original floorboards. We solved this problem with liberal amounts of mud and water, which we worked into the pores of the patch job to resemble aging. Finally, we rebuilt the ruined fireplace to further conceal the damage. This time we built it up off the floor to lessen the chances of another such fire. We finished our repairs just in time to return to our sleeping areas for the morning inspection.

When Colonel Yuse and his party entered the wardroom for the inspection they walked all around the fireplace, examining it intently. The floor under it was so weak that the weight of the inspection party on adjacent boards tended to tip the fireplace slightly toward them. (It reminded me of the portraits whose eyes seem to follow the viewer all around the room.) I do not think the commandant really

A Curtis JN4-D "Jenny," the model in which a young John Kinney first experienced the thrills of flight. During his thirty-three years as an aviator, he would log over six thousand hours in more than sixty makes and models of aircraft, including jets, helicopters, and seaplanes. *Author's collection*

Kinney's classmates prepare to launch him into Oakland Bay after his first solo flight. *Author's collection*

Second Lieutenant
John F. Kinney, USMC,
in dress whites,
Hawaii 1941.
Courtesy G. Urwin

Wrecked F4F-3 Wildcats on Wake Island. Kinney was his squadron's
engineering officer—with no repair manuals and very few spare parts.
National Archives

Japanese officers inspect Wake's last Wildcat, in which Captain Herb Freuler shot down the Japanese pilot who had sunk the *Arizona*. *National Archives*

Two years and three months later, American bombers hit Japanese positions on Wake Island. *National Archives*

Kinney's first prison camp in Woosung, China, as it looked in 1945. In his second camp, in Kiangwan, he was able to use his formidable mechanical skills to improve his fellow POWs' plight, creating a radio, a hot plate, and other ingenious items from scratch. *Courtesy W. Taylor*

Kinney in a Chinese Communist uniform, happy to be away from the Japanese. In forty-seven days, he traveled approximately a thousand miles through and behind enemy lines. *Author's collection*

Members of the Chinese Communist unit that rescued Kinney, in action against the Japanese. *Author's collection*

The author's escape group on the day the Chinese Communists turned it over to the Nationalists. Left to right are Liu Young, the Communist interpreter; a Communist officer; John McAlister; Louis Bishop; a Communist intepreter; Richard Huizenga; James McBrayer; a Communist officer; Kinney; and two Nationalist officers. *Author's collection*

Two of the more senior second lieutenants in the Marine Corps, John McAlister, left, and Kinney, back in the United States in 1945.
U.S. Marine Corps

This Grumman F-9F Panther, from the squadron Kinney commanded in Korea, wore out sixteen 20mm cannons on its 445 combat missions. Kinney's solutions to the Panther's maintenance problems helped prove that jets could be reliable attack aircraft. *Department of Defense*

After his Korean War service, Kinney was recognized as an expert on jet attack planes. His recommendations helped lead to the classic A4 Skyhawk. Pictured is an A4M. *McDonnell Douglas Corp.*

Kinney shortly before his retirement from the Marine Corps in 1959 as a brigadier general. *Department of Defense*

The author, second from left, as a civilian test pilot for the Corvus missile program. *Vought Aircraft Co.*

Kinney and his wife, June, in China in 1979 with Liu Young, one of his rescuers. *Author's collection*

cared that we were using the room, but there was much excited finger pointing and jabbering about the stove. Major Devereux, seeking to justify its existence, proudly pointed to the permit posted on a nearby wall. The interpreter finally explained to him that the Japanese characters that Colonel Yuse had scribbled onto Devereux's request had said that the stove was *not* authorized. After a few thousand more words the commandant directed us to deliver the stove to the prison office.

As soon as Colonel Yuse and his staff left, six prisoners heaved the still-wet, and extremely heavy, mud-and-brick structure off the floor and headed across the prison yard toward the office with it. They looked for all the world like so many pallbearers. Before they reached their destination one of the men stumbled under the load and the whole thing came down in a heap, and that was the end of our fireplace.

In addition to warmth, our other most basic need during our early days in prison was food. The Japanese used Chinese labor to prepare the prisoners' food, but we quickly realized that we would fare much better if we could get our own cooks into the picture as soon as possible. We believed that our own supervision would be more efficient, and our control of the distribution would undoubtedly be more equitable. We did not have much luck convincing Colonel Yuse until after the arrival of the North China Marines. But we felt that our food would improve when we did get Americans, both civilians and Marines, into the galley. Of course, improvement is a relative concept. Our daily ration consisted of one cup of cooked rice, two cups of soup, and three cups of weak tea.

Even with Americans overseeing the preparation and distribution of our food there was still griping. For instance, the food for each barracks was carried from the galley in large buckets. Each man in the barracks presented his bowl for filling in a prearranged sequence. That way, if there was any food left over after everyone had received his ration, seconds were served out as far as they went. Then the next time there was enough food for seconds the distribution began where the previous one had ended. This occasionally led to arguments as to whose turn it was to be first in line for the extra food. There were also occasional charges of favoritism with regard to how the soup was ladled out. Someone might accuse the ladler of purposely not stirring the soup. That way any small pieces of vegetables or other nutrients fell to the bottom, where they could be dished out later to special friends of the server.

Another big problem for us was in the area of sanitation and personal hygiene. The latrines contained ten individual stalls, which provided a little bit of privacy, and had large earthenware pots under the floors to receive our waste. Neighboring Chinese farmers came into the camp every few days to remove this "night soil" for use as fertilizer on their farms. The prisoners gave them a wide berth as they jogged out of the camp with a "honey bucket" hanging from each end of a pole balanced across their shoulders. The Japanese issued toilet paper at the rate of only twelve sheets per man per year. Not only was this a ridiculously inadequate amount, but the eight-inch-square paper they *did* give us was only about as soft as 00 sandpaper. In the face of this shortage some of the men used newspapers, when they were available, but most of us kept a small can of water and a rag handy for such purposes. We washed the rags as best we could after each use so they would be available the next time we needed them.

On February 9, 1942, I was summoned, along with Commander Cunningham, Captain Tharin, and Captain Freuler, to Shanghai for some undisclosed reason. On the way out of camp, Marine Warrant Officer Paul Chandler slipped me some money and asked me to buy him some peanuts if I got the chance. Once we reached the city we were again under the control of the Imperial Japanese Navy and we experienced slightly more humane treatment than we had at the army facility at Woosung. The most obvious improvement was a chance to take our first bath since leaving Wake, almost a month before. In addition to the obvious psychological benefit of again being reasonably clean, this gave us a chance to get warm at least once a day. Up to this time, my feet had been cold continuously since arriving in China. The food was also a little bit better, and for two days we ate regular meals at the Cathay Mansions Hotel (now the Peace Hotel) in downtown Shanghai, where we went for questioning.

None of us had any idea of what to expect under Japanese questioning. We had not been through any indoctrination such as military personnel serving in later wars received. We had not received survival training. There was not then any emphasis that when captured one should only give his name, rank, and serial number. In fact, so little importance was attached to serial numbers that I doubt if very many of us even remembered what our numbers were. (In contrast, everyone who had been issued a rifle probably knew *its* number!) There was no such thing at the outbreak of World War II as "The Code of Conduct for POWs," so the only guide we had was common sense. We would not knowingly give out any information to the enemy that might help him.

All of us selected for questioning were pilots, and it very quickly developed that the Japanese were very interested in the performance of our aircraft now in service as well as those being built. The Japanese admiral in charge of this interrogation operation knew nothing about airplanes and seemed content to stay that way. He left all of the actual questioning up to a naval lieutenant. Our standard answer to all of his questions was, "In the United States, they only tell the pilot what he needs to know to fly his own plane. We don't know anything about any other planes." Surprisingly, after we had each repeated this over and over again, the lieutenant seemed to believe that we were indeed very poorly informed.

Unable to get any useful information from any of us, the lieutenant switched tactics and began to explain to us what he already knew about American planes. I guess it reinforced his low opinion of us to be able to educate us in this fashion. He and the admiral gloated as they showed us a recent issue of *Aero Digest*, complete with three-view diagrams of American warplanes. These plans were complete with manufacturers' performance specifications, and we expressed our amazement at their good fortune to have this information since this was the first any of us had seen of it. Then they produced pictures of the Douglas and Boeing hangars, and early prototypes of our B-17 bombers.

Our interrogation sessions, after we had exhibited our "ignorance" about most American aircraft, were not especially taxing. The two Japanese officers treated us humanely and seemed to respect the fact that we, too, were officers and professional soldiers. Perhaps they would not have been so polite if they had been dealing with enlisted men, but for whatever reason I began to feel *almost* at ease. It didn't take much effort to divert the Japanese lieutenant from questioning us to boasting about the superior features of his country's aircraft. He was particularly proud of the dive brakes on Japanese dive-bombers.

While we were in temporary residence in the Shanghai prison we received the sad news that Singapore had fallen on February 15, 1942. We also learned that the huge liner *Normandie* had burned and turned over on its side in New York Harbor. Our captors delighted in passing bad news on to us.

At the prison we met a British naval officer, Commander Sheppard from the British embassy. As he waited for repatriation, he passed his time studying the Japanese language, learning not only to read it but to write it. He said that Japanese was much easier to master than Russian and advised us that in case we were interested the best book on the language was written by an Italian couple named Vaccari and was titled *Japanese-English Conversation Grammar*.[3] I didn't think at the time that I would have any use for this bit of information but filed it away in my memory anyway.

On our second day at the Cathay Hotel, right before the Japanese shifted our interrogations to the Shanghai prison, the Japanese lieutenant offered to take us to a market where we could buy some items. Our money supply was limited to what Chandler had slipped me, but the lieutenant offered to exchange it for Chinese dollars for us to use at the market. This put me in a minor quandary. I had thus far observed nothing in the nature of the Japanese that engendered the slightest amount of trust. The troops back on Wake, after all, had systematically stolen everything of value from us. I seemed to have no choice but to accept the lieutenant's offer. I could give him the money voluntarily, or he could simply take it from me. I grudgingly turned it over, not knowing whether I would ever see it again, but he was true to his word and returned shortly with Chinese dollars. I felt a little sheepish about holding such suspicions about him. I guess if he had wanted our little bit of money he simply could have taken it without bothering to make up a story about exchanging it for local currency. At the market I bought some peanuts for Chandler, a pound of hard candy, a Japanese notebook, and—fortunately, as it turned out—the aforementioned Japanese-English language book. The prices were reasonable, and I even had some money left over.

The Japanese admiral warmed to us enough to tell us what an accomplished bird hunter he was and to promise to provide us a full dinner of Chinese pheasant before we returned to Woosung. In spite of the amicable feelings we had experienced during our little interlude at Shanghai we all realized that a sufficient amount of food would likely be one of our most serious problems as prisoners of war. So although we certainly hoped that the promised dinner would indeed materialize we were not going to skip any meals in anticipation of it. On the day before our scheduled return to Woosung we ate our regular lunch in the Shanghai jail just in case the admiral reneged. Happily for us, he was as good as his word. We were his guests at the Cathay Hotel for a magnificent meal. In spite of having already eaten at the jail we dug in with considerable gusto. The food—although not in great quantity—was better than we had enjoyed in quite some time. We did not leave a crumb.

Since our interrogation sessions had not proved to be very profitable to the Japanese we returned to the prison at Woosung on February 26, coming once again under the control of the Japanese army. I delivered the peanuts and the leftover money to Chandler and parceled out the candy to the surviving enlisted men of VMF-211. Each man got only one piece of candy, but even that pitiful amount was greatly appreciated. In fact, one of the men very sincerely asked my opinion on how to get the most value from that single piece of hard candy. He finally settled on using it to sweeten and flavor his tea. He let about half of it dissolve before carefully retrieving it and saving the second half for another time. Sadly, this man later died in the camp.

Everyone appreciated the peanuts, but their effect on those who ate them was not entirely beneficial. We later decided that they had either been inadequately roasted or perhaps had absorbed moisture in the humid climate. Whatever the reason, everyone who ate them came down with severe diarrhea. Of course, our digestive systems had been denied rich food for so long that that might also have been a contributing factor to the sickness that followed.

I put my other purchases to good use, too. I used the notebook to record the events of the defense of Wake while the memories were still fresh. I recorded the names of the men of VMF-211 in it and also used it to begin a list of useful Japanese words and phrases.

Lieutenant McBrayer and I began daily study sessions in the Japanese language book. We had no idea how long we would be the guests of the Greater East Asia Co-Prosperity Sphere, so learning some of the language might prove helpful. Newspapers occasionally found their way into our camp, and being able to read them would help keep us current on the progress of the war and other world events. It would also be nice to understand what our guards were saying about us.

We began our study much like kindergarten students beginning to learn to recognize English letters and words—we made flash cards. We took the cardboards that came in the cigarette packages we received from the Japanese. Each ten-cigarette package had two of these cardboards, and it did not take long to lay in quite a supply. We found that fifty characters of Katakana, the simple characters, enabled us to write most of the words we were learning. We eventually discovered, however, that such a simple task as reading a newspaper required the knowledge of some eighteen hundred such characters. Our progress was slow, but our daily lessons helped to pass the time and keep our minds off the cold and our hunger.

These basic uses for the language book quickly gave way, in my mind, to plans for escape. I would have to convince McBrayer or some other North China Marine to make the attempt with me, so as to take advantage of any geographical knowledge they might have. At first that was not so easy. These men still held out hope that the Japanese would live up to accepted international custom and exchange them as diplomatic prisoners instead of holding them as prisoners of war.

While I had been away from Woosung, the prison staff had instituted a work program for the enlisted men. The Japanese work orders were originally intended for all prisoners, including officers, but Colonel William W. Ashurst, a North China Marine and our ranking officer, reminded the commandant that according to the 1929 Geneva Convention Relative to the Treatment of Prisoners of War, only enlisted men could be expected to work. Officers, because of their exalted status, *could* work, but only if they volunteered.[4] Ashurst quickly disabused Yuse of any idea that we would voluntarily work, but suggested, as a way for the commandant to save face, that the American officers would volunteer to supervise various work projects.

The first of these work details did not get off to a very auspicious start. The guards assembled the men, divided them into three work groups, and passed out shovels, hoes, and picks. The camp commandant issued lengthy instructions, which the interpreters relayed simply as, "Now dig." After puzzling over this for a bit, most of the men dutifully, but very slowly, began to remove dirt from the area in which they were standing. Another problem then arose. Where should they deposit the newly dug dirt? The guards *finally* got the Americans to understand that the object of this work project was to make the field level. They were to cut down the high spots and fill in the low spots. Knowing the intent of the project did not make it get done any sooner or any better. With no incentive to work, the men instead made conscientious efforts to stretch the task out for as long as possible. The Japs were not amused.[5]

On March 11, 1942, only a couple of weeks after my return from questioning in Shanghai, news of an escape swept through the camp like a prairie fire. Commander Cunningham, Commander John B. Wooley (Royal Navy), Dan Teters (the construction superintendent on Wake), Commander Columbus D. Smith of the U.S.S. *Wake*, and Smith's young Chinese servant, Liu, were gone! They had made their getaway under cover of darkness by digging a small trench under the electric fence behind Barracks 3 with a stolen shovel and then wriggling under. The guards did not discover their absence until morning roll call the next day. By then they had a six-hour lead on any pursuit, and a thick fog had rolled in. Their considerable head start and the dismal weather both worked in their favor. The make-up of the escape party further enhanced their chance of success. Wooley and Smith were old China hands who knew the area around Shanghai very well, and Liu would be of great value as an interpreter.

The escape reflected poorly upon Colonel Yuse. The only thing that could be worse for him, in this culture where "saving face" was of such great importance, was if his soldiers failed to recapture the runaways. The commandant immediately brought in dogs to track the escapees. A guard retrieved some clothing that the men had left in a barracks and brought it out to the hole in the fence so the dogs could get the scent of their prey. After dutifully sniffing the clothes, one of the "bloodhounds" took one look at the fence and turned and went directly to the galley. Perhaps he was as hungry as we all were. Most of the others seemed to know what was expected of them and led their handlers off across country.

We were all glad to hear of this escape and hoped that Commander

Cunningham and the others would make it to friendly lines, but at the same time I felt as if they had beaten me to the draw. Whether this first group made good its escape or not, the Japanese would be more vigilant against any future attempts, and that was bad news for me. Maybe I had been too complacent up until now, too cautious in planning for my own getaway.

A couple of days after the escape, Japanese soldiers escorted Cunningham, Wooley, Teeters, and Smith back into camp. They were trussed up as we had been immediately after our capture on Wake, with their hands bound behind their backs and loops of rope snugly around their necks. Guards had told us quite proudly that the Americans had been recaptured within a day of their escape, but up until now we had refused to believe it. Here was irrefutable proof. Nobody got a chance to talk to any of them to see what had gone wrong with their plan, and the guards soon whisked them away to another prison in Shanghai.

The Japanese reaction to the escape attempt was increased vigilance, as I had feared, and a second electric fence. This one enclosed just the seven barracks, the wash racks, and the latrines, although there were gates through which we could get to the other buildings, located within the outer fence. On the back side of the barracks, the new fence passed so close to the buildings, within a couple of feet, that it was almost impossible to walk between the fence and the buildings. Our guards told us that in order to conserve electricity they turned on this fence only after evening roll call, and they turned it off again after morning roll call. We found out, tragically, that this was not always the case when Corporal Carroll Boucher was electrocuted while trying to throw some onion plants over the fence to a friend for transplanting. Somehow he got too close to the fence, and the shock threw him to the ground. Those nearby immediately called for a doctor, and within seconds Dr. William T. Foley, the navy surgeon on duty with the North China Marines, was at Boucher's side trying to resuscitate him. He worked over him for an hour before finally admitting that he could not bring him back. A senseless death.

A few days later Colonel Yuse ordered all the prisoners to assemble in the open and presented us with another rambling list of camp regulations, similar to those that had been posted on board the *Nitta Maru* and reproduced here verbatim:

NOTICE

(I) War-Prisoners should comply with the following regulations:

    (I)   War-Prisoners should absolutely comply with the orders issued to them by the personnel of the Camp (including the orders of the guard).

(2)   War-Prisoners should make obeisunce to the Imperial Japanese soldiers and officials in the military service.

(3)   War-Prisoners should keep the premises as well as the barracks, particularly the latrines, in sanitary condition and should keep their bodies clean.

(4)   War-Prisoners should not smoke except at the smoking place, in the barracks or premises, where the ash-trays are fixed and at the same time, should not carry the matches with them exceeding the number permitted.

(5)   War-Prisoners should be obedient to the instructions issued to them by their adjutant and section leader.

(6)   War-Prisoners should submit the propositions or petitions in order, to the officer of the day (the week) in case you would like to do so.

(7)   War-Prisoners who violate the Regulations or commit any act of violence or attempt to escape or disobey the orders and instructions issued to them by the personnel and guard of the Camp, should be heavily punished with the imprisonment, confinement, etc.

War-Prisoners who disobey the orders fo restraint issued to them by the personnel of the Camp (including the guards), attempting to escape or committing acts of violence might be shot or stabed to death.

(8)   War-Prisoners should not approach the electric barbed wires across three metres as they are charged night and day.

(9)   War-Prisoners should not go out of the premises across the road (including the road) surrounding the barracks except when they are going to the hospital for medical examination or to the kitchen for work.

(2)   War-Prisoners who attempt to escape or those who allow their fellow-war-prisoners to escape should be punished as follows:

(I)   Those who, in spite of their being able to foresee the attempt to escape, do not ~~inform inform~~ dissuade them and do not inform the section leader of that fact should be punished with the confinement not exceeding thirty (30) days.

The adjutant and other war-prisnoers should be punished with the confinement not exceeding ten (I0) days.

(2)   Those who are found unsuccessfuly in the attempt at escape should be punished with the confinement not exceeding thirty (30) days.

The section leader and the other war-prisnoers should be punished with the confinement not exceeding seven (7) days.

(3)   Those who allow their fellow war-prisoners to escape while they are outside the Camp under the control of guard should be punished with the confinement not exceeding thirty (30) days including the section leader.

The adjutant should be punished with the confinement not exceeding ten (IO) days.

(4)   Besides, the above-mentioned war-prisoners should be punished under the Article 8 of the Order of Punishment according to their crimes.

(3)   War-Prisoners who violate the Regulations when they are outside the Camp under the control of guard, if so recognized, should be punished with the confinement not exceeding three (3) days including the section leader, and at the same time, they should be prohibited from going out after that.[6]

Colonel Yuse then insisted that we each sign the following pledge:

1.   I will not attempt to escape from the control of the Japanese military authorities.

2.   I will exercise proper care in the preservation of all property issued to me by the Japanese authorities.

3.   I will be obedient to the orders and instructions issued by the camp authorities at this internment camp.[7]

The idea of promising not to try to escape was ludicrous, and none of us agreed to sign any such document. Colonel Yuse told us that we would stand in formation until we signed, and after a few hours some prisoners began collapsing from weakness. Finally, Colonel Ashurst, in an attempt to prevent further harm to the prisoners, told Colonel Yuse that we would sign if he could first add a statement at the end of the pledge. The commandant didn't care what Ashurst wrote on the paper as long as it was followed by the signatures of all the men under his command. The document, as finally signed, contained a disclaimer just above our signatures: "Signed in accordance with a direct Japanese order, under duress and with the threat of terminal punishment."[8]

I signed with the others, but I certainly did not consider any such agreement to be binding on me under the circumstances, and continued to plan some way to escape. It did not take long to see that others obviously felt the same way. On March 27, just ten days after signing our "agreement," four North China Marines calmly walked away from a work detail outside the fence and were gone. This brightened things for all of us left behind even though it would probably mean increased watchfulness on the part of the guards. This time there was no official mention of their recapture. It was only two years later, when Dan Teeters returned to our camp after serving his jail sentence for escaping, that we learned that these escapees had been retaken a couple of weeks after making their break. The only other escape attempt in 1942 was made by Platoon Sergeant Raymond L. Coulson and Navy Corpsman A. T. Brewer, but the Japanese caught them both almost immediately.

I continued to study my Japanese-language flash cards so I could hope to read the occasional newspaper that found its way into camp. This was the only way we had of finding out what was going on outside the prison, and this type of knowledge was vital to any plans for escape. Getting out of the camp itself would be the easy part. The difficulty would come, as Commander Cunningham and his comrades had found, in reaching friendly lines. Before I tried to escape, therefore, I had to have some idea of in what direction and how far I would have to travel in order to reach safety. Before long, however, the Japanese began to send in newspapers printed in English—they were *Japanese* newspapers, but printed in English. They wanted us to be able to read of Japanese victories in the Philippines and elsewhere to further depress our morale. One of these papers had an account of how Japanese forces had captured Wake on *December 11, 1941*! They would not even admit to their own people that we had held them off for almost two more weeks.

Just in case we didn't read of their successes, they presented the camp with AM radios, one for each barracks. They were adjusted to pick up only the Japanese-sanctioned station in Shanghai, but they were better than nothing. During the regular daytime broadcasts we listened to Russian news (in English) that covered the European operations, and news from the Vichy French (also in English) that gave the Japanese propaganda version of Pacific operations, all of which we took with more than a grain of salt. McBrayer and I immediately began to try to convert these radios to pick up short-wave signals from farther away.

We enlisted the support of Sergeant Frederick B. Mohr, a North China Marine, who had brought a set of earphones and other miscellaneous radio hardware into Woosung and buried it for just such a venture as we had planned. With the North China Marines still holding out some hope of a diplomatic exchange, we decided that I would be the one to operate our secret radio so as not to jeopardize their status. Sergeant Mohr, however, was glad to help and designed a circuit with another tuning condenser and a tube base with a shortwave coil that allowed me to remove a standard tube and insert the adapter that made the radio into a shortwave set. Of course, I couldn't very well listen in to these shortwave broadcasts by way of the barracks loudspeaker to which the radio was hooked up. Sergeant Mohr came through again by providing an old speaker frame, and I fashioned a paper cone for it and installed it in the barracks. With this speaker in place I rigged a quick disconnect for both speakers.

At night, after lights-out, I disconnected the speaker and hooked up the earphones and a makeshift antenna, inserted the adapter, and listened to the news from New Delhi and San Francisco. This was how I first heard the news of Jimmy Doolittle's bomber raid on Tokyo on April 18, 1942; the American landings at Guadalcanal on August 7, 1942; and the general progress of the rest of the battles in the South Pacific. My shortwave set helped me to learn to dissect the Japanese version of the news more accurately and to confirm earlier interpretations of what we heard on the AM radio.

During this period the Japanese ordered our enlisted men and civilians to polish expended brass artillery shells intended for reloading. Colonel Ashurst immediately protested, citing the provision of the Geneva Convention that forbade POWs from being forced to do anything to aid their captors' war effort. The commandant assured Ashurst that the shells these men were polishing were not going to be used against the Americans but were intended to be used to fire only ceremonial salutes. Ashurst really had no bargaining position, so twenty to thirty prisoners began to report every day to the shell-polishing area outside the fence to do the work. Their immediate supervisor seemed happy that they showed up at all and set a quota of only two shells per day. The prisoners did not work with much diligence, however, and most finished only about one shell per week. Perhaps at least as perplexing to the Japanese as the slow pace at which these Americans worked was how clumsy they seemed to be. They were forever dropping the shells or somehow bumping them so hard against table legs as to dent them beyond reuse. The shell polishing continued for quite some time, although it served more to dispel the boredom of the men assigned to it than to provide any real service to the Japanese war effort.[9]

Another prisoner work assignment was in a Japanese army truck repair shop a few miles away. Again Ashurst protested, and again his protests were of no avail. Just like the prisoners on the earlier field-leveling and shell-polishing projects, the men working in the garage also surprised the Japanese with how little productive work they were able to accomplish. Those assigned to this detail realized what a golden opportunity it was for sabotage. They "fixed" a number of the Japanese trucks so that they were soon beyond repair altogether. The prisoner-mechanics turned their situation into an advantage at every opportunity. During the cold weather they often stole truck tires and cut them up to fuel the stove in the shop. This was the only way they could keep warm. When a truck driver came for his vehicle and saw that it was missing a tire, he simply had the POWs steal a tire from another truck and put it on his. This system worked pretty well throughout the coldest part of the winter.

These workers also stole anything else they could possibly smuggle into camp. They even managed to steal alcohol that was used in the shop as a cleaning solvent for greasy parts and tools. The most common method of getting this alcohol back to camp involved taking a piece of truck tire inner tube, sealing one end, filling it with alcohol, and then sealing the other end. At the end of the day they would fasten these contraptions around their waists under their clothing and nonchalantly stroll back into camp right under the noses of the guards. Of course, even a little bit of alcohol in a man with so little food in his system as most of us had produced intoxication very rapidly. The Japanese had very little patience with the booze smugglers, but one quick-thinking Marine saved himself what would probably have been a severe beating by convincing camp authorities that he needed the alcohol to rub on his rheumatism.[10]

These minor acts of sabotage encouraged all of us to do likewise, but we had to be careful not to push the limits of our guards' patience. Beatings, some severe, were not an uncommon occurrence at Woosung. In one instance, Lieutenant Huizenga borrowed some tools to make some minor improvements or repairs in his quarters, and for some reason this did not sit well with Isamu Ishihara, Colonel Yuse's sadistic civilian interpreter. He took a club and beat Huizenga into unconsciousness.

Against this backdrop of shortage and ill treatment we sought amusement wherever we could find it. I knew that as long as I could keep my sense of humor there was hope for the future. I had to look pretty hard at some situations in order to find something to smile about, but sometimes it paid off. Navy Lieutenant (j.g.) James B. Robinson wrote the following poem about Colonel Yuse:

There was a camp commander named USELESS,
    He was old and bald and toothless.
When he was young he suffered a very bad fall
    And for the rest of his life he was juiceless.

A half century later, it does not seem all that hilarious, but at the time we were quite fond of repeating it to each other.

Sometimes we even found humor in our recollections about the battle for Wake. One of the men recalled that during the battle he saw two men carrying a wounded comrade on a stretcher toward the hospital. As they were carrying this heavy load all three men heard the drone of more approaching Japanese bombers. The "wounded" man instantly jumped off the stretcher and outran the other two to the safety of the underground hospital bunker.

One day while several officers were digging in the plot that was to be our garden, they heard someone in the barracks calling, "Captain Platt, Captain Platt." When Platt responded, the man inside said, "Telephone." This was so ludicrous it just about doubled everyone up. None of us by this time had even heard a telephone in two years.

As the days got longer and the temperature got warmer the prison population of flies and mosquitoes mushroomed, and there was no way to avoid the incessant buzzing and biting. Not only were they bothersome, they also posed a very real threat to our health. The flies, for example, were thick around the latrines, and there was nothing to stop them from visiting the galley immediately after the honey pots. Malaria-carrying mosquitoes were also more than just a nuisance. Our windows had no screens, and there were never enough mosquito nets in camp to be effective. Colonel Yuse, instead of requisitioning sufficient screens and nets, decided that the key to this pest-control problem was for the prisoners to manually exterminate all of the unwanted flying creatures. I am sure that the colonel's apparent concern for our health was not due to any humanitarian feelings toward us but rather to the thought that a healthier prison population was also one from which he could conceivably extract more labor. Secondarily, if we somehow eliminated the flies and mosquitoes from the prison compound, they would also be less likely to infest his own quarters and those of the rest of his staff.

Camp authorities ordered each prisoner to turn in a specific number of dead flies and mosquitoes every day, but even though we all realized that we would benefit, it was often hard to muster the necessary energy to go bug hunting. Soon the Japanese offered a bounty—one cigarette for every ten flies. This reward system produced immediate results, as even those prisoners who did not smoke could always use extra cigarettes for trading purposes. The Japs were soon paying out so many cigarettes that they decided they were being too generous. So they upped the ante to one cigarette for every *hundred* dead flies. This took some of the steam out of the men. A hundred flies was just too much for only one cigarette. Still, there were some enterprising prisoners who persisted. One man crafted a giant twelve-by-twelve-inch fly swatter and then went out to the latrines to hunt. He almost always was able to kill several flies with each swat. Some of the North China Marines thought to look in the shades and reflectors of the overhead lights and were rewarded with hundreds of tiny corpses ready for harvesting. We were never able to completely eliminate the problem, but our efforts certainly did no harm.[11]

On June 9, 1942, we suddenly got word that Warrant Officer Chandler, four other Marines captured at Shanghai at the outbreak of war, and the British embassy personnel were going to be repatriated. They left almost immediately, and after Chandler's return to the United States, he and the other Marines did an outstanding job of writing to the relatives of the Woosung POWs. For most families, mine included, this was the first accurate information about their loved ones they had received. One sad note was that it was now obvious that the Japanese had no intention of releasing the rest of the North China Marines. The bright side was that McBrayer and Huizenga now wholeheartedly embraced the escape planning that I had been engaged in from the start. Their rudimentary knowledge of the Chinese language would be of inestimable value once we got out of the camp and headed for friendly forces. We might not have to rely on sign language to seek help from the locals. If I could also learn a little Japanese, our chances for success would improve even more.

I continued to monitor my secret radio and release bits of information to the others so there would be a general sense of the progress of the war. By the late summer of 1942 we were all aware that Japan's phenomenal early success had stopped and that the United States had begun the long fight back. It helped our morale to have this optimistic information. In fact, we began to bet with one another as to when the Allies would reach certain milestones in the progress of the war. When would Turkey finally enter the war against Germany? When would American and British forces invade German-held France and liberate Paris? How about the Philippines? When would MacArthur recapture them? Of course, none of us had any money to cover any of these bets, but we all promised to pay up after the war. (I paid off over forty dollars' worth of my losing bets, but I never collected a penny from those I won.)

When the war started going badly for the Japanese they took away the radios that they had presented with such fanfare earlier. They also conducted more frequent, and more thorough, searches of our quarters. During one such search they found my earphones, without which I would not even be able to rig up a primitive crystal set with which to pull in even the Shanghai station. I think some of the guards who understood English must have overheard some of the prisoners discussing war news that came in over my set, and this led camp authorities to conduct these searches.

We also lost our newspapers, but not before we saw an article by a recently returned Japanese diplomat from temporary internment in the United States. He complained bitterly about his treatment, stating that the oppressive Americans had even expected him to cook his own bacon and eggs! When we read this our diets were down to about five hundred calories per day, and none of them came from bacon or eggs. To say that we were less than sympathetic to this man's plight would be an understatement.

At the same time that the camp commandant suspended our newspapers he ordered every prisoner in the camp to commence the study of the Japanese language. This seemed rather pointless to me since we no longer had anything to read. It also just rubbed me the wrong way to be ordered to do something like that, and I could not bring myself to comply. Not only did I discontinue the studies that I had begun on my own, I made a conscious rebellious effort to forget everything I had already learned. I realized later that I hurt myself more by this attitude than I gained in the satisfaction of not following the orders of the enemy.

Camp discipline tightened up even further when orders came down forbidding the playing of cards, which had occupied a part of every Sunday for some prisoners. A lot of the men had taken the same cigarette package cardboards that McBrayer and I were using for our flash cards and made decks of playing cards from them. The ban on card playing seemed to be nothing more than a petty attempt to lower our morale even further. Naturally, it was passively resisted.

One method the inveterate card players used was to station a lookout who would shout a warning at the approach of any guard. Of course, the warning had to be something that would not inspire suspicion in the guard when he heard it, so the lookout would shout "Air bedding." This was a likely call, since we did have to shake out our blankets and hang them in the sun periodically. We could only wash them on hot summer days, so we aired them when we had the chance instead. Whenever a guard entered the compound and headed for the first barracks you would hear the call, "Air bedding." This was passed from barracks to barracks and was the signal to hide everything not authorized and to shake out a blanket or two just to make things look legitimate. This system worked for about a month, until a guard somehow got into the compound without being spotted by the lookout. He burst in upon a card game, grabbed all the contraband cards, and yelled "Air bedding!" After that we learned to change our signals more frequently.

In the fall of 1942, Colonel Yuse, who had never seemed to me to be the picture of health, died of an apparent heart attack at the age of sixty-four. His replacement was Colonel Satochi Otera, whose luxuriant mustache earned him the prison nickname "Handlebar Hank."

By this time, too, through the efforts of the Swiss consul general in Shanghai, Edouard Egle, the camp began to receive fairly regular shipments of food and clothing from the International Red Cross. A truck arrived in camp every couple of weeks with supplies. Red Cross reports showed that a typical shipment might include five hundred pounds of ham, which would not have gone very far to feed fifteen hundred men even if we had actually gotten any of it. I remember that after one of these meat shipments arrived the guards called the mess officer and each of the barracks adjutants out and lined them up in the galley, where, under the watchful eyes of the visiting Red Cross representatives, they got to see all this food. It was all for show. As soon as the requisite propaganda photographs were taken and the visitors had been ushered out to their waiting vehicles and were out of sight, the guards removed all the meat from our camp. Sadly, Mr. Egle was completely taken in by the Japanese charade. He and others of the International Red Cross honestly believed that the donations of food they had worked so hard to arrange for us literally made the difference between life and death for many prisoners. The truth is that we saw little, if any, of this food. It wound up instead on the dinner tables of the camp's Japanese officers and guards.

As our second winter in China approached, Mr. Egle was able to send in a great deal of clothing to us. Sweatshirts, corduroy trousers, and coats were among the apparel items we used to augment the Japanese army uniforms that had been issued to us. We welcomed the clothes and could certainly have used the Red Cross food.

On December 6, 1942, we moved to another camp, called Kiangwan, about ten miles away and closer to Shanghai. We heard different rumors as to the reason for the transfer. Some said our new camp was right between two Japanese airfields so that Allied bombers would be hesitant about attacking either one of them out of fear that some of their bombs might fall on us. Others believed that it was just so we would be closer to the site of a new work project the Japs had in mind for us. One thing was certain. Very few prisoners held any hope that our living conditions would improve at the new site.

7

Kiangwan Prison

The camp at Kiangwan, although similar in general layout to the one at Woosung, incorporated several changes. Instead of a simple electric fence, an eight-foot-high brick wall surrounded the compound and effectively reduced communication between any of us on the inside and Chinese civilians on the outside. An electric fence was mounted on top of this wall—which not only made it less likely that a prisoner could get over the wall to freedom but also meant that we were not as likely to accidentally electrocute ourselves, as Corporal Boucher had.

By this time the Japanese had modified our living arrangements slightly. We still lived in the same run-down sort of buildings as before, but officers now occupied small rooms in one end of each barracks while the enlisted men continued to reside in large bays. This situation allowed me a lot more privacy; I had only two roommates—Navy Ensign James J. Davis, Jr., and Marine Lieutenant Robert W. Greeley.

By the time of our transfer to Kiangwan we had been prisoners for almost a year, and it had been a very difficult year. We spent most of the time merely trying to survive, both physically and emotionally. Early hopes that the war would be short and we would all soon be free had faded by then. Most of us never doubted the eventual outcome of the war, but we had resigned ourselves to what could very well be a lengthy period of confinement, and we began to search for ways to actively alleviate our unfortunate situation. It was time to quit feeling sorry for ourselves and do something about it!

Just before Christmas, my second as a prisoner of war and my first in China, we received our first individual Red Cross packages. It was tremendously uplifting to have this tangible evidence that we had not been forgotten, that people in America cared about us and were doing what they could to ease our difficult situation. Typically each box contained a can of powdered milk, a couple of cans of Spam, two or three cans of corned beef, a can of powdered Nescafé instant coffee, a can of hardtack, a few bars of concentrated chocolate, a small can of butter, some small cans of jam, several packs of cigarettes, sometimes a box of prunes or raisins, and a can opener.[1] The boxes weighed about eleven pounds each, and none of us would have accepted eleven pounds of gold in their stead. Not only did they have a beneficial effect on our morale, their contents quite literally helped save the lives of some of our sick comrades. Had these packages arrived earlier in my confinement I might have been tempted to consume the contents in one huge feast, but I realized that I might not see another such windfall for quite some time and budgeted myself accordingly. Some of the prisoners could not resist, however, and gorged themselves on the relatively rich fare, only to become very, very ill. Most of the men formed small groups and pooled their supplies. For example, five prisoners might share in the opening of one man's ten-ounce can of corned beef. Then, a few days later, another member of the group would share his. This enforced conservation and made the food seem to last longer. Over the course of the next two and a half years we each received several more Red Cross food parcels. There is no telling how many we would have received if the camp guards had not pilfered the shipments on a regular basis. I believe that the Japanese officials held out for their own use at least as many Red Cross packages as those they allowed to get to the prisoners.

For prisoners with the nicotine habit the American cigarettes in the Red Cross packages were almost as welcome as the food. Some even contended that smoking dulled their appetites to the point that they were better able to cope with the short prison rations. I was not a smoker, but I found the cigarettes valuable as a trading medium. I could always find someone willing to trade some of his rice or other food for a couple of smokes.

Most of the Red Cross food items were packaged in tin cans and were relatively fresh. The exception was the chocolate bar, which was in standard paper wrapping. The first time I took the wrapping off one of these bars I saw that it contained hundreds of small worms. What a disappointment! It had been so long since I had tasted something like chocolate that I thought there must be some way to salvage it. Seeing that most of the other men had made similar discoveries, we got together and worked out a plan for eating the worm-infested delicacies. The method that evolved was to unwrap the chocolate bar and shout, to make the worms crawl to the far end of the bar, and then take a small bite off the near end. We then carefully wrapped the remaining chocolate back in its paper and repeated the entire process the next day. Of course, there had to come a day when the last bite had to be taken. When this day arrived we would shake the bar hard and gulp it down. We were *very* hungry!

The food supplied by the Japanese continued to be of very poor quality. For example, the rice we got was apparently the sweepings from the floor of some Chinese warehouse or had been threshed on the ground and then swept up without any attempt to separate out the dirt and rocks from the rice. This led to both good and bad results. The positive aspect was that we tended to eat slowly to avoid swallowing this debris, but the bad side was that many prisoners inadvertently chomped down on bits of rock and broke their teeth. We even suspected that the Chinese, who sold the rice to the Japanese by weight, might have intentionally inflated the weight by adding these bits of rock and dirt. Whatever the cause of the contaminated rice was, we had to figure out some way to deal with it, and once again it was an officer from VMF-211 who developed a fix.

We rotated mess officers every few months, and when Herb Freuler served in this capacity he designed a very ingenious device for separating the rocks from the rice. It was a wooden sluice box, very much like those used by the gold miners of the nineteenth century. Within the box was an inclined ramp with intersecting cross bars every few inches. To operate it one introduced rice with water at the top of the incline and the mixture flowed down across the slats. The pebbles, since they were heavier than the grains of rice, settled out faster and lodged against the baffles while the rice and water flowed on over them. It was then a simple matter to scoop out the rocks and repeat the process until all of that day's rice ration had been sluiced. The Japanese were quite impressed with Captain Freuler's ingenuity, and the prisoners were grateful that they now had less of a risk of damaging their teeth.

Late in 1943, the Red Cross was able to begin sending in monthly supplies of cracked wheat to augment the rice that was such a staple of our diet. The wheat came from an accumulation of American famine relief supplies destined for China a few years earlier. In fact, I remembered making contributions toward this effort long before the United States entered the war. The Japanese overran much of China before the wheat could all be delivered, and a considerable amount of it wound up in warehouses in Shanghai. It was almost five years old and full of worms when we got it, but it was an important source of calories for us. One cup of cracked wheat, boiled, contained about two hundred calories. We each ate a cup of it for breakfast each morning, and it became the most important part of our diet. The cooked worms were hardly noticeable after a while, even though they were easily seen in the daylight. The squeamish among us, and there were fewer and fewer of these the longer we were imprisoned, solved the problem by eating theirs in dark corners. Lieutenant Woodrow M. Kessler of the defense battalion began to notice a sort of hierarchy of squeamishness among the prisoners that depended, at least in part, on how long they had been held captive. A relative newcomer to prison life would go hungry rather than eat the weevil-infested cracked wheat. A man with a little more time in captivity would try to separate the bugs from the wheat before eating. A long-timer, and by this time most of us from Wake were long-timers, ate it all without hesitation. The weevils, after all, were full of protein, and we needed all of the protein we could get just to stay alive.[2]

The Red Cross also took steps to see that flour was sent into our camp. With this accomplished, several of our officers approached the camp authorities with a request that we be allowed to build an oven so we could bake our own bread. Our navy engineering officers, Commander Elmer B. Greey and Lieutenants (j.g.) James B. Robinson, Bermont M. Williams, and Robert C. Walish, had already thought through how they could build such a structure. They had even come up with one they could erect without using any precious (and almost impossible to obtain) reinforcing steel. They designed the entire oven to be built of bricks and cement. Colonel Otera gave his consent, and, with no shortage of skilled craftsmen among the prisoners, the Wake Island construction workers got to work. At the same time, prisoners in our makeshift tin shop began to make bread pans large enough to each hold two three-by-three-inch loaves of bread. When construction was complete, our cooks were able to produce sixteen hundred of these little loaves per day—enough for each prisoner to have one. With the addition of this bread to our diet our menu now consisted of: breakfast—one cup of cracked wheat; lunch—one loaf of bread, one cup of soup, and tea; dinner—one cup of rice, one cup of soup, and tea. I estimated that our daily intake of calories had now reached about 525.

Besides the food packages, the Red Cross people were also able to send in small stoves. Each was about two feet high and eight inches square. Our captors allowed us to set these up throughout the barracks. Included with the little stoves was some sheet tin with which to construct stovepipes. The civilians from Wake turned these out for us, and their primitive shop was later the source of some much-needed tools and other supplies.

Although we appreciated the fact that the Japanese allowed the use of these little stoves, their generosity extended only so far as to letting us use them for two hours per day. Of course, this was better than nothing, but it also meant that to get maximum benefit we had to do something about the fuel we were using. The Red Cross sent in some coal, but like the food parcels most of it was appropriated—stolen—by the prison staff. By the time the prisoners got any at all it was in the form of small chips and dust that tended to drop through the grates when we tried to burn it. Somebody came up with the idea of mixing mud with the coal to form balls about the size of baseballs to give us workable-size chunks. Too much mud in the mixture meant inefficient fires that would not stay lit. Too little meant that the coal balls fell apart and fell through the grate before we could extract the maximum benefit from the fuel. This all took a great deal of effort, and several men worked full-time just to provide coal balls for the cookstoves. What little we got for our barracks stoves was the leftovers from the galley.

Lieutenant Huizenga was one of several POWs who decided that there must be some better way to make these coal balls. If there was just a sufficiency of materials and tools perhaps a machine could be built to do most of the work. He began to work on such a machine, with the approval of camp officials, but was continually hampered by a dearth of proper materials. What he really needed to develop the necessary pressures for his machine was steel, and the closest thing he had to that was some tin scraps left over from the Red Cross stovepipes and some miscellaneous pieces of wood. His plan called for a hopper, tubes, slots, and levers, but he was never able to get a workable model from all his efforts.

The lack of good coal was only part of the problem with our little stoves. Each of these coal fires required a considerable amount of air to get started, and they were likewise very difficult to keep going. If we were to benefit fully from our limited stove time we had to figure some more efficient method of burning the coal. I decided that if there was some way I could rig up a mechanical blower, we would be able to start the fires in the stoves and get heat more quickly. Any such project required tools and materials, neither of which was in great abundance within the walls of Kiangwan prison camp. I would have to steal them or make my own. I first took a piece of a hacksaw blade from the prison tin shop and made a handle for it by mounting it between two pieces of wood and wrapping them tightly with string. I then sharpened the back of the blade on a whetstone so that the resulting tool could be used as a knife on one edge and a saw on the other. Next I "borrowed" a pair of pliers from a Japanese workman's tool kit. I made a hammer from a tree limb, and I pulled nails out of the barracks walls and sharpened them to use as drill bits. I was at a loss as to how to come up with a tin shears and finally had to make do with an ordinary scissors.

After assembling my tool kit I began scavenging for materials. I found that by taking more nails from the walls I could fashion them into rivets to join pieces of scrap tin into more useful sizes. I took eight empty tin cans from a Red Cross food packet and cut the tops and bottoms off, using my scissors/tin snips to cut longitudinally through the cans. Next, I unrolled them into flat pieces and riveted them together into a section about three inches wide and fifty inches long to use for the air duct. I cut some plywood, made of Philippines mahogany, from the barracks walls up in the attic and used it to make the drive wheel and the sides of the blower. Other materials were scraps from the electric fence that I found around the compound, small pieces of bamboo, and a leather shoelace that served quite well as a drive belt. Some of the construction was on a trial-and-error basis, but when I got it completed it was one of the most useful devices we had. We used it to start about twenty stoves per day during the fall and winter.

My air blower was not the only homemade device intended to make our condition a little more bearable, nor was I the only one tinkering. Throughout the camp prisoners began to make their own hibachis, electric water-heating devices, hot plates, bed warmers, and other such little luxuries. Our Red Cross stoves were of considerable benefit, but there were never enough of them for everyone in camp. To solve this problem we came up with small, individual heaters in which we could burn coal, wood, or anything else combustible and get enough heat to warm up a bowl of rice or toast a piece of bread. We made these little hibachis by nesting two different-size cans together, filling the space between them with mud, and cutting an opening near the bottom for draft. We used nails or scraps of wire to form grates over the top, and we were ready to cook. After one or two uses the mud between the walls became very hard, almost like ceramic. My blower also came in handy in starting these and keeping them going.

One man, I think he was one of the enlisted Marines, saw a way to tap into the camp's electrical system for his own benefit. Exposed wires ran along the barracks ceilings on insulators. This Marine managed to scrounge a couple of lengths of wire about ten feet long, and he scraped the insulation off each end, fashioning one bare end of each wire into a hook. He then carefully peeled a little bit of insulation off each of the wires along the ceiling—the "hot" wire and the ground wire. Next he drilled a couple of small holes through a short board, placed it on top of a bucket of water, and stuck his two wires through the holes and into the water below. When he then hooked the other ends of his leads onto the appropriate places on the overhead wires the current flowing through the bucket soon produced hot water.

Hot plates, because they were electric and did not depend on an unreliable supply of fuel, became popular in camp after we learned how to secretly use the enemy's electricity. Some of the prisoners were able to smuggle commercially manufactured hot plates, or at least the heating elements, into camp after buying them from

Chinese laborers with whom they came in contact on various work details. Some even bribed Colonel Otera's chauffeur into taking part in this trade by hiding various items of contraband under the seats of the commandant's car. The colonel would have had a fit if he had known that he often rode into his camp directly over a hot plate heating element destined for a prisoner. Like most of the others who had them, I insulated my heating element with mud. I disguised it by putting it into a hollowed-out book. When I wanted to heat something, I simply took the book from the shelf, opened the front cover, and there was my hot plate. When I finished and it had had a chance to cool down a little, I closed the book and put it back in its place.

The cold Chinese winters and the shoddy, threadbare blankets we had led me to another little invention—an electric bed warmer. This little device was simplicity itself. I managed to steal an extra light socket, a light bulb, a switch, and a couple of pieces of wire. Then I took an empty tin can from one of my Red Cross food parcels, punched a number of holes in it with a nail, and mounted the light socket in one end of it. When I wanted to use it I hooked the wires into the overhead electric lines just as we attached the water-heating device. The heat from the light bulb dissipated through the holes in the can and soon had my blankets warm. My bed warmer worked so well that I accidentally burned myself a couple of times when I brushed up against it. I also learned that thirty minutes was about the limit of its usefulness. After that the blankets started to smoke.

As the number of homemade electrical hot plates and various other electrical gadgets increased, the power consumption reached astronomical proportions. There were frequent blackouts due to all the power being drained off. When that happened our quarters went black, the guards' quarters went black, and the electric fence became impotent. As far as Colonel Otera was concerned the only legitimate uses for electricity in the camp were for the electric water pump, the floodlights, the lights in the barracks—both prisoner and guard quarters, the lights in the prison offices, and the electricity for the prison fence. The engineers at the Shanghai power company noticed that camp usage was much higher than it should be and came out to investigate. They found that the camp was drawing about as much power as the entire city of Shanghai, and Otera ordered a shakedown. Guards came through the barracks collecting illegal conveniences, although they never found my hot-plate-in-a-book.

The confiscation of our contraband appliances was a setback, but not a complete defeat. Mr. Compton and some of the other civilian electricians from Wake began to monitor the camp's only electric meter closely. When it began to indicate excessive use they reversed it for a while so the meter readings were in line with estimated usage. Prisoner electric use soon reached preconfiscation levels as the men replaced their lost appliances and relied on the electricians to rig the meter. In fact, the meter probably ran backward most of the time. The Shanghai power plant still showed excess use *somewhere*, but was no longer able to pin it on the prison camp.[3]

Our lives improved further when we finally received our first mail from home. Some of the letters did not reach us until several months after they had been written, and I am sure that the folks at home wrote a lot of letters that we never received at all. American censors cautioned our families not to write anything that might give the Japanese any hint of low spirits among American civilians. Japanese censors, Ishihara and the other interpreters, also read every word. This second reading slowed things up considerably. It is always a little more time-consuming reading something in a second language, but much of the delay within the camp was deliberate. Sometimes mail arrived in camp and just sat, uncensored, in Ishihara's office until he or his assistant got around to reading it. It was not unusual for this delay to be three or four months, and I am sure that the little bit of outgoing mail that we were allowed to send was similarly held up.

In spite of the mail's rather sporadic delivery, we were always eager to hear from home. Mail has always been important to servicemen, but it is immensely more so for prisoners of war. It is hard to believe just how important this was to our morale. It let us know that our families knew we were at least still alive. Of course, some prisoners received bad news from home, such as the notorious "Dear John" letters. A girlfriend, or maybe even a wife, had gotten tired of waiting for his return and decided to marry someone else. News like that was always devastating and would sometimes be the last straw in breaking a man's will to survive.

The people in the International Settlement in Shanghai sent in some of the books and recreation gear they had to leave behind when they were being repatriated to England and the United States. The books enabled us to start some classes that helped to pass the time. The teachers were usually officers, who, as a rule, had more formal education than most of the enlisted men, some of whom had left high school before graduation. The courses had two goals. The mental gymnastics required of the teachers would keep them sharp, and the students would learn things that would help them when we all finally got back to the United States. What seemed like such a good idea did not last very long in practice. There were never enough basic supplies—even pencils and paper were rare luxuries—to conduct effective classes. Even if that had not been the case, the initial enthusiasm soon wore thin because the men were just too tired at the end of the day to do very much more than eat their meager evening meal and rest.

I was able to use the cover story of teaching a class on celestial navigation to perfect some of my own escape gear. For a while I had considered an escape plan in which, once I got out of the prison itself, I would steal a small boat and sail it eastward until I met up with American forces fighting their way toward Japan. I had already decided that getting away from the camp would probably be the easiest part of any escape attempt. More difficult would be locating a boat without getting caught, and the *most* difficult part of the entire plan would be determining my position once at sea so I could reasonably hope to reach American-held islands. For this I needed a sextant, and, like many of the other conveniences we had at Kiangwan, I would have to build it myself out of whatever scraps of wood and string I could find within the prison compound.

One day when my roommates and most of the other men were away from the barracks, I climbed up into the attic with my little homemade saw and removed a section of plywood from the attic ceiling. Next I located a wooden stick, an empty thread spool, a piece of string, and a scrap of tin. I fastened the wooden stick—my sighting bar—to a quarter circle of plywood, cut the spool in half for my sighting aperture on one end of the stick, and fashioned a tin sight on the other end. The string, with a weight on one end, became the plumb bob, and I was ready to calibrate and test my sextant. After leveling the sighting bar it was a relatively simple task to mark off a ninety-degree line with the plumb bob and then further subdivide that angle into smaller and more useful graduations.

Even after interest in the various classes flagged the supply of books did not go unused. We soon had a regular library, well stocked with the works of Charles Dickens and Mark Twain as well as the more contemporary Pearl Buck, Sinclair Lewis, and Erle Stanley Gardner. I guess a lot of us read for pure escapism, leaving behind for a while our dismal prison existence as we rafted down the Mississippi with Tom Sawyer or Huckleberry Finn or solved convoluted murder mysteries with Perry Mason. Books we never would have considered reading under normal circumstances we now devoured. The library was so popular that the men literally read the covers off many of the books, and prison officials had to send them into Shanghai for rebinding.

Also among our library's holdings were quite a number of back issues of *Fortune* magazine with all sorts of interesting information. I remember one among them that contained an article called "The Wonders of Diet." It covered fad diets (circa 1936), and the relative food values of various items. There was, for example, the vegetarians' claim that a no-meat diet could still supply all the necessary vitamins and minerals. "And," the claim went on, "you avoid the danger of eating animal flesh, which may be diseased and full of putrefying bacteria." I guess none of us were in too much danger of acquiring any of this "putrefying bacteria" while we were guests of the Japanese army. The author also discounted the baked-potato-and-buttermilk diet and the raw-tomato-and-hard-boiled-egg diet, neither of which seemed likely to threaten any of us any time soon. The piece went on to discuss the basic daily caloric needs, which it illustrated with a full-page, full-color chart. One pound of butter, for example, contained all the calories one needed for a full day. Of course, you could also find these calories in a wide variety of other food items if you did not care to eat a pound of butter. You could instead have two small sirloin steaks, sixty-four heads of lettuce, twenty-four bananas, six pineapples, or forty-four dishpans full of spinach. I am not sure how useful this information was to us. At this time we were trying to grow spinach, cabbage, and beets in a little garden to supplement our diet. We might not harvest a total of forty-four dishpans of spinach out of our entire garden, and if we did it would have to feed several hundred men. The bananas and pineapples were just as unlikely to find their way into our diets as the two sirloins, but still it was nice to dream.[4]

The athletic gear we received was enough to equip a couple of softball teams and included basketballs, footballs, and volleyballs. The able-bodied men made up teams, and when the weather was nice on Sunday afternoons and the men were not too worn out from working all week we had regular games. The good-natured rivalry that developed on the playing field boosted morale. Even those prisoners who were too sick or overworked to participate in the games themselves enjoyed sitting on the sidelines and cheering on their favorite teams.

The Shanghai people also sent in some safety razors and hair clippers, and we put these to immediate use. We were all grateful for the chance to have our heads closely trimmed—perhaps even shaved—to cut down on the possible nesting sites for lice. This also gave us a more military look, and was therefore a morale plus. Each of us received a safety razor and one double-edged blade. When that one blade got dull there was no quick trip to the corner drugstore to buy replacements. That one blade had to last. I kept the one I received sharp for over two years by regularly honing it on the inside of a drinking glass.

Red Cross food packages, stoves, mail from home, books, and softball equipment improved the quality of our life in prison but in no way made it tolerable to me. I never stopped thinking about some way to escape. After the Japanese had confiscated our radios at Woosung and stopped the flow of newspapers into the camp we had no information on how the war was going except what the guards told us. And, of course, they told us only about their own victories. I had to have a radio of some sort, and if the Japanese would not provide one I would just have to make my own. This was not as farfetched as it might sound. After all, I was part of the generation that grew up with radio. It was not unusual for boys in the 1930s to build their own primitive radios—crystal sets—and although I had never built one before I determined to build one now.

It seemed to me that the major problem to be solved was in constructing some sort of earphone or speaker. I cautiously broached the subject to some of my fellow prisoners—I didn't want too many people to know what I was up to lest the guards get wind of it—and they all told me that I was wasting my time trying to build an earphone. I was not convinced. Besides, what did I have to lose by trying? As a boy I had often taken apart the receiver of our old crank telephone just to see what it looked like, so I had a good idea of what materials I needed. Since most of the men I asked about it were less than enthusiastically supportive of my effort, I decided to work alone as much as I could. The fewer people who knew about it the fewer there would be to tell me it would never work. There was also a smaller risk of word accidentally getting to the guards.

I began accumulating parts for my clandestine radio by having one of the enlisted men who worked in the truck repair shop steal me a speedometer magnet and an ignition coil. The magnet and the miles of hairlike insulated wire in the coil gave me the basic ingredients for the electromagnet I would have to have. I then took a Red Cross–supplied Nescafé powdered coffee can as the housing. This would be sturdy enough to support all the parts of my earphone and was inconspicuous in case the guards staged a shakedown.

Actual construction took a long time, but time was the one thing that was abundant. I worked on the radio only when there was no one around. Some of the prisoners got excited at the least hint of something like a radio, but their enthusiasm sometimes worked against us. They might, for example, talk among themselves about it within earshot of a guard who, unknown to them, understood English. It would not be long, then, before the entire camp was shaken down in a search for the elusive radio.

It was not easy to find a time or a place to work on the earphone where I would not be interrupted. I did a good bit of the work on it in the latrine, carefully wrapping each of two nails with five thousand turns of wire. Sometimes the wire broke, and I had to carefully peel back the insulation, splice the pieces together again, and reinsulate the repair before going on. After six months of tedious work the earphone was finished—I hoped.

I had been working on the crystal set at the same time and had finally reached the point of selecting the crystal itself. I had picked up several pieces of different kinds of rock inside the prison compound and even tried using coal. I drove a nail into the wall in one of the stalls in the latrine and connected it by a wire to a stake driven into the ground nearby. Finally the day arrived when I was ready to test my crystal set. I hooked it up to the ground wire and used the tin roof of the latrine as an antenna. But it didn't work. I was discouraged and frustrated—because I didn't know whether it was my crystal set that wasn't working or my earphone. I was stymied. I would have to take someone into my confidence to ask for help.

I approached Lieutenant McBrayer and told him what I had been working on. He was not surprised to hear about it, and shared my disappointment when I told him that I had not yet gotten it to work. I asked him to have Sergeant Mohr check my schematic drawing to see if I had left something out somewhere, and I also asked for suggestions as to what to use for a crystal. A couple of days later he reported back to me that my drawing was basically sound and that neither he nor Sergeant Mohr had any ideas for a crystal.

I knew that I was probably very close to hitting upon the correct solution, so I took yet another fellow officer into my confidence. Herb Freuler was a graduate chemical engineer. Maybe he could help. When I told him what I was up to he was taken completely by surprise. He had had no idea that I had been working on such a thing, but promised to try to come up with a suitable crystal. About a week later he came up to me with a devilish gleam in his eye. "I believe that if we melt some sulfur with lead, we can get a crystalline substance that might work." That was the best news I had heard since I started this project, but it only led to my next question: "Where do we get the sulfur?" Herb was ready for this question, too. He handed me a folded-up piece of paper in which were two spoonfuls of sulfur that he had liberated from the Japanese medical supplies. It just might work!

I divided the precious sulfur into two smaller packets so in case my first effort was unsuccessful I would still have some left for a second attempt. As secretly as I could I put the sulfur and some lead shavings into a small glass bottle over a charcoal fire to melt. When the mixture cooled I broke the bottle and examined the resultant glob. It had little bright spots in it—a good sign! I reassembled everything and retreated into the latrine, my special lab, to see if it worked. I began picking up some very faint, indecipherable sounds, and I was ecstatic. I was fairly certain that if I doubled the windings on the electromagnet in my earphone I would have an acceptable radio. After I made this modification, which took almost another month, I was again able to listen in on the outside world.

One of the first items of news I picked up was the surrender of Italy in September 1943, and I continued to follow the progress of the war through the Allied landings at Normandy in June 1944, the Battle of Leyte Gulf in October, the huge losses at Iwo Jima and Okinawa in the spring of 1945, and Germany's surrender in April of that year. I relayed these news items to a select few prisoners, who were very careful where they repeated the information. The crystal set helped make our long imprisonment more endurable, and it was invaluable to me in my escape planning.

With our move to Kiangwan, the Japanese put most of the enlisted men to work building a recreation area, or so the Japanese called it, for about a year. We referred to it as Mount Fuji. The men worked in all kinds of weather, digging earth and hauling it in straw baskets or pushing heavy railcars up a steadily growing incline. This was quite an ordeal for the men, especially those who were sick. One temporary benefit from this work was the chance to trade with the Chinese laborers who were also employed on the project. A lucky prisoner might be able to get such things as an occasional egg from the civilians.

The negative aspect of this trade was that Ishihara got wind of it and determined to stop it. His method was both simple and fiendish. He would single out a prisoner, or a small group of prisoners, for questioning with regard to this illicit trade. He wanted to know who else was involved. If the prisoner refused to answer, as was almost always the case, Ishihara administered the water treatment to loosen his tongue. The victim of this particular brand of torture found himself strapped to a plank that was inclined about thirty degrees. His head was at the lower end. A guard then draped a wet towel over his face and poured water on it. The prisoner would then be unable to breathe, and any attempt to do so would force water into his lungs. A few seconds of this brought the victim close to suffocation or drowning. Ishihara then removed the towel and resumed his questioning, and the whole process was repeated until the Jap guard got his answers or until the prisoner was unconscious. The end result was that trading with the Chinese was substantially reduced.[5]

After some time it was pretty obvious that Mount Fuji was not destined to be a recreation area but was instead the backstop for a Japanese army rifle range. The Geneva Convention expressly forbade the use of prisoners of war for such projects, but as usual, our protests fell on deaf ears.

Three U.S. Army aviators joined us in Kiangwan. First Lieutenant Howard Allers and his two-man crew had been flying a B-25 equipped with a three-inch gun when the Japanese shot them down over China. All such newcomers to camp as Allers and his crew were eagerly sought out by the rest of us because they could fill us in on the progress of the war. The lieutenant was able to tell me, for example, that one of my classmates from my days at Washington State

College had been involved in the Doolittle raid on Tokyo. Captain Ross Greening had been the one to come up with a cheap bomb-sight—which cost about twenty cents to produce—that went into each of Doolittle's B-25s so the Japanese would not be able to recover the new, more precise Norden bombsight from any planes they might happen to down.[6] In a more general vein, these newcomers were able to cheer us up by telling us how the nation's industry was turning out ships and planes and tanks in unprecedented numbers.

Allers and his crew had destroyed what was left of their aircraft to keep the enemy from making any use of it, but Lieutenant Allers had a badly mangled foot. When he arrived at Kiangwan he had received almost no treatment for it, and the muscles had contracted to shorten his foot. Dr. Kahn and Dr. Foley performed surgery on his foot in a section of Barracks 1 that they had previously received permission to turn into a sick bay. They were able to stop the spread of infection and save the foot from amputation, but the primitive conditions under which we all lived made a complete recovery impossible. Allers was able, by 1945, to walk without crutches or a cane, but his foot never returned to normal.

Lieutenant Huizenga also turned his considerable engineering talents to the needs of the sick bay. The Japanese finally allowed the Red Cross to send in a pedal-powered dental drilling machine of the type used in World War I, and Huizenga built a wooden reclining dental chair to go with it. He also turned out several sets of crutches for those who needed them.

Ensign Louis Bishop was another American flier who entered Kiangwan in 1943. He had gone through flight training at Pensacola in the class ahead of mine. He later took leave from the navy to join the American Volunteer Group in China as a member of Claire Chennault's Flying Tigers. The Japanese had shot his fighter down over Hanoi in May 1942 and had kept him imprisoned there until he joined us. He was in very bad shape. He had beriberi, and his weight was down to about eighty pounds; he was a walking skeleton. Our doctors immediately put him into our sick bay and worked to save his life.

The greatest threat to Bishop's life was starvation. If the doctors could put some more meat onto his bones he would probably recover. Bishop was so wasted that his eyes actually bulged out of his face when he saw someone carrying an entire bucket of rice into the sick bay from the galley. The most he had seen at any one time for the last several months had been a cupful. The Japanese made no allowances of extra food for sick prisoners, so we had to do it ourselves. A few grains of rice from each healthy prisoner's ration would be diverted to the sick, thereby doubling the amount of nutrition they received. We all knew that any one of us could be in the sick bay instead of those who were there, and there was no grumbling over giving up a few grains of rice to help our comrades. We knew that they would do the same for us if the tables were turned.

After three months, Bishop was back to normal, or as normal as any of us could be in our surroundings, and told us all about the operations of the Flying Tigers. I must admit I felt a twinge of envy when he told us that for every enemy plane that a Flying Tiger pilot shot down he earned a five-hundred-dollar bonus. I guess there was no way we could control how the Nationalist Chinese government of Chiang Kai-shek spent its American aid dollars.

Not many American air crews came into our camp. We wanted to believe that this was due to their superior skill in avoiding the fire of the less-able Japanese pilots. We found out with the next crew, about a year later, that the scarcity was due to a lack of operations in this theater.

During 1944, two P-40 pilots arrived who had been shot down while escorting a B-24 raid on Hong Kong. They had relaxed their vigilance after the release of the bombs and had pulled back to assess the damage when Japanese fighters jumped them. Another B-25 crew also joined us that year. These men had been on their first mission against the Japanese Shanghai-to-Nanking rail line. I began to think that some of these losses were due to the fact that our pilots were going through their training too fast, that they did not have time for as complete an orientation as they should have. This type of loss didn't do much to help our morale, but we had to realize that it would take thousands of new pilots to win the war.

I never lost my desire to escape, but I knew that any such venture was fraught with difficulties. It began to seem as if my best chance was not to sail a stolen boat eastward, since even with my home-made sextant attempting to hit any specific island within the vast expanse of ocean was remote. Escaping overland also called for some way of figuring out which way I was going, and it seemed that some sort of small compass would be more valuable than the bulkier sextant. I again had one of the enlisted men bring me a small piece of magnet from the truck repair facility. With that in hand it was relatively simple to make an easily concealable compass. I took a small piece of wood and carefully split it longitudinally. Next I hollowed out one of the halves to accept the magnet snugly. Then I mixed up a little bit of rice-and-water paste and carefully put the stick back together again. Then, when the Japs shook down the camp looking for contraband items, all they would see would be a stick of wood and not a potential escape tool.

Operation of the compass was simplicity itself. I just tied a small piece of thread to it so that when I held the thread the stick was free to turn until it pointed toward magnetic north. This method gave very good results, but it took too long for the stick to stop oscillating. Another method was to set the stick in a small puddle of calm water. Within just a few seconds it would align itself in a north-south direction. After trying it out several times I rounded the "north" end of the stick so that on a dark night I could tell by feel which end of the stick pointed north and which end pointed south. After all, once I got into the open Chinese countryside the compass would be most useful on those dark nights when I was unable to navigate by the North Star.

Our camp at Kiangwan was close enough to a couple of different airfields that we sometimes observed various types of Japanese aircraft using Shanghai as a refueling or rearming stop. One day we saw the disappointing sight of one of our prized B-17s landing at one of these airfields and then taking off a short time later for Japan. If it had been on its way to bomb Japan we would have cheered it, of course, but it was not. It had apparently been captured, probably in the Philippines, and was now wearing Japanese colors. It was another blow to our morale.

By the middle of the summer of 1944 we began to hear American bombers and fighters in the sky over Shanghai at night. They were hitting the Japanese airfields in the vicinity of our camp. Within a few months the attackers were more bold, striking in the daylight when we could see as well as hear them. It was quite a morale boost to see the bombs falling and our guards running around like so many chickens with their heads cut off. When the planes appeared our guards chased us all into our barracks and threatened to shoot anyone who came back outdoors before the raid was over. If they thought the planes were close enough they fired at them with their rifles, and they occasionally snapped off shots at any prisoners who ventured too near the windows to cheer.

By the spring of 1945 it began to look more and more as if my prison camp days might soon be coming to an end. The news reports coming in on my crystal set indicated that friendly forces were inching ever closer to the eastern coast of China on their way to Japan. We could see increased air activity in the Shanghai area as American B-29s and P-51s seemed to raid targets almost with impunity. My evaluation at the time was that the next series of amphibious landings would likely be in China, and that boded well for the recapture of Shanghai and the eventual release of all of us in Kiangwan.

I also began to see that the Japanese war machine was reduced to using a variety of makeshift training devices for its latest recruits. I remembered that in the United States, in some of the last peacetime training maneuvers, our forces had sometimes painted the word *tank* on the side of a car or truck because of the shortage of tanks. I was now seeing the same thing again. The Japanese troops training around Shanghai often used two-wheeled pushcarts to simulate their tanks. What is more, the trainee learning demolition techniques was often armed with nothing more than a bundle of sticks tied together with grass rope to represent an explosive charge. He would hide along the path the "tank" was on and then dart out and place the "charge" directly under it before rolling off the trail to the other side. Sometimes these soldiers stayed with their "bombs," practicing for suicide missions. Their training, like ours had been, was now being adapted to doing the best they could with what they had.

Different units rotated through this training on a regular cycle until late in the spring, when we saw a slightly different evacuation of the training camp. This unit seemed to be taking everything movable from the camp when they left. They disconnected the faucets from the wash racks and took them. They removed barracks doors from their hinges and took them. They even went so far as to force entire window frames out of the walls and take them. Finally, when they had loaded everything they could onto two-wheeled pushcarts, one of the soldiers went around breaking out all the glass in the remaining windows. And he was very thorough. When he could not reach some of the higher panes, he swung a teapot that successfully extended his reach. This scorched-earth tactic left little doubt that this training camp would not be used again. It also made me wonder what changes were in store for the prisoners.

8

Escape

Rumors began to circulate in camp that the Japanese were going to move all the prisoners farther north in China to keep them out of the way of any possible American landing near Shanghai. Some even mentioned the possibility that we might wind up in Japan. The rumor gained currency when Captain Tharin, who was serving as mess officer at this time, received instructions from camp officials to have the galley bake up a large quantity of hardtack. This almost certainly meant that we were about to begin a long period without fresh bread, cooked cracked wheat, or rice. One of our less brutal guards, a Formosan whom we had nicknamed "Popeye," confirmed the rumor.

The news of the move was a topic of much speculation throughout the camp. The fact that we were moving at all seemed to be a clear indication that the progress of the war had taken a decided turn against the Japanese. The boundaries of their fabled Greater East Asia Co-Prosperity Sphere were contracting day by day. Most of us viewed this development as a sure sign that the end of the war could not be very far away, although there were some among us who also raised the fear that our guards might simply murder us all if American forces got too close. As far as I was concerned, the move presented me and a handful of other interested inmates with our best chance for a successful escape. If we did not get away soon we would be farther than ever from friendly forces. The main questions, of course, were how and when. A lot would depend upon our mode of travel once we left Kiangwan.

The debilitated condition of most of the prisoners precluded any long road marches, so it seemed likely, what with increasing losses of Japanese shipping to American submarines, that we would travel by train. Lieutenants Huizenga and McBrayer and the rest of the

North China Marines had come from Peiping to Shanghai in early 1942 by train and were more familiar with the Chinese rail system than I was. We would obviously not be traveling by first-class passenger coach so I asked for a description of other Chinese rolling stock. I learned that their boxcars were not much different from those in the United States outwardly, except they were considerably smaller. They had wooden floors, sliding steel doors at the center of each side, and, unlike any freight cars I had seen at home, small windows at the ends of each side.

On May 8, 1945, the guards came and took a work detail to a rail siding nearby to prepare the cars for our use. When these men returned we grilled them for more details on the construction of these cars since our best chance for escape would be to leave the cars somehow en route. The prisoners on the work detail had shoveled out the horse manure left by the cars' previous occupants and installed barbed-wire screens to separate the center sections, where the sliding doors were and where the guards would ride, from the ends, where we would ride. Exit by way of these doors therefore was highly unlikely, and we also learned that the windows had iron bars across them that were set into heavy timber frames. Perhaps, depending upon the condition of the wooden floors, we could somehow cut our way out the bottoms of the freight cars. We did not have long to ponder over the difficulties facing us, because we received our orders to move the very next day.

Our evacuation of Kiangwan prison camp was to resemble closely that of the nearby Japanese army training facility. Camp authorities even instructed us to take the doors from our rooms with us. Amid all the commotion of everyone gathering their meager bundles of clothes and bedding, I was also busy dismantling my fire-starting blower and packing it for future use. It had done great service for a long time so it was definitely worth carrying with me. (Even if I somehow managed to escape before the train reached another camp, the other prisoners could use it.) I then secretly began putting together my escape kit. It included my homemade combination knife and saw, a stolen screwdriver, my canteen, my homemade compass, some Russian cheese, half of a chocolate bar, two sulfa pills, two aspirins, ten matches, and a Chinese-English dictionary of useful phrases that we called a "pointee-talkee." It was a piece of paper upon which was written such phrases as "I am an American pilot. I have just escaped from the Japanese." In use, when we met with a Chinese we would point to this phrase on the "pointee-talkee." The Chinese, who more than likely would not be able to speak English, could then read the Chinese translation immediately below the phrase we had pointed out. He might then point to a phrase in Chinese, such as, "I will help." We could then read the English translation directly above the Chinese, and in this way we hoped to be able to communicate with any Chinese we met along the way. I put my escape kit into a small knapsack that I had made and tore out the important pages of my notebook and put them in my pocket. I was as ready as I would ever be.

On the morning of May 9, we hauled our few possessions, including our straw-filled mattresses, in two-wheeled carts to the railroad siding. The boxcars were basically as Huizenga and McBrayer had remembered them, although many of them had jagged half-inch-diameter holes randomly spaced along their sides—the handiwork of General Claire Chennault's Fourteenth Air Force fighter pilots. This observation reinforced our notion of the superiority of American military power, but it also caused us to wonder if American pilots would attack the train while we were on it. All the more reason to escape from it as soon as I could.

When we got to the train our guards split us up into the groups that would occupy each car. Four of us—Lieutenants John McAlister, McBrayer, Huizenga, and myself—had determined to escape, and since we were all from the same barracks and all of the same rank we felt pretty sure the Japanese would assign us all to the same car. Then, with only a minimum amount of maneuvering, we also wound up in the same end of that car. Our most likely method of escape, we had finally agreed, was to cut an opening in the floor of the car, drop to the roadbed underneath, and wait for the train to pass by. Therefore, as soon as I got aboard I snuck my screwdriver from my escape kit and tested the wooden floorboards. To my delight I was able to work the blade of the screwdriver all the way through the rotted boards in just a few seconds. This was good news. We should be able to break through the floor very easily when the time came.

While I turned these things over in my mind fortune seemed to smile once again when someone noticed that one of the windows in our car did not have the customary bars across it. It was blocked only by a few strands of hastily strung barbed wire. After a hurried consultation we decided to abandon our original escape mode and go out through this window some time after dark. There were too many variables that might hinder an escape through the floor. First of all, going out through the floor of the moving car meant that probably only one of us could go at a time. That person would have to find some handholds on the car's undercarriage and hang on until the car stopped somewhere or until it was going very slowly. We were afraid that if we tried to go out this way at any other time we risked bouncing off the ties and into the paths of the car wheels. On the other hand, if we waited until the car slowed down considerably there might only be enough time for one or two of us to escape at once. That meant that we could probably never hope to link up with one another for the overland trek to friendly lines. No, going out the window at night seemed like the best bet. With luck, no one would miss us until the train was several miles away from where we left it.

Of course, there was still the small matter of getting out the window without the guards in the center of the car seeing us. There was a five-gallon can for a toilet in each end of the car, and it was positioned near the barbed-wire separation between the prisoners and the guards. We were able to convince the guards in our car—without too much trouble—that they did not want to be right next to one of these cans when a prisoner was using it. "You don't want the smell of POW crap in your face," we suggested. We, of course, had a solution to this delicate problem and that was to place the can in the end of the car, away from the guards and close to the unbarred window. Our guards even accepted a further suggestion that we screen this privy off with one of our barracks doors and a blanket so they would not even have to see a prisoner relieving himself. The guards seemed pleased that we were being so considerate of them by making these adjustments.

Huizenga and McBrayer, having traveled this route before, remembered that we would enter an area of rolling hills by the time we reached Nanking, a couple of hundred miles northwest of Shanghai. In these hills the little underpowered locomotive that was pulling our train would have to slow down often, and our best chances to jump without risking broken bones were during these times. We calculated that we would likely reach this area during the night of our first day's travel.

Our progress was slower than we had anticipated. We did not reach Nanking until the morning of May 10. Since there was no railroad bridge across the river there, the locomotive and the cars had to be ferried laboriously over to the north side. Our captors took this opportunity to show the people of the puppet government of Wan Chin Wei how powerful they were by marching us through the city, the same kind of display that the foul winter weather had prevented back in January 1942 at Shanghai. Here were hundreds of American prisoners of war—prisoners of the Imperial Government of Japan.

It was almost dark as we reboarded the cars on the other side of the river, and once again our guards made sure that we hung blankets over all the windows so the light from the lanterns in our cars could not be seen from the outside. This blackout measure suggested that the region through which we were traveling might be populated by friendly guerrillas or at least peasants who would help us once we were off the train. It also meant that the sliding doors of the boxcars would be closed, so guards in the cars behind ours

would not be sitting with their legs dangling out and in a position to
see us running away from the tracks once we got out of our car.

Even if the guards in our car did not discover us going out the window, and even if no one else saw us, there were several inanimate dan-
gers to contend with. We would have to trust to blind luck, for
instance, that when we jumped from the train we would not hit one of
the frequent telephone poles or bridge members adjacent to the tracks,
because even at a relatively slow speed such a collision could be devastating. None of us wanted to start our trek through unknown terrain
with any broken bones. We knew that we just had to take that chance,
but we also knew that the danger would be lessened if we jumped at a
slower speed, so we tried to gauge the speed of the train by the frequency of the *clickity-clack* of the steel wheels over the rail joints.

It was almost time. We knew that as soon as the Japanese discovered our absence they would start back along the tracks, trying to
find the place where we left the train. Because of that we decided
that the first man through the window would only push the barbed
wire back but not remove it entirely. Otherwise, a search party could
find the barbed-wire strands along the track and know where to
begin their search for us. We also planned to leave the car in pairs.
The first man out would hang on the outside of the car until the second man was through the window. Then both would drop to the
ground together and the process would be repeated with the next
two men. The first pair would work its way north, and the second
pair south, until they linked up.

About three hours after leaving Pukow the train slowed, but then
speeded up again shortly. We had evidently topped a small hill and
were now rolling along again at a fairly good rate. We could not
afford to wait much longer to make our break. If the train got into
some level country it would not be slowing down as often, and our
chances of success would be much less. While we were getting ready
to make our move an Air Corps officer near me grabbed my arm and
said, "John, I know what you are planning, and it is too dangerous.
You have survived this long. Don't risk being killed now. The war
will be over soon and you will get out alive." I would not be talked
out of it. I had waited too long. When he saw he could not dissuade
me he said, "If you try to escape, I'll grab you and attract the attention of the guards." I could not believe my ears. How dare he threat-
en to deny me my chance at freedom! I knew he was serious. He was
undoubtedly doing what he thought was best for me, but I was still
furious. I finally promised him I would not try to escape, and I lay
down as if to sleep.

Huizenga and McAlister would now go first. We consciously
paired a North China Marine with a Wake Islander so each group
would contain a man who was somewhat familiar with Chinese

geography and language. Huizenga rolled his few extra clothes and some straw into his blanket to make it look like he was sleeping and then headed for the can. As soon as he got out the window his foot slipped against the sliding door and caused it to bang loudly against the side of the car. The guards quickly peered into each end of the car and made a quick count, but Huizenga's dummy must have fooled them in the dim light of the oil lamp, because they soon sat back down.

McAlister got out next without any undue commotion and then it was my turn. I filled my blanket with straw, checked to make sure that the well-meaning Air Corps officer was asleep, gathered my knapsack and shoes from where I had stashed them near the can, and eased my way out the window. Getting through the small opening was made easier by the fact that intermittent bouts of malaria over the last three and a half years combined with my meager prison diet during the same time had left me fifty-five pounds lighter than I had been before my capture. I had to be careful not to scratch myself on the barbed wire as I went out, because a cut could get infected very quickly, and I had no idea where or when I would be able to locate any kind of medical treatment if I needed it. I tried to be quiet when I got out, but I think I made more noise than Huizenga had. I also found, once I was out, that there were no convenient handholds on this side of the car where I could wait for McBrayer to join me. I hung on for a few seconds until my feet brushed the cross arm of a track signal, and then I pushed away. I rolled down the loose stones of the embankment and then sprinted for the darkness. By the time the last car passed me, the car full of soldiers and dogs, I was about fifty yards away from the tracks.

I ran for about ten minutes, but the night was overcast, with no stars showing through to guide me, so I soon had to stop to get some sort of a fix on my location. I took my wooden compass out of my knapsack and put it into the water of a rice paddy, but it just would not settle down. Something must be interfering with it, I thought, and then decided that the various metal items in my knapsack were probably too close to the compass. I put the knapsack down about ten feet away and bent over the compass again. All of a sudden I heard dogs barking and men slapping at the paths with bamboo sticks. The Japs must have already discovered that I was gone. Maybe if I just laid still the dogs and men would not find me, but as the noises got closer I realized that any dog worth the name would find me very quickly unless I moved away from there. I took off at a run in the direction that I assumed was west. After about a half hour the dog noises were still behind me but were growing more faint. It was then that I realized that in my haste to escape the dogs I had not picked up my compass *or* my knapsack. "Damn," I swore softly to myself. My entire escape kit was lost. I could not even think about going back for it, because even if there had been no dogs on my trail I could never have found it again in the dark.

By now the clouds began to break up, and I was able to locate Polaris to the north and Venus to the west. As long as I had these familiar markers I would not need my compass. The clearing night sky also allowed me enough light to distinguish various geographical features of the countryside. I could now travel along the dikes separating the rice paddies rather than trying to make my way through the water. I kept moving west until I came to a river. The river did not look particularly troublesome. It seemed neither too wide nor too swift for me to cross. As I tried to get to the water, however, I encountered deep gooey mud, almost like quicksand. I would have to find another crossing point.

I headed north, parallel to the river, for a few hundred yards and then tried again to find a crossing. This time I scared up a flock of snoozing geese who set up such a terrible racket that I thought everyone within miles must have heard it. Several more attempts met with the same results. My God, there were a lot of geese in China! After a few more hours I decided that I must wait until daylight so I could best determine which way to go. I had finally quit hearing the dogs, and I was tired from my exertions.

I worked my way into a wheat field and decided to rest there until dawn. In the morning I would seek out a friendly Chinese to ask for help. By then the Japanese would probably have alerted troops and police in the area, so I would have to be very wary of who I approached for assistance. Although I was quite tired from my night's activities, I found it hard to sleep. I was excited at having gotten away from the train, but my elation was tempered by the fact that I had not been able to link up with McBrayer or the other escapees. The uncertainty of what fate still held in store for me weighed heavily and sleep was impossible. I ate a few kernels of wheat and hid myself near a trail while I waited for the sun.

After it got light I observed from my hiding place a couple of Chinese walking along the trail. I watched them carefully, looking for some outward sign that I could trust them to help me. Both men were slender and both wore the traditional peasant garb of a rumpled gray, denimlike jacket, cap, and baggy pants. There seemed to be no way to gauge their political leanings by just looking at them, so I decided to risk approaching them. I stepped onto the trail, and when they got nearer I tried one-third of my entire Chinese vocabulary on them. Pointing to myself I said, *"Mei guo fi ji,"* which I hoped meant "I am an American aviator." My sudden appearance seemed to startle them and they appeared fearful. Maybe my Chinese was worse than I thought. Then they stepped back away from me and made chopping motions with their hands at the backs of their necks. They *had* understood me and were now telling me that the Japanese would cut off the heads of anyone they caught helping an American pilot like me. My next two contacts exhibited the same reaction, and I began to wonder if I would find anyone to help me.

Finally, I stopped a younger man walking along by himself who seemed interested, and after my stilted introduction of myself and some smiles, I showed him the pointee-talkee. Before I could use it, however, he took it out of my hand and read the whole thing at one time, which of course made no sense to him. He still seemed friendly, however, and took me back into the wheat field to hide. When he left I was not sure whether to trust him or not. He might be going to turn me in or he might be going for help. His demeanor was so different from that of the first four people I had met that I decided to risk trusting him.

After about a half hour my newfound friend returned with an older man dressed in a long dark gown and a straw hat. He also took the pointee-talkee and read the entire thing. This time I was able to point to the phrase that said I wanted to go to Chungking, and he seemed to understand and beckoned for me to follow him. We went to a group of four small huts surrounded by a wall. The huts were made of mud plastered over reeds. The only wood in the structures were tree limbs that bridged the tops of the dwellings and upon which the roofs were laid with more reeds. They reminded me of the American Indian huts along the upper Missouri River that George Catlin had painted over a hundred years earlier.

While the lady of the hut offered me boiled water—she called it "tea"—and some partially cooked doughlike dumplings, I tried to communicate with the man by way of sign language. (He had kept my pointee-talkee.) He let me know, as of course I already realized, that my prison clothes made me stick out like a sore thumb amid the Chinese peasantry. I therefore traded my trousers and shirt for a kimono and a straw hat. My Japanese army shoes, which were fairly sturdy, had the major drawback of leaving telltale tracks for anyone who was on my trail, so I swapped these for some straw slippers that were so short my heels stuck out the backs of them. My host then rubbed dirt on my face to try to camouflage my pale skin and motioned for me to follow him again. I trusted him. His actions were friendly and I doubted if he would have gone to all the trouble to disguise my features if he intended to turn me over to the Japanese. We returned to the wheat field, where I hid for the rest of the day.

I kept down during the day and did not see any Chinese at all. What I did see, and what scared me half to death, were two Japanese soldiers not fifty yards away. I watched them closely, but they did not seem to be searching for anyone and they eventually moved off. I had a lot of time to think as I lay hiding, and it occurred to me that the time of year was on my side because the wheat was already tall enough to conceal me but still green enough to bend back into place when I moved through it. Had it been earlier in the season I could not have hidden so easily. Closer to harvest time the stalks would have broken as I passed through, marking my trail for anyone to follow.

After the sun went down, a Chinese boy—I assumed he was one of the sons of the older man—led me to another of the mud huts, where I was soon joined by a man who spoke a little bit of broken English. Our conversation was long and tedious. I wished that I had kept the pointee-talkee. Nevertheless, by repeating the word *Chungking* and making walking motions with my fingers I finally conveyed to him my intention to get to Chungking. He agreed to help me, and the couple occupying the hut fixed me a place to sleep across the foot of their bed.

The next morning my would-be helper returned to discuss the trek to Chungking. First, he scratched the figure "$10,000" in the dirt of the floor to let me know that this was the amount of payment he expected to receive for helping me. I nodded my agreement and said that he would get the money when we got to our destination. When he left to finalize preparations, the man of the house escorted me back through the wheat field to a cemetery where I could hide until nightfall.

As I surveyed my immediate surroundings I could not help but notice that the Chinese method of internment was yet another area where their culture differed from ours. This cemetery contained about thirty burial mounds, each one about four feet high and eight to ten feet in diameter. It seemed that an awful lot of potential farmland in this starving nation was being used up for burial mounds.

During the day, still another young Chinese man brought me more of the boiled-water tea, and by sign language let me know that my chances of survival were very slim unless I could learn to speak at least a little Chinese. This was real incentive, and with the help of my visitor I soon learned the Chinese words for such simple things as "rice," "tea," "doctor," and "medicine."

That night my $10,000 friend informed me that he and four companions would take me to Chungking. This seemed fine to me, even after he told me that it meant another $10,000 *for each of them*. I agreed. How could I afford not to? Besides, the exchange rate between the Chinese dollar and the American dollar was such that I figured I could easily earn the requisite amount. He must have read my mind, because he now insisted that the payment be made in U.S. dollars, not Chinese money. This was a staggering amount, but again I had no choice. How does one put a price tag on freedom?

With the business details out of the way, my prospective traveling companions decided to celebrate with some Chinese white lightning made from broom corn. It was closer to gin than anything else I had ever tasted, but I had to be very careful. I could not afford to offend them by not drinking with them, but at the same time my physical condition after over three years of prison rations would not tolerate very much alcohol. Besides, I wanted to stay alert. There was something about this group that I just didn't trust.

On the thirteenth, I went to another cemetery to hide, and while I was there another man joined me to pass the time and teach me some more Chinese. He seemed to be afflicted with elephantiasis; his legs looked like nail kegs, each one about ten inches in diameter. The lesson this day was sprinkled heavily with political indoctrination. I learned, for example, that Chiang Kai-shek was "number one," indicated with the thumb, and Soong Mei-ling, his wife, was "number two," indicated with the index finger. Likewise in our brief geography lesson, China and the United States were "number one" and "number two." The little finger, standing for the number five, was the lowest ranking digit. In this case, "number five" was *Zippon* (Japan). My tutor constantly drilled me on who was number one and who was number five. He didn't get any argument from me over who was number five.

I made only slow progress in my Chinese-language lessons, and I seriously doubted if I could ever learn enough to get across China by myself. Huizenga and McBrayer had made mention of Chinese bandits in some of the areas, but I did not remember that there was another political party or strong force in addition to Chiang Kai-shek. I never learned the Chinese word for "Communists" and assumed that I was learning all the important words I would need for the area through which I must travel. I tried very hard to soak up everything my teacher put before me.

That night I got some bad news. My guide-for-hire said that he and his friends would not be able to take me to Chungking after all. He said there were too many unfriendly people on the route—bandits, I supposed. He did promise, however, that another man would lead me out of the immediate area. I wasn't sure what to think about my chances. I had spent three days in the same general area and made myself known to several Chinese without making any progress toward friendly forces. Now my best hope of getting to Chungking had told me that he could not help me.

A guide arrived about midnight, and we started off toward the river. This time there was no deep, gooey mud or mad, honking geese. The guide knew where there were stepping-stones, and we got over the river with no trouble. We walked all night until we arrived at a small, isolated mud hut that looked like an igloo, except that it was made of blocks of mud instead of ice. The guide crawled in and awakened the sleeping couple inside. Then, after a short conversation, he left me there and returned to where we had come from.

During that day, the fourteenth, my new hosts made me feel as welcome as our language barrier would allow. The woman went out into a field and came back with some roots to use for fuel while she boiled up a batch of crude tea. Someone had apparently done a very thorough job of indoctrinating the Chinese peasants to boil all drinking water to prevent typhoid and other diseases. They seem to have failed, however, in getting the message across that the dishes and bowls should also be washed once in a while. The bowl in which my tea was served looked as if it had not been washed in a hundred years. Nevertheless, I was grateful for even the small amount of energy present in this concoction.

That afternoon, the igloo's male inhabitant led me off toward the west. It was difficult for me to keep up with him and keep my short slippers on my feet at the same time, but I was not about to ask him to slow down. The more distance I put between myself and the Japanese, the better I liked it. Toward evening we came upon another cluster of a half dozen mud huts inside a protective wall. Milling about within the central courtyard were some horses and a few Chinese in wrinkled blue uniforms.

Inside the first hut I saw about a dozen more such men gathered around a table and looking at a cartoon map of Japan. The diagram showed U.S. bombers releasing their cargoes on the home islands while battleships and submarines offshore added the weight of their guns and torpedoes to the destruction. I was obviously among friends, and in response to their greeting I called into play some of my newly found Chinese phrases. "Chiang Kai-shek," I said, raising my thumb. You could have heard a pin drop. "Soong Mei-ling," I continued, holding up my index finger. Still total silence. One more try. "Zippon," I said, indicating the number-five ranking with my little finger. Still not much reaction. I could not figure out what was wrong. I had tried to pay attention to my tutor back in the wheat field. Could my pronunciation have been so bad that these soldiers did not even recognize what I was trying to say?

I was too tired to worry about my communication difficulties right then. I had gone for over twenty-four hours without sleep, and a good portion of that time I had been walking at a fairly rapid pace. I was taken into an adjoining room and instantly fell into a deep sleep. After a couple of hours a Chinese woke me up and told me that he could speak some English. I quickly discovered that his English was only a little better than my Chinese, but we were able to communicate after a fashion. Over the course of the next hour I relayed to him my recent history. I told him that I was an American pilot, that I had fought against the Japanese on Wake Island and had been captured there, that the Japanese had taken me to a prison camp near Shanghai, and that I had escaped from a prison train moving into northern China. I stressed the fact that his country and mine had a common enemy in Japan. If he could help me reach American forces I could again fight the Japanese and help drive them out of China.

The "interpreter" seemed to accept my explanation of who I was and why I was in his village. He then left the hut for a few minutes and came back with some food—a raw chicken. As hungry as I was—and I was *very* hungry—I did not relish the idea of eating raw meat. And to make matters worse, I didn't really care that much for *cooked* chicken! I did not know much about Chinese peasant culture, however, and I was afraid of offending them if I did not eat it. I certainly did not want my life to depend on people I had insulted by refusing their offer of a raw chicken. Even though the very thought of it made me ill, I did my best to eat a small portion.

By the time I had finished, the interpreter said, "We go now," and led me outside. It was almost dark, and there were almost fifty mounted soldiers in the little village compound. I would be going with them. They all wore the same blue uniform, but their weapons were a hodgepodge of British Enfields, U.S. Springfields, and some Japanese rifles. When the interpreter showed me to the horse I was to ride I was able to see that the tack also reflected a less-than-modern quartermaster system. My saddle was merely a steel frame covered with heavy quilting to protect both me and the horse from chafing. Simple ropes served as bridle, reins, and stirrups. I didn't care what this gear looked like as long as I could now ride instead of walk.

As soon as everyone mounted we left the little cluster of mud huts and headed east. East? I had just come from the east, and it had not been an easy trip for me. Now we were going back in the same direction. Before we had gone far my stomach began to bother me. The jogging motion of my horse combined with the raw chicken I had eaten caused me to have to stop and dismount several times with severe stomach cramps. While I was doubled over from one of these attacks a soldier gave me some seeds to eat, probably poppy seeds, and they acted like paregoric in stopping the cramps.

At about eleven o'clock that night we stopped within two hundred yards of the rail line between Nanking and Peiping. It gave me an eerie feeling to be back so close to where my escape began. At least this time I was surrounded by friendly soldiers with rifles. As we sat there about two hundred Chinese peasants met us. Each carried a bamboo yoho pole, the kind with which they often balanced rather heavy cargoes slung from each end. Some of the soldiers rode toward the tracks, and when they returned a half hour later we all retired another hundred yards or so and waited.

Soon I heard the sounds of an approaching Japanese locomotive and the *clickity-clack* of wheels. When the train reached a spot opposite our point of observation there was a tremendous explosion on the track. We could hear the screeching of wheels and the banging and tearing of metal, and almost before the wreckage could even come to a complete stop the peasants rushed forward under a guard of cavalry to pillage the contents of the freight cars. About twenty of the cavalrymen, my escort, and I then rode off toward the west again as I marveled at this Chinese supply system.

For most of the rest of that night we traveled west in such a way as to save as much wear and tear on the horses as possible. We rode for about twenty minutes, then dismounted and led the horses for about the same length of time before mounting and riding at a very rapid pace for another twenty minutes. When we stopped it was still dark and my companions showed me a place to sleep.

When I woke up the sun was bright and the horsemen were gone. They had apparently taken me as far as they could, so I continued my westward trek on foot and with the guidance of only a lone farmer. At a rest stop that day another peasant farmer showed me a gasoline cap from the drop tank of an American fighter plane. This evidence reinforced the feeling that I was now among friends who knew my background. Later still my guide and I met another man who pointed farther to the west and said, "Two friends." He must mean that Huizenga and McAlister were ahead of me. After all, they were the only others I was sure had gotten off the train, because they had left before I did. I had no way of knowing whether McBrayer had gotten away after I left. Still later we met another friendly fellow who also pointed to the west, but he said, "Four friends." I didn't think I had heard him correctly. Four? He held up four fingers and said, "Four like you." I continued to puzzle over this until that evening when we reached another mud hut compound occupied by men in the same rumpled blue uniforms and carrying the same motley collection of rifles that I had observed before. Upon being ushered inside I immediately saw the "four like me." Sure enough. There were Huizenga and McAlister. McBrayer was there, too, along with Ensign Louis Bishop, our Flying Tiger friend. He had not originally planned on escaping and had not known of our escape plans until they were under way but had observed the four of us get away, so on the spur of the moment he followed suit. It was quite a relief to be among my friends again after six days, and I was happy that Bishop had also gotten away.

We all had stories to share with one another about our own individual escapes. Lieutenant McBrayer told me that I had made so much noise on my way out the window that the guards had the train stopped until they could count all the prisoners and reassure themselves that everyone was still aboard. Luckily, the dim light of the kerosene lamps in the car did not reveal the straw dummies we had left behind. When the train began moving again, McBrayer pulled himself through the window and dropped to the ground alongside the tracks and remained motionless until the train had passed on by. Then he realized that there was a Japanese blockhouse and sentry station not twenty yards away on the other side of the tracks. He spent the next couple of hours slowly crawling through a drainage ditch that paralleled the tracks until he was far enough away from the enemy camp to risk going overland.

It was not until many months later that any of us learned that two Wake Island civilians escaped the night after we did. Bill Taylor and Jack Hernandez had also laid in some emergency tools and were able to get out the window of their car as we had done. Unfortunately, Hernandez broke his leg in the leap from the train, and Taylor, weakened by his long confinement, was unable to carry him very far. They both soon decided that at least one of them should keep going, so Taylor left his friend in as comfortable a position as he could and then headed west. Hernandez was recaptured and remained in enemy hands for the rest of the war. Taylor twice ran into Chinese sympathetic to Japan who attempted to hold him, and twice he was able to get away, once with bullets whistling over his head. He finally reached Yenan, where he was welcomed by none other than Mao Tse-tung himself.[1]

Soon after my reunion with my fellow escapees, Huizenga and McBrayer cleared up the mystery of my earlier chilly reception by the first group of Chinese soldiers I had encountered. After recapping the internal political dispute between Mao Tse-tung's Communist followers and Chiang Kai-shek's Nationalist forces, they told me that these blue-uniformed men were members of the Chinese *Communist* New Fourth Army and had therefore not been terribly impressed when I had boldly told them that Chiang Kai-shek was number one.

This group of soldiers included an interpreter who was much more adept than any of the others I had met, and he was able to shed more light on my recent experiences. When I told the other Americans about my difficulties getting across the river that first night, the interpreter told me that I was lucky I had run into those noisy geese along the riverbank. Otherwise, he said, I would have crossed the river and found myself right in the middle of a Japanese army strong point. We all also learned that if we had made our break from the train about twenty miles earlier we would have found ourselves among a bandit group known as the Silver Swords, who would probably have killed us just for the sport of it.

Being with Huizenga, McBrayer, McAlister, and Bishop was almost like being home again. I had spent six days in a foreign land without being able to communicate effectively with anyone. Now, not only were there four more Americans to talk to, but the Chinese Communists provided us with two good interpreters. We were all anxious to continue our journey. I had recovered from my raw chicken, but Bishop, who had been sick while on the train, was still too ill to travel very far, so we only moved to the nearby village of Hotan.

Our newfound Communist friends fitted us out with blue uniforms like the ones they wore, complete with the distinctive blue-and-white sunburst emblems for our caps, and I finally got some straw slippers that fit. Lieutenant Huizenga's feet were bigger than anyone else's in our escape party, and so far he had not been able to find any Chinese footwear that would accommodate him. Seeing the problem, one of the Chinese officers called all of the village's tall men together and sat the tallest one down next to Huizenga. This man removed one of his slippers and Huizenga tried it on. It fit. The man then removed the other slipper and made a present of them to the American. It was the tale of Cinderella's glass slipper in reverse. All that Dick could do in return was to shake the man's hand and thank him.

By this time, news of Germany's surrender had reached China and there was much celebration in every village. With the collapse of Japan's European allies—Italy had surrendered back in 1943— maybe China would soon be rid of its foreign invader, too. We Americans were in great demand to make speeches on the occasion. The celebrations followed a familiar routine. Things would get under way with a salute to the flag. Then some high-ranking military officer would address the crowd, and a district political commissar would follow him. Then one of us would make a speech. The five of us took turns doing this. It was a relatively easy task since no one in our audience understood one word of what we were saying. I remember that when it was my turn I uttered a few words and let the interpreter relay my thoughts to the crowd. While he was doing that I had a few seconds to think up whatever it was I was going to say next. One aspect of our talks became routine. We all ended each little speech with a plea for greater effort to achieve a speedy victory over our joint enemy, the Japanese.

Bishop finally felt better by the nineteenth, so we started out for the headquarters of the New Fourth Army with a detachment of cavalry. Our destination was about fifty miles east of the Tientsin-to-Pukow railroad at a place called Makipa. The intervening territory was swarming with Japanese patrols, so it was good that we had an armed cavalry escort. I still did not like the idea of spending so much time in the vicinity of where we had escaped, but there was nothing I could do about it. Our method of travel was to approach to within about three miles of any known Japanese positions before nightfall. At dark we would saddle up and ride at a gallop until we were well past the enemy line. Then we would revert back to the ride-and-walk method of travel that was less tiring for the animals.

We arrived at Makipa on May 21, 1945. When we got there, Chinese army officials sent a message to the nearest American military personnel, two observers several hundred miles away, notifying them of our escape and asking for instructions. While we waited for a reply our hosts took us on tours of their nearby military and industrial installations. I will never forget the method they employed to make gunpowder. A donkey, walking in a never-ending circle, was the motive power for a three-foot-long, eighteen-inch-diameter stone roller that blended the ingredients. The Chinese, of course, had invented gunpowder hundreds of years earlier, and I could not help but think that I was watching the original method of manufacture.

I also visited a shop where the workers were carefully reloading spent .30-caliber cartridge cases with the newly manufactured powder. The cases looked as if they had been fired dozens of times already, but that made little difference. They had previously collected a supply of copper and brass doorknobs from some of the more prosperous houses in the area and had diligently worked that material down into sheets that they could form into primers for the shells. Our host, a Chinese general, must have sensed my incredulity, because after my tour was over he insisted that I fire some of the remanufactured rounds. I did, and in spite of my initial skepticism at the rather primitive manufacturing techniques, they seemed to work fine.

Another shop was the site of artillery manufacture. The operation of this shop was most interesting in that teams of donkeys, walking around a wooden cog wheel, provided the power to run the machines. This power was belted to an overhead pulley gang device like those in American shoe shops of the 1930s. The power then branched off to turn lathes and milling machines, although in some cases humans provided the power for lathes. The process of rifling the barrels of the small mountain howitzers being built there was slow and laborious. A crude jig held the barrel forging, which had a predrilled hole through it, vertically. A gang of workers manhandled a huge weight to the top of a pile driver guide and released it so that it would hit a spiral drill bit and drive it into the barrel blank. (I recalled this operation with pleasure a few weeks later when, in the United States, I was asked to talk to a group of reluctant shipyard workers.)

On another of our excursions we visited an army field hospital. From the outside it looked pretty much the same as many of the other mud huts in the vicinity. When we entered it, however, we found an underground area well equipped to perform delicate operations. The medical personnel had strung a parachute up near the ceiling to keep dirt and other debris from falling onto the patients and into open incisions during surgery. While we were there a beautiful woman doctor drew fluid from a patient's lungs with such an air of competence that I had no doubt she was capable of any task.

Although our visits to armories and the hospital were enlightening, we kept insisting that we wanted to be taken to any nearby airfield so we could be flown out. We knew that such fields could not be far because the P-51s that we had witnessed raiding Shanghai would have to have refueled somewhere. The Communists insisted, however, that there were no such airfields within their area of operations. They finally decided that we should go toward the northwest, into An Whei Province, where they could turn us over to some Nationalist Chinese troops. There were airfields in their areas, and they could take us to them.

Whenever we came into a new district in our travels, the political commissar and the general in charge invited us to share a meal with them. In these cases, the two officials, the five of us, and a senior interpreter would sit around a square table. The meals generally consisted of rice, soup, some kind of meat, and eggs, each of which was placed in its own separate bowl in the center of the table. We each had a cup for drinking toasts of Chinese liquor, and a pair of chopsticks. Then all of the diners would begin eating out of the common bowls of food. It did not seem to bother anyone that their dining companions were continuously dipping their freshly licked chopsticks back into the bowls of food for more.

When we passed through villages along the way we saw that the populations enthusiastically greeted their blue-clad defenders. They waved from the fields or quickly gathered around and furnished tea if we stopped for a few minutes. Parents brought their small children to the leader so he could praise them. It seemed almost like an old backcountry election campaign in the States.

As we moved across country we managed to end each day's march at one of the walled villages that were so common. The weather was warm by that time of year, so the villagers insisted on taking enough doors off the hinges of their houses to make each of the Americans a raised sleeping platform. Usually these doors were double doors about seven feet high and eighteen inches wide. The villagers placed them on bricks or other suitable material to elevate them up off the ground, and they were quite comfortable beds after a long day's ride or walk. Comfortable, that is, if you slept on your back. Our bedding consisted of either a quilted saddle blanket, if we happened to be mounted that day, or a quilt from one of the houses in the village.

Our sturdy door-beds served another purpose if we had horses and were near a stream that had to be crossed. We could usually cross on a boat, but getting the horses into the boat was sometimes difficult. Part of the problem was solved by using the doors as loading ramps for the horses. Then, when all were aboard, the soldiers returned the doors to the villagers and off we went.

The Communists insisted that we would need money after they turned us over to the Nationalists, and so they gave each of us twenty thousand Chinese paper dollars. We tried to refuse the money, even though we had none of our own, because up to now we had not had to pay for anything. Everyone had been eager to help us, and whenever payment was required for anything our escorts paid it. They brushed off our protestations, and almost filled up our small knapsacks with money.

Coming from a farm background, I could not help noticing the different farming techniques the Chinese used. In harvesting rice, for example, they went into the rice paddies and cut the rice by hand. Then they returned to the paddies to search carefully for any heads that they might have missed the first time or that they might have dropped. The third step occurred when they collected the roots, dried them out, and used them for fuel in their cook fires. The Chinese method of separating the grain from the straw and chaff was also very different from what I had seen at home. They spread it along the streets and allowed all the regular traffic, horses and people, to trample it down until the grain and chaff were loosened from the heads. After collecting it, they waited for a windy day so they could toss it all into the air and allow the wind to blow the chaff to the side. Then they gathered up the chaff for animal feed and used the straw as roofing for their houses. Viewing this process again brought home to me how much more wasteful we seemed in America. Rice growers simply left both the straw and the chaff in the field, where they burned it in place before plowing it under in readying the field for the next crop.

Because of my interest in their small farms, the Chinese often asked me for suggestions on how to use American-type tractors and other machines to make their tasks more efficient. My experience driving tractors and operating mechanical threshers back in Endicott was that we Americans tended to tolerate a lot more waste than did these simple Chinese. In fact, it seemed to me that we wasted more than some of these families actually harvested. More than that, however, was the fact that the rice fields were too small in most cases to make the use of machinery profitable. In the United States it was the rare farmer who had less than 120 acres, whereas over here that amount of land would have indicated a very rich man. I could only tell the Chinese that we used machines in the United States because we did not have the available manpower that they did, and that they should continue to use their way until there was a consolidation of land.

The diet of most of the villagers in this area reflected the fact that their two most prevalent crops were rice and wheat. They ate a lot of rice and sometimes varied this fare with a dough made from wheat flour. For meat, they often raised their own eels in pits about a foot in diameter and three feet deep; it was not an especially appetizing sight whenever I looked into one of these pits and saw the black, slimy creatures crawling around inside. Most families also had a few chickens, but they rarely ate them. They were too valuable as egg producers to eat.

On June 12, 1945, our little caravan finally reached the village of Mengcheng, where we were to meet up with the Nationalist Chinese soldiers who would convey us to an airstrip. From there we could fly out of China and home. A representative of Chiang Kai-shek's forces, a major, met us in the village, and we ate a final meal with our Communist hosts. Then, after a final group photograph, we thanked them and headed for the center of a huge field, sort of a no-man's-land, where the Nationalists would officially receive us into their care.

The transfer occurred about noon as the five of us, along with one Nationalist Chinese officer and one Communist Chinese officer, started out for the center of this large plain. There were at least a thousand Communist troops deployed along the east side of the field, wary of any trick the Nationalists might try to pull off. We said our final good-byes at the middle of the field, and the Communist representative returned to his troops as we continued walking westward. As we neared the Nationalists' lines we saw that they, too, were poised and ready for anything the Communists might do.

A Nationalist general greeted us warmly as we entered his camp and told us that the first order of business had to do with our clothes. It would not do to have us traveling in the uniforms of the Communists, so we each traded our blue clothes for green Nationalist uniforms, complete with fancy waist belts and ornamental buckles. It seemed odd to me that both sides used the same cap ornament, the blue-and-white sunburst.

We had traveled for a month in territory dominated by the Chinese Communists. Throughout that time our treatment had been excellent. The Chinese fed us, clothed us, medicated us when we needed it, and gave us money. They led us through Japanese lines when necessary and opened up their hospitals, schools, and factories for our inspection. They obviously hoped that what we saw would cause us to give favorable reports to American authorities when we finally reached home, but they did not stress this as their reason for showing us these things. I think that in large part they were just proud of what they were accomplishing with limited means and wanted us to see it, too. We left them with fond memories, dozens of photographs, and, from one of their teachers, a letter that we promised to send on to a friend of his in Chicago after we reached America.

As we continued to travel toward ultimate freedom, I noticed definite differences between our treatment while with the Communists and our treatment among the Nationalists. Food was one area of great difference. Whereas with the Communists we usually ate our rather plain fare in the company of no more than three Chinese, our dinners now were much more elaborate. Sometimes as many as twenty others ate with us now, and the meals were fancier. Instead of everyone dipping into the four common food bowls with their bamboo chopsticks, we now used two sets of chopsticks. We used a silver pair to transfer food from the common bowls onto our individual dishes. Then we picked up our bamboo pair to carry the food from our dishes to our mouths.

During our initial banquet there was also much toasting with *gam pai*, a local whiskey that had quite a kick. After each toast the drinkers turned their cups upside down to show that they had indeed drained the contents. It all seemed innocent enough, and I am sure it was, but before long it became obvious that the five of us would soon be insensible because of the way the toasts were being made. For instance, each of the twenty or so Chinese might rise to make a toast to the five Americans. Then, as we all drained our cups, only the Chinese who had made the toast drank with us. At this rate each of us would have to drink twenty cups of this "white lightning" to each of their one. We quickly began playing their own game as we each stood up, in rapid succession, and offered a toast to all of them. That way they were at a five-to-one disadvantage for a while, and we were able to at least hold our own until the middle of the banquet.

Our evening of socializing finally ended with a postbanquet visit to a Chinese opera. During the night, when the Chinese must have figured we would all be asleep, we noticed that we were not alone in our quarters. Our visitors were carefully going through each of our knapsacks. We were carrying lots of photographs, many of which showed Chinese Communist combat operations; the letter to Chicago; and the Chinese dollars, but everything was in its proper place the next morning. We pretended to be asleep during the search process and only hoped that they would not find anything among our meager possessions that would cause them to renege on their promise to take us to an American airfield. We did not discuss the episode with our host the next morning. We figured that he already knew about it anyway; perhaps he had ordered it.

We left the village the next morning, five Americans and one Chinese interpreter. Our mode of travel with the Nationalists was not much different than it had been with the Communists. Sometimes we walked. Sometimes we rode horses. Our mounts now had the more traditional leather saddles, and I was amazed at how much more noise they seemed to make. Not only did the leather squeak, but it even seemed that the horses' hooves made more noise than before. Another big difference was with regard to care of the animals. We constantly rode at a fairly rapid gait. We never dismounted to lead the horses for a while, giving them a chance to rest. Of course, this meant that we had to change horses more frequently. We also noticed that the Nationalists were reluctant to travel at night or in the rain, nor did they volunteer to cross through Japanese lines. Instead they would say that it was impossible to do so and we must go around.

One novel method of transportation we had not encountered with the Communists was the sedan chair. Part of our route was over mountain trails, and the best mode of travel was in these chairs. And it was here that we were glad that we had accepted the money that the Communists had so insistently proffered. We had to use some of it to pay fifty Chinese dollars per day to each of the coolies who carried our chairs. Some of the coolie teams had trouble keeping up with the others, so we often became separated. We soon devised an unusual method for making sure that everyone stayed on the same trail. We were all eating apricots as we traveled, and the interpreter, in the lead chair, would throw his pits out every so often to mark the trail. Then, as each successive man passed this point he would add his apricot pits to the pile. By the time the last man passed by there was no mistaking that he was heading in the right direction.

At one of the first major command stops we encountered a prolonged period of rain. The Nationalists were in no hurry to continue; for them, escorting us was just another day's assignment. For us, however, each day that we did not travel was one day more until we reached American lines. Every time we suggested that we move on, the Chinese commander told us, "You cannot travel in the rain." We tried to assure him that we could. "Our troops are fighting in this kind of weather," we told him, "and so we don't mind traveling in it. It is urgent that we proceed." He finally gave in and we continued.

After covering 150 miles we met an American officer, First Lieutenant William T. Miller. He sure was a sight for sore eyes! He directed us to an army weather communications station near the village of Linchuan. At Linchuan, a Captain Glass welcomed us and prepared to notify higher authorities of our successful transit across much of China. We gave him our names and ranks, but none of us could remember our serial numbers. There had never been much stress placed on knowing them anyway. Glass sent the information he had on to Major General Albert C. Wedemeyer's headquarters in Kunming, which then notified the casualty branch of the Marine Corps. On June 21, 1945, my parents received the following message from the Commandant of the Marine Corps: "We are happy to inform you that your son, Second Lt. John F. Kinney has escaped from the Japanese. He is now safe . . . in free China but still within Japanese lines."

Arrival at this outpost gave us our first real feeling that we were going to succeed, although our travels were not quite over yet. The airfield that had been servicing this station was pockmarked with bomb craters, and the recent heavy rains had turned the area into a veritable marsh. It was impossible for a plane to land to pick us up. Captain Glass arranged for us to be picked up at an airfield eighty miles away if we could be there by June 23. The eighty-mile distance was as the proverbial crow flies and did not take into account the steep mountain passes and other difficulties to be encountered along the way.

We had to hurry to meet the pickup date, and the weather did not seem to want to cooperate. Again the rains slowed us down. We even received a report that the airfield toward which we were hurrying had been inundated by floodwaters but that two thousand Chinese laborers were making repairs as fast as possible. When we finally rounded the last turn in the mountain trail before the airfield we saw the most beautiful sight imaginable. Sitting on the field was an Army Air Corps C-47 just waiting for us. Major Richard V. Hill of army intelligence greeted us warmly and took movies of us as we joyfully boarded the aircraft.

It is difficult to describe the elation we all felt as the wheels of that big plane lifted off on the first leg of the long flight back to the United States. As we settled in for the ride I could not help but wonder whether my enforced period away from flying had seriously eroded my skills. I eventually went forward and chatted with the flight crew for a while, and when the army pilot asked if I wanted to take the controls for a while I had no hesitation. I was pleasantly surprised to discover that even after my years of confinement I retained much of my instrument flying proficiency. We finally landed at Liangshen for refueling and an overnight layover, and the next day a five-hour flight brought us to Kunming and General Wedemeyer's headquarters. I was now *really* free!

Over a period of forty-seven days I had traveled about a thousand miles through and behind enemy lines, although certainly not all in a straight line. I had covered various parts of this distance on foot, on horseback, by donkey, by boat, and in sedan chairs. During this time all five of us regained our health rapidly, and when we reached Kunming we were in fairly good physical condition.

At Kunming we had a succession of debriefing conferences where we provided as much information as we could on the strength and disposition of the enemy—as well as that of the Chinese Communist army units. We related what we could about the defense installations in the Shanghai area so that military planners could schedule them for future air raids. We were, of course, able to provide very detailed data on the conditions in the prisoner-of-war camps. We provided the names of POWs in our camp and the names of those who had died. We discussed the morale in the camps, of both prisoners and guards, and did what we could to determine the probable effect that psychological warfare would have on the camp guards. We were also able to correct a previous misconception of the prison camp at Kiangwan. American military intelligence had apparently labeled that camp as the site of a Japanese ammunition storage depot and had slated it for a future bombing attack.

On July 2, 1945, we each received travel orders back to the United States. Actually there were two sets of orders. One was for the general priority for air travel, but in case there was any difficulty we could show the second set, marked SECRET. We would be traveling in plain khaki U.S. Army uniforms but with no military insignia. Our cover story was that we were employees of the Department of the Army. An officer at Kunming answered our questions about the need for such circumspection by telling us of a similar case to ours when such secrecy was *not* employed. An Army Air Corps officer was shot down in China, but, with the help of a lot of different Chinese, was able to escape and return to U.S. forces. When he returned to the United States he was besieged by reporters who wanted to hear all the thrilling details about his escape. In telling them what they wanted to hear he even mentioned the exact routes by which he traveled and gave the names of many of the Chinese civilians who had helped him. The Japanese soon learned these details and sought reprisals. They attacked and destroyed many of the villages that the flier had mentioned and executed several of those who had helped him get away. Needless to say, Chinese in that area were extremely skeptical about offering any further help to Americans. When I heard this story, I immediately thought back to the reactions exhibited by the first Chinese I had contacted after my escape from the railcar. The chopping motions to the backs of their necks now made a lot of sense.

We finally left Kunming aboard a big Air Transport Command C-54 headed west. Our route took us to Myitkyina, Burma, then on to

Calcutta and Karachi in India and Abadan, Iran, before reaching Cairo, Tripoli, and Casablanca. We spent a few days at Casablanca—resting, eating as much as we could, and waiting for a plane that would take us directly to Washington, D.C. There were some flights to the States that went through Miami, but we would have had a more difficult time preserving our anonymity from reporters there. We finally boarded another C-54 and flew to the Azores, then on to Newfoundland, and finally to Washington, D.C. I once again stood on American soil on July 9, 1945.

9

Peace, Another War, and Peace Again

When we reached Washington I was immediately promoted to first lieutenant and attached to Headquarters, United States Marine Corps. I spent most of my first two weeks in the United States at the Pentagon giving information to the intelligence sections of the army and the Marine Corps as well as the Office of Naval Intelligence, the Office of War Information, the Office of Strategic Services (forerunner of the Central Intelligence Agency), and the War Crimes Commission. We went over the same material I had provided at Kunming, but in much greater detail.

Although I was naturally extremely glad to be back home, there were a couple of sour notes surrounding my homecoming. I found out, for example, that until my recent elevation to first lieutenant I had been the most senior *second* lieutenant in the entire Marine Corps. The Navy Department had issued orders for my promotion to first lieutenant to take effect as of December 2, 1941, but they had never reached me aboard the *Enterprise* or later on Wake. And, since I had not formally accepted the promotion, it had not become official. But that was not the worst of it. The Navy Department placed great reliance on an officer's periodic efficiency reports when considering him for further advancement. The rating system for Marine second lieutenants was on a scale of zero to five. These scores were then multiplied by the number of months in that particular rating period to arrive at an overall ranking for that officer. An outstanding officer would receive a rating of five, although a grade of four was still considered excellent. The only time a commanding officer assigned a score of one to a man was when he was a total foul-up. It meant "unsatisfactory." If for some reason an officer's superior did not observe his performance during a given rating period, that officer received a rating of zero. Therefore, even though my commanding officer, Major Putnam, had submitted glowing reports about my performance during the defense of Wake, both he and I had then been guests of the Imperial Japanese Army for over three years. During all that time, and certainly through no fault of my own, my efficiency reports contained zeros, which meant that my evaluation was lower than the hypothetical officer who received consistent unsatisfactory reports. This system reduced my standing in the Basic School class of 1939 from 4½ all the way to last—108! I had lost 103½ numbers. Men with whom I had attended Basic School were now lieutenant colonels—three grades above first lieutenant.

A civilian assistant to the Commandant of the Marine Corps informed me, as if I had been unaware, that there was a war on! It just would not do to promote those who had been in prison camps until they returned and attended Marine Corps schools and had their qualifications for promotion recertified. I guess there was a fear that we would all come home mentally unbalanced or emotionally wrecked and therefore be unsuitable for promotion to higher rank.

The next disappointment concerned the war bonds that I thought I had been accruing since 1941. In September of that year, Captain Bob Galer and I had each signed payroll deduction forms that authorized Warrant Officer George Stahl to have $62.50 withheld from each month's check for the purchase of a $75 war bond. Now, almost four years later, Marine Corps Headquarters told me that it had no such record. During my upcoming leave I decided to track down Stahl, who was now a paymaster stationed in my home state of Washington. Luckily, he remembered the allotment request and wrote an explanatory letter to the Commandant of the Marine Corps. My pay records were then updated to reflect the bond deductions along with the three percent earnings thereon. Although I was glad to get this mess untangled, I was still miffed at the lack of promotion.

Lieutenant McAlister and I were summoned to a press conference at the Pentagon. I guess our status, not as escaped POWs but as former defenders of Wake Island, was what spurred the interest, because neither McBrayer, Huizenga, nor Bishop was invited to participate. I took advantage of this opportunity to ask a few questions of my own. In the brief time since my return I had read everything I could find on the battle for Wake, and virtually every account omitted any mention of the contributions of Commander Cunningham. A great many of the articles never even mentioned his name but gave all the credit to Major Devereux. Although I certainly did not intend to take any well-deserved credit away from Major Devereux, I remained baffled by the apparent neglect of Cunningham's role. When I asked the assembled reporters why this had happened they said that when the war started they had gone to the Navy Department to find out who was in charge at Wake. Someone there told them that there was a navy commander assigned, but that they did not know whether he had arrived yet. With this piece of noninformation they next went to Marine Corps Headquarters, where they learned that Major Devereux was in command of the defense battalion on Wake. After that all the published accounts showed him to be in command of all defense activities there.

Near the end of the picture-taking, question-and-answer session one of the reporters asked us what we thought of the movie *Wake Island*. We could not answer since neither of us had seen it, so they arranged a special screening for us. I found it to be entertaining as a movie, but short of the mark when it came to telling the real story of Wake Island. I was barely able to stifle a laugh when I saw the obsolete Japanese biplanes attacking the island. I guess there was no reason, however, for the moviemakers to be any more up-to-date than had the navy intelligence officers on the *Enterprise* when we were on the way to Wake. A little more disturbing to me was how the movie portrayed Commander Cunningham. Although the characters in the film all had fictitious names, it was easy to see that the role representing Major Devereux was clearly that of the hero. The island commander in the film is rather weak and indecisive and is conveniently wounded during the first day's raid, clearing the way for the commander of the defense battalion to take complete control. Commander Cunningham, of course, was not wounded at all and played a much greater part in our defense of Wake than that with which he was generally credited. After sitting through the screening I didn't think that *Wake Island* would ever be considered in the same light as *Gone With the Wind*, but it seemed to be helping to sell war bonds, so my rather negative comments to the reporters never saw publication.

While in the Washington area I received orders to report to an Aviation Flight Refresher Course at the naval air station in Corpus Christi, Texas. Before leaving Washington, however, I took and passed a flight physical at the naval air station at Anacostia and also flew a check flight. My flying skills had not noticeably deteriorated during my enforced inactivity, and I had no difficulty with the check flight. I did notice one tremendous difference between flying in 1945 compared to flying in 1941, and that was the increased amount of radio transmissions that cluttered the air. It seemed as if hundreds of pilots wanted to talk at the same time. It was almost impossible to get a word in edgewise, even when requesting a clearance for takeoff or landing. I had flown into this very area before the war under actual instrument conditions on a filed flight plan during which there had been little traffic control. Pilots then flew at their pre-scribed altitudes, and the scarcity of air traffic made further control unnecessary. Radar was unheard of. No one forecast any danger of midair collisions since everyone believed that it was impossible for two airplanes to be in the same airspace at the same time.

After my successful check flight I was granted sixty days' leave and immediately headed across country. I arrived at my parents' home on July 29 and spent a fair amount of time catching up on what the rest of my family had been doing since my capture. The lit-tle bit of mail from home that had reached me in China did not con-tain very much detail. They had received a letter from me as recently as May, but when they showed it to me I saw that it was one I had written eight months earlier. Nor, I am sure, had I received all the letters they had written. My dad had been working in nearby Colfax, and when the war started he volunteered with a local civil defense militia. After working all day, he often spent his nights guarding the reservoir or other strategic targets against possible sabotage. My older brother, Lindsay, was not able to serve in the military because of an earlier fractured elbow that had left his arm stiff. He still made a contribution to the war effort, however, by his work as a mining engineer. Clair had gotten a job with Trans World Airline as a co-pilot, but as soon as the war began he entered the Naval Reserve as a lieutenant and flew navy transports. I was very proud of all of them.

I also found an enormous pile of mail waiting for me when I got home, and more continued to arrive. There were approximately four hundred letters from people all over the country who had read of my escape. They all had relatives at Kiangwan, although they were not all men whose names I recognized, and they were desperately seek-ing information on their conditions. It would have taken my entire sixty-day leave to have answered each one individually, but knowing how anxious my own parents had been about my fate the whole time I was a prisoner, I searched for a way to send some encouragement to these people. I prepared a form letter and had it approved by Marine Corps Headquarters in Washington. I did not want to hold out any false hopes, but at the same time I did not want to give the impression that the prisoners I had left behind were doomed, either. I described our rather meager living conditions and our less-than-imaginative diet, but I also assured them that camp morale remained high and that none of us had ever given up hope that the United States would eventually win the war. The war could not last much longer, I assured them, and I saw no reason why all of their imprisoned loved ones could not regain their health in a relatively short time after their release, as I had. Finally, I added personal notes to each of the letters going to families of men that I had known in the camp. With the help of Red Cross volunteers I eventually answered more than six hundred letters.

While I was on leave I discovered that radar was not the only dramatic technological improvement since my capture. Along with the rest of the world I learned in early August of the frightful power of the atomic bomb when Air Corps B-29s attacked Hiroshima and Nagasaki. There was now no way that Japan could continue the war in the face of these awesome weapons, and she finally surrendered.

By the end of July 1945, I received a change of orders. It was no longer considered necessary for me to attend the refresher course at Corpus Christi. Instead, I would go to the Overhaul and Repair Facility at the Marine Corps air station at El Toro, California. I barely had time to get married before reporting.

At El Toro, I checked out in all of the latest aircraft. The Wildcats we flew at Wake had long since been superceded by faster, more maneuverable, better-armed planes. I was not only the civilian personnel officer, but I was also to be a test pilot for the Assembly and Repair Facility. While I settled into this peacetime routine I heard from Lieutenant McAlister that he and Captains McBrayer and Huizenga (they *had* been promoted while in captivity) had received orders to Marine Corps schools to determine if they, as ex-POWs, were qualified for further promotion. When I mentioned this to my commanding officer, he arranged for orders sending me to the Marine Corps schools at Quantico, Virginia, in February 1946.

While stationed at Quantico, I also had the responsibility of commanding the Marine Corps Aviation Technical School, where some of the instructors and I built the first jet engine test cell in the navy. Private contractors later constructed similar facilities for other installations, but ours was the first, and it did not cost the taxpayers a dime!

For the next few years I worked very hard at my craft. I had noticed that we were losing many aviators when they encountered adverse weather because they were not trained or were not willing to fly through the clouds. The best way for me to avoid a similar fate, I reasoned, was to earn the highest instrument qualification possible. I also wanted to become proficient in as many different aircraft as I could.

I received orders to attend the Air War College at Maxwell Field, Alabama, in July 1949. While there I seemed almost driven to prove to myself and to everyone else that my time in the prison camps had not hindered my flying skills. The postwar budgetary cutbacks did not provide for very much flight time for military fliers. By this time the number of aircraft in the navy's inventory had also fallen to less than one third of 1945 levels, and most Marine Corps pilots were lucky if they got four hours a month in the air. Somehow I was able to fly P-51s, C-47s, B-25s, and just about everything else I could get my hands on. It was a pilot's dream come true. My hard work and determination paid off, and my reputation soon reached the point that I was chauffeuring VIP visitors from Washington to Maxwell in an Air Force B-25. This caused some consternation among my Air Force classmates; some of them wondered why a Marine lieutenant colonel—a rank to which I had been promoted in 1948—was flying Air Force brass around in an Air Force plane.

I graduated in May 1950, and while I was en route to my next duty station, on the West Coast, I heard the news that North Korean troops had crossed the thirty-eighth parallel into South Korea. That small Asian country, administratively divided in 1945 to facilitate the surrender of Japanese troops at the end of World War II, was now the scene of another war. The Marine Corps immediately canceled what was left of my leave and assigned me to be the operations officer for Marine Air Group (MAG) 12.

By the time I arrived in Japan the first phase of the Korean War was about over. The North Koreans had pushed what little opposition there had been aside and had almost reached the southeastern port city of Pusan. Jet fighters from the U.S. Air Force were doing all they could to support ground forces, but as the North Koreans pushed closer and closer to Pusan they captured many of the airfields from which those planes had been operating. That meant that some American planes had to fly all the way from bases in Japan to do their work. The longer flights meant that desperately needed air support was sometimes late in arriving, and when the planes did appear they were not always as effective as they might have been because they had to sacrifice weight of armament in favor of carrying the necessary extra fuel. As a partial solution to this frustrating situation, many of the squadrons parked their jets and began flying World War II–vintage propeller-driven P-51s (now called F-51s).

The second phase of the war began when General Douglas MacArthur, commander of the United Nations forces, landed Marines and soldiers at the west coast port of Inchon on September 15 and cut off the North Koreans' supply lines. The landing was a great success, and within a few days planes from MAG-12, under the operational control of MAG-33, were operating out of the Kimpo airfield, near the South Korean capital of Seoul.

By the end of September, almost all of the invading North Koreans had been killed, captured, or chased back into North Korea. Thus United Nations forces had attained their original goal, that of reestablishing the border at the thirty-eighth parallel. Since this threatened spread of communism had been contained rather more easily than some had thought possible, General MacArthur now received permission to cross into North Korea and liberate that country entirely from the Communist menace.

MacArthur's staff began planning immediately for another amphibious assault. The target this time was Wonsan, on the east coast of North Korea about seventy-five miles north of the border. This time, however, the North Koreans were better prepared than they had been at Inchon, and they seeded the harbor at Wonsan liberally with Russian-made mines. As it turned out, South Korean troops captured Wonsan on October 10, so a seaborne assault was not necessary, although a slow and tedious sweep of the harbor was required before it could be used to support land operations in the area. Within a few days, I was at Wonsan with MAG-12.

By now United Nations forces were sweeping northward almost as fast as they could travel. As they neared the Yalu River, the border between North Korea and Communist China, Chinese officials grew more and more concerned about the rapid collapse of their North Korean friends. They let it be known that not only did they oppose the presence of UN troops in North Korea, they would certainly not allow these forces to cross into China. Very few American leaders took these warnings seriously. General MacArthur even predicted that we would all be home by Christmas. Such was not to be the case. In late November, China entered the war with thousands of fresh troops, including, I later learned, some of the very men of the New Fourth Army who had helped me escape from the Japanese in 1945.

The entrance of Communist China marked the beginning of the third phase of the war. The original enemy, North Korea, was virtually destroyed, but the new foe was almost overpowering, and United Nations forces began reeling southward. In particular peril were the Marines and soldiers operating near the Chosin Reservoir, about a hundred miles north of Wonsan. Badly outnumbered by the Chinese, the Americans began to retreat toward the port of Hungnam and a sea evacuation on December 1, 1950. Planes from MAG-12 took part in the almost constant umbrella of air support that accompanied this movement, and the evacuation was finally completed by December 24.

By January 1951, MAG-12 had redeployed to one of the many airfields around Pusan. There, on the twenty-seventh, Colonel Boeker C. Batterton, the group's commanding officer, called me into his office to tell me that Major General Field Harris wanted me to prepare a new Table of Organization (TO) for the First Marine Air Wing. This request took me by surprise since General Harris had perfectly capable personnel officers on his staff who could do the job, but orders are orders and I flew over to Japan that day to meet with the general. After brushing off my polite suggestions that his own staff people prepare the table for him, Harris insisted that I was the one he had in mind for the task, and I flew back to Pusan and got right to work on it.

As it turned out, this rather unusual request was a blessing in disguise for me. Over the next couple of days as I worked up General Harris's TO, I also gave a lot of thought to other aspects of the air war. This was the first conflict in which both sides employed jet aircraft, but some of the American planes were having problems. The Marine Corps' only all-jet squadron, VMF-311, had Grumman F9F Panthers that were constantly in need of maintenance. Their unreliability had caused them to be temporarily grounded while problems were resolved, and in the meantime F-51s and F4Us went back into production as a stopgap measure.

I turned in the TO that General Harris had requested on January 30, and used that opportunity to speak out in defense of jet aircraft. General Harris was, of course, aware of all the problems the jets were having, and he also knew that wartime offers no leisurely timetables within which to come up with solutions to those types of problems. That, after all, was why the World War II–vintage planes were still being used. Nevertheless, I continued to plead my case until finally the general asked me what my recommendation was. "Give me command of VMF-311," I told him confidently. "I'll make it go. I have the mechanical background. I've been to the Allison J-33 engine school and taught jet maintenance at the Marine Corps Technical School." General Harris said that he would consider my request and I returned to Pusan once again on February 2.

I assumed command of VMF-311 on March 11, 1951, and now had to back up my earlier claims. My new squadron's planes did not seem to have an exceptional amount of problems when operating from aircraft carriers or from well-established airfields, but there were problems now. The main difficulty was contamination in the fuel. The primitive conditions at most of the hastily constructed Korean airfields played havoc with our engines. Planes taking off blew up so much dust that others had to wait several minutes before following them into the sky. This caused the squadron maintenance men to wage a constant battle to keep airborne contaminants out of the fuel. The fuel itself was often simple aviation gasoline pumped from rusty fifty-five-gallon drums instead of the more sophisticated jet fuel available on the carriers. The gasoline lacked any lubricant qualities for the high-pressure fuel pumps in the Panthers.

The maintenance crews of VMF-311 were outstanding. To make the available fuel a little more compatible, they mixed it with heated oil. They made plugs for the vents on the wingtip fuel tanks and fashioned removable screens for the intake ducts. But contamination was still getting to the high-pressure fuel pumps, and pilots were continually frustrated by the red warning lights on the instrument panels of their planes. It was very exasperating because until we found the actual source of the problem we could not propose a solution. Finally we decided to see if the fuel filters were working properly by adding a dye to the end of the filter and then watching for discoloration downstream from there. Pay dirt! There was leakage around the seals. The filter body, provided by one manufacturer, was too large for the filter, provided by another manufacturer.

Having identified the problem, we now felt that we could not wait to clear the usual red tape. We did not have time for manufacturers in the States to redesign the filters and send new ones out to us. We had to have those F9Fs in the air again. Remembering all the scrounging I had done in my POW days, I hit upon a temporary solution. All we had to do was make some neoprene gaskets for each end of the filter bodies. The closest source of any of this material was at Taegu, about sixty-five miles away. Fortunately, one of my Air War College classmates was stationed there; he provided me with three sheets of it, and we had more than enough to make our seals. From then on we hardly ever had a fuel-control problem.

The more I flew the F9F the more convinced I became of the future of jet attack aircraft. It was a jewel to fly compared to any of the propeller aircraft I had ever flown—and I had flown most of them by this time. The jet engine did not produce torque in the aircraft so the pilot could roll in on a target without slipping and skidding all over the place. This greatly enhanced gunfire accuracy. Of course, the jets used a tremendous amount of fuel, and that is what had caused military planners to go back to the World War II–vintage propeller planes in Korea where they had to fly long distances to their targets.

By May of 1951, Russian-built MiG-15s began making their appearance in the war. The Chinese pilots usually took off from airfields on the north side of the Yalu and, after doing whatever mischief they could over northern Korea, returned to their safe havens knowing that we would not penetrate Chinese airspace to go after them. Then, the next time there was a bombing raid on targets in the north, the MiGs would be back to try to break it up. Lieutenant General Earle E. Partridge, commanding the Fifth U.S. Air Force, decided to try to neutralize the MiGs by luring them up with VMF-311's F9Fs as bait. He figured that when the MiGs saw our Panthers they would be inquisitive since these planes normally did not fly that far north. We would then try to draw them up to chase us. I told General Partridge that it seemed like a good plan, but our limited fuel capacities meant that we could not stay on station for more than about fifteen minutes once we arrived over the Yalu. He said that was fine because he had F-84s and F-86s standing by to finish off the MiGs and F-51s and ADs to attack the airfields.

On May 9, my squadron was the lead element in what was one of the largest raids of the war. Three hundred American jets and propeller planes targeted the North Korean airfields at Sinuiju, on the south side of the Yalu. When we arrived over the target enemy planes took to the air from bases on the Chinese side of the river, but they seemed puzzled and did not cross the river to challenge us. So although we did not get a chance to attack any MiGs, neither did they get in the way of a very successful bombing raid. The only near casualty in the squadron occurred when one of the Panthers flamed out, but the pilot was able to restart the engine and catch up with the rest of us.

My squadron was very busy during this second summer of the war. We provided cover for Marine and army infantry units during the Chinese spring offensive that began late in May. In addition to this close air support we also flew escort missions to protect the B-29s farther north. This heavy activity contributed to the squadron's 2,241 flight hours for the month of June 1951.

By the end of August 1951, Colonel Ben Robertshaw of the Division of Aviation requested my transfer to Washington to be his assistant. Marine Corps Headquarters shared my enthusiasm for the future of jet attack planes, and when I reported to Colonel Robertshaw he told me to begin drawing up specifications for such an aircraft. It was in this capacity, I believe, that my greatest contribution to the Marine Corps occurred. I worked hard on the specifications, talking to anyone with specialized knowledge, and sometimes working into the night. The aircraft that began to take shape in the specifications I was preparing was a fast, lightweight, jet attack bomber with a high power-to-weight ratio. It would have to be able to operate from aircraft carriers without employing folding wings, and it must be capable of delivering at least a thousand pounds of ordnance—bombs, rockets, machine-gun fire—against ground targets. The Korean War had demonstrated beyond any doubt the value of a plane designed for the close support of ground combat elements.

While I prepared the specifications for this new aircraft, a senior designer at Douglas Aviation named Ed Heinemann was working on a new lightweight fighter design. After Major General Clayton Jerome approved my specification on behalf of the Commandant of the Marine Corps and Captain James Russell did the same for the Chief of Naval Operations, it became evident that Heinemann's new fighter was the logical starting place for building the new attack bomber. After reviewing his presentation, I prepared a letter for the Marine commandant's signature recommending that Douglas be awarded a contract to produce a prototype.

Douglas got the contract in June 1952, and the first plane—named the A4 Skyhawk—was ready for testing two years later. By the fall of 1956, A4s were arriving in the fleet, and by early 1958 my former executive officer in VMF-311, Lieutenant Colonel Sam Richards, took delivery of the first squadron of A4s for the Marine Corps at the First Marine Air Wing base at Iwo Kuni, Japan. Ultimately, almost three thousand A4s were manufactured before the last one rolled off the line in February 1979, and they have proven to be durable, hardworking, effective aircraft.[1]

Following a stint as safety officer for the Marine Corps Reserve, where I helped Marine Reserve pilots make the transition from the piston-driven ADs and F4Us to Grumman F9Fs, it was back to Pensacola for more flight training for me. By this time I had flown most of the fixed-wing aircraft in the Marine Corps inventory, but now I was going to learn to fly helicopters.

At the end of my training I received helicopter pilot designation #3808 in 1957, and soon had orders to take command of MAG-16, a helicopter unit in the Far East—Japan, Okinawa, and the Philippines. I have to admit that I was a little apprehensive about spending time in Japan. My experiences with her military people between 1941 and 1945 had not exactly been pleasurable. Actually, I had spent a little bit of time in Japan during the Korean War and had found the people of Japan to be quite friendly, and two incidents occurred that showed another personality trait—honesty. One day I took a jeep into Osaka to pick up a few things. Unable to lock the jeep, since it had no doors or top, I risked leaving some of my earlier purchases in the vehicle while I made a few more shopping stops. They were never disturbed. Another time, also in a jeep, I had crammed a small package into my left front trousers pocket, climbed into the jeep, and driven off. The small parcel worked itself free and dropped out of the jeep and onto the road. A Japanese man saw it fall, picked it up, and then chased me down on his bicycle to return it to me. When I offered him some small monetary reward for his honesty he refused. This was certainly a much more refreshing side of Japanese culture than I had experienced at Woosung and Kiangwan.

I logged over a hundred hours of helicopter instrument flight time in Japan, including medical evacuations in zero visibility with zero ceiling. I learned a lot about those special birds. Of course, no aircraft has an unlimited lift capability, but helicopters seem to be particularly subject to variations in load distribution, altitude, temperature, and humidity. I found that most pilots did not often appreciate the interplay of all these factors. They simply flew by the seat of their pants in many instances. For example, a pilot with orders to transport a certain number of troops simply had them all clamber aboard with their gear. Then, if he was unable to get airborne he ordered passengers to get off one at a time until he could fly the others to their destination. This was certainly not a very scientific approach to flying, so I decided to see what I could do to improve things.

By early 1958 I had devised an easy-to-use checklist for all helicopter pilots in MAG-16. It made use of simple manufacturers' charts for each type of craft. The pilot plugged in values of temperature, humidity, fuel weight, and a few other variables and in less than three minutes could arrive at a safe maximum payload. By calculating the weight of consumed fuel he could then estimate a higher lift capacity for the return trip if necessary. Of course, there had to be some quick way to gauge the temperature, and three such instruments were available. One was called an electrical psychrometer and sold for $107. The second was a sling psychrometer for only $4.78. I soon located a third possibility, a simple Japanese-made wet-and-dry bulb thermometer that cost only $.40. After instituting this new procedure we never had a single accident due to overloaded helicopters, and our payloads were always at the maximum permissible limit.

We also did a considerable amount of public relations work with the Japanese while I was there. A good bit of it was rather standard—making donations to orphanages and so forth—but not all of it. I once took some of their highway engineers up in a helicopter so they could see from the air the amount of traffic congestion on their roads and begin to figure some way to alleviate it. Another time, at Japanese request, I flew down to Osaka, about 150 miles away, to check the feasibility of making a helicopter landing on the roof of the Osaka Hotel. It seems that the emperor was scheduled to visit that city soon, and such a landing would save a lot of time.

All of these positive relations went only so far. Some orphanage officials once invited me to participate in an appreciation day; one of the other guests was the Japanese ace Saburo Sakai. When some photographers asked to get a picture of the two of us I was unable to comply. He had shot down something like eighty-five Allied airplanes during the war, and I just could not quite forgive and forget quite so soon. (I met him again in 1991, and by then I did not have any trouble in shaking his hand.)

Early in the spring of 1959, I received advance notice that I was to be ordered to Washington. By that time colonels with as many years of service as naval aviators as I had were no longer required to maintain their flying proficiency. This was intended as a cost-saving measure, but it pretty clearly indicated to me that the rest of my military career was to be behind a desk instead of in a cockpit. Not only that, but the promotion fiasco during my prison days meant that I was not likely to gain flag rank.

I still felt that I had a lot of good flying years ahead of me and had begun to put out feelers for flight jobs in private industry. In fact, before my tour with MAG-16 I had even contacted Pan American Airways about returning to work there. I probably had more flying time in jet aircraft than any of their pilots, and I felt that I could put this experience to good use as an airline pilot. My leave of absence from 1938 was still in effect, but certain other things had changed. The airline pilots were unionized, and they did not welcome the idea of my stepping directly into the cockpit without first working my way up through their ranks. The people at Pan Am offered me a job, but it was at the bottom of the list. Or I could work as an instructor pilot. Or I could have a supervisory position in maintenance—that section of the company from which I had taken leave so many years before.

I also had other options to explore. My friend—and Medal of Honor winner—Bob Galer had retired from the Marine Corps already and was vice president of Temco (Texas Engineering and Manufacturing Company) in Dallas. He told me that one of the designs his company was working on at its Garland, Texas, plant was a radar-seeking air-to-ground missile called the Corvus, and that if I decided to leave the military I could come to work as a test pilot on that project. Since this was a way to keep flying, I decided to leave the Marine Corps.

Galer had told me that the airplanes Temco would be using to test its missile system were Douglas A3Ds and A4Ds that the navy was providing at no cost. Therefore, I decided it would be a good idea to qualify in these planes before I left the service. This presented a bit of a problem, although it was certainly not insurmountable, because I was no longer attached to a fighter squadron but commanded MAG-16, a helicopter unit at Oppama, Japan. However, my responsibilities included attending monthly Air Wing meetings at Iwo Kuni, home of Sam Richards's A4 squadron. After deciding to accept Temco's offer I made sure that I allowed time during my monthly visits to begin accumulating flight time in one of Sam's Skyhawks. Returning from Japan, I was able to wrangle an assignment to attend A3D pilot ground school at Whidbey Island, Washington, and I made several observer flights with factory test pilots in early production A3Ds.

Following an honorary promotion to brigadier general, I retired from the Marine Corps on June 30, 1959, after more than twenty years of service.

I reported to the Temco test facility at Point Mugu, California, anxious to begin this new phase of my flying career. I would miss many things about the Marine Corps, but I tried not to dwell on them as I looked forward to the challenging and exciting work that I was sure lay ahead of me.

There was nothing particularly hazardous about flying either of the two planes assigned to the Corvus project (one to launch the missile while the other observed). An element of danger entered the picture with the liquid-fueled missile itself. The two-part propellant was so volatile that even the electrolyte for the battery was carried in the wing of the launch airplane and not introduced into the missile until it was cleared for launch. The apprehension level noticeably increased by the time the missile was ready for firing. I was never absolutely sure—at least not for the first several launches—that the missile would not somehow malfunction and blow the wing of the aircraft off. Because of this uncertainty, we flew two hundred miles out over the Pacific and came back to attack a radar station on San Clemente Island, about fifty miles off the coast. That way, if there was a premature detonation there at least would not be any casualties on the surface, and an overflight of the missile was not likely to reach all the way to Los Angeles. However, bailout of the pilot of the A4D—or the entire three-man crew of the A3D, if it was the launch vehicle—would mean a rather uncertain future in the cold Pacific.

To minimize the effects of exposure in case we did have to ditch, each of us wore rubberized immersion suits—secured at ankle, wrist, and neck to keep the frigid water away from our skin as much as possible—over our flight suits. These suits worked fairly well as long as they remained intact. The other pilots and I realized, however, that upon scrambling out of a crippled plane there was a certain risk of snagging the suit on any number of sharp edges that might be present in the aftermath of a wing's blowing off. If that happened, of course, the suit would be almost worthless, and our only hope would be to be rescued very quickly after we hit the water.

Eventually we got new double-slick wet suits, made specifically to our individual measurements, that were about a quarter of an inch thick and were supposed to keep a person warm even though wet. This made us feel a little better about our chances of surviving a dunking, but there was also a negative effect of these suits. They were extremely hot. This was partially alleviated by having long zippers installed in the legs and sleeves so we could open them for a little air circulation until just before we were ready for takeoff. Of course, this also necessitated similar modifications to our flight suits. Even with the zippers, however, I remember sitting in the cockpit many times waiting for the missile to be tuned up and the range cleared and sweating so profusely that the leather band on my wristwatch became soaked.

The early days of the test program saw a fair number of failures before we even reached the stage of actually firing the missile. This was not totally unexpected, since the new technology that works properly *every* time is very rare. After the engineers worked out some of the problems we finally began to have some successes, destroying the radar facility on San Clemente. I sometimes wondered what would have happened if the guidance system in the nose of the missile had not worked properly and the projectile had overshot the target and headed for Los Angeles. Thankfully, that never happened.

About the time we began enjoying rather consistent success the navy canceled the project. Since the position for which I had been hired no longer existed, I took a job as assistant to the electronic test manager at Sikorsky Aviation, a helicopter manufacturer, in Bridgeport, Connecticut. Although this job did not turn out to be as interesting as I had hoped, it was easy to see the growing importance of helicopters in both military and civilian applications. I therefore returned to the West Coast as a test pilot—and, later, manager of flight operations—for Hiller Aircraft Company, another helicopter manufacturer.

Stanley Hiller, Jr., had flown a helicopter of his own design back in 1944, and he had founded United Helicopters, Inc., in a converted wine warehouse in San Francisco to manufacture them while still in his teens. By 1950, Hiller was outselling every other helicopter manufacturer, and with the outbreak of war in Korea that year he was quick to convert his popular Model 360 to military configurations. Along with the Model H-23 that followed, these helicopters were extremely effective as airborne ambulances and saved the lives of thousands of American servicemen by getting them from the battlefields to the hospitals quickly.[2]

By the summer of 1963, the American military buildup in South Vietnam had not yet reached the helicopter-consuming levels of later years, and sales of the Model H-23G were lagging. Marketing specialists Bill Callary and Phil Johnston began looking for some kind of a gimmick to improve sales. They thought that one of Hiller's little helicopters might be fast enough to break the existing speed records for such craft, and if that could be accomplished it would certainly be a positive selling point for prospective customers both at home and on the international market. The preliminary plan was to set records in each of two weight classes by removing the landing gear and flying the heavier class first, and then, after burning off enough fuel to reach the lower weight, flying the lighter weight courses. This all seemed like a great idea to me, and since I had something of a reputation for getting things done on a shoestring, Stan Hiller asked me to look into the matter and prepare a list of what we would need.

I checked out a Cessna 172 from the flying club at nearby Moffett Field Naval Air Station and flew to Edwards Air Force Base, the nearest feasible location for staging our tests. By the time I returned I had compiled quite a list of items that we would have to have to make a run at the records. Considering the company's cash flow problems at the time, it was by no means guaranteed that the attempt would be made at all unless I could find some way to cut corners on the costs. For example, we would have to hire surveyors to lay out the courses. There would be a straight-line course twenty-five kilometers long with intermediate markers at the three-kilometer and the fifteen-kilometer points, and there would be a hundred-kilometer circular course around the control tower. This closed course would have to have a dozen or so easily visible markers to keep the pilot on course, and each of the markers would have to have a ground observer. We would have to install a radar reflector in the helicopter and pay for at least three hours of radar control time. Since we were trying to set records in two different weight classes, we had to have scales available. Officials of the Federation Aeronautic Internationale would have to observe and certify the record attempts. And, assuming we were successful, we would have to pay for a celebration party for all of those involved when it was all over.

Mr. Hiller convinced army officials to pick up the cost of surveying the courses and using the radar. They also agreed to let us use one of their H-23Gs to make the attempt. We solved the problem of building course markers by using piles of burning automobile tires. (This was, of course, before the advent of the Environmental Protection Agency.) We rounded up official observers to man the markers, and even though they worked without pay they still required lodging and food for the few days they would be at the air base. We borrowed scales for weighing the helicopter both before and after the record attempts, and acquired barrels and pumps for our hundred-octane gasoline in the same manner.

We had hoped that I or one of our own pilots would fly these speed attempts, but the army, in light of its considerable support of the project, insisted on its own pilot. The army assigned Captain Bertram G. Leach, a Korean War veteran only recently returned from a tour of flying helicopters in Vietnam, and on October 31, 1963, he reached speeds of just over 123 miles per hour for three kilometers and twenty-five kilometers. Since this exceeded the previous records for these distances, the little Hiller set four world records that day—two in each weight class. The next day, Captain Leach flew the closed course at almost 122 miles per hour in his first attempt and almost 120 on his second. Each of these eclipsed the existing records by about 15 miles per hour.

Unfortunately, even these world speed records were not enough to guarantee Hiller Aviation's success. The little helicopter came in second to the Bell 47G-3B1 in British trials for a general purpose helicopter in 1964, and was underbid by the Hughes OH-6 the following year in U.S. Army trials to decide on a light observation helicopter.[3]

When Hiller merged with Fairchild Aviation in mid-1964, I left Hiller and spent the next fifteen years as a missile planner for Lockheed.

In 1970, on the twenty-fifth anniversary of my escape, I decided to rebuild some of the gadgets that I had made as a prisoner. For most of the items that went into my crystal set I was able to use the same kinds of materials I had used in the camps. There were some minor changes. I found that the speedometer magnets in the Japanese army trucks were finer than those in more recent automobiles. I also had to use a substitute for the metal Nescafé can, since that company no longer uses the same type of can. The best substitute, ironically, was a can of current Japanese manufacture. I never was able to find any 0.002-inch shim stock for the earphone diaphragm. The closest I could come to that was the end of a beer can, although it was much thicker. I used a modern-day transistor radio to test my earphone and found that it was workable and demonstrated the principle involved, although a store-bought fifty-cent earphone would have been much more sensitive.

I also built a copy of the blower we used to start our little stoves in the prison barracks. After completion, I donated it and the crystal set to the Marine Corps Museum at Quantico, Virginia.

Epilogue

I reached the mandatory retirement age of sixty-five in 1979, and left Lockheed. Following this second retirement, my wife and I decided to visit China. I wanted to see if I could still locate the scenes of the events of 1945 that had been so meaningful to me. In Shanghai, our guide told us that there was no use trying to find the prison camps of Woosung or Kiangwan. They had long since been flattened and the area put into agricultural production. There was nothing visible to indicate the prior uses of that particular portion of Chinese real estate.

Gone, too, was the smell of the "honey buckets" that had been such a prevalent, and disagreeable, part of life in the countryside. Although many Chinese still used "night soil" to fertilize their fields, they no longer carried it through the city streets on poles across their shoulders or in the "honey carts." Some farmers had also begun to use commercial fertilizer to increase their crop yields. A certain amount of land consolidation had occurred during the intervening decades, and that had lent itself to the use of farm machinery, something that was not viable during my first visit. In the small fields, however, there had not been as much change. The farmers still cut the rice by hand and laid it out in the street for the traffic to loosen the grain from the heads. By 1979 the next step in the procedure had been updated in that some farmers made use of big gasoline-powered fans to generate the wind necessary for separating the chaff. They no longer had to wait for a windy day to do this.

I found very few of the mud huts that had been so common during my walk through China and that so often had provided shelter for me and my fellow escapees. Instead, most of the houses I saw were of brick and mud with crude tile roofs.

During this trip I asked our China Travel Agency guide if there was any way to locate Liu Young, the interpreter who had been so helpful in 1945. I really did not think that there was much hope of this. A lot had happened since I last saw him. Perhaps he had been killed in Korea. Or maybe he had died in the fighting between the Communists and the Nationalists. Maybe he had simply passed away from other causes. Or maybe he had survived all of those things to retire to anonymity. After all, it had been thirty-four years. Our guide did not offer much encouragement either, but after returning to Peking from a visit north to the Great Wall we were met at the train by Liu Young.

Our scheduled visit to China was nearly over by this time, but I spent a long and enjoyable evening with my old friend. He showed me on my present-day map of China the key locations of my 1945 adventure, and when my wife and I flew out of Peking for Shanghai he arranged for me to have a window seat and to take pictures from the air. I hoped that our flight would take us over the same route we used in 1945. I am not sure that it did, but I was able to spot one area that I believe was the place where I jumped from the train.

Retirement has afforded me the time to keep up with some of my friends from Wake through *The Wig Wag*, the regular newsletter of the military survivors of Wake, and I have attended three of their yearly reunions. Some of them stayed in the Marine Corps, as I did, and many of them have had very prosperous careers.

I do not fly anymore. My last *real* flight occurred in about 1970 in a Skybolt that a friend of mine from my Pan Am days had built. He wanted me to teach him aerobatics, and I agreed—even though it had been thirty years since I had flown anything similar. I had grown quite accustomed to jets, which require very little rudder, and when I tried a slow roll in the little Skybolt I fell out into a dive. I had to pull more Gs than he ever thought the plane could withstand to recover, but we made it.

At about this time I was also the vice-president of a flying club at Moffett Field, near San Francisco, where I was able to fly a Cessna 172 and a Navion occasionally. The price of aviation fuel, however, soon got to be too high, and I gave it up.

The nearest thing to flying I have done since was at a reunion of VMF-211 in 1992. There I was offered the chance to spend some time in a flight simulator for the Marine Corps Harrier. It was just like the real thing. I felt as if I were actually in flight. My only problems were that my eyesight has begun to fail a little due to cataracts, and that made it difficult to see close enough for the instruments and the long distances required for landing. I miss flying, but cannot think of going back into it because of my eyes.

Since retiring I have often been asked what it is that makes a good engineer (my degree from Washington State College is in engineering), a good pilot, and a good leader. I have had plenty of time to reflect on these questions, and I find that there is no simple answer. I believe that some of the characteristics of success seem to be inborn. In my case, I had a natural curiosity about how things worked. This inquisitiveness is probably what led me to study engineering in the first place. The training I got in college, as well as what I picked up from Ray Darden and others along the way, prepared me to look for ways to improve things. I put this to good use in the prison camps.

A good pilot should have something of the engineer in him, too.

He needs to understand completely the aeronautical characteristics of his aircraft. This includes the mechanical, hydraulic, and electric systems as well as the communications and electronics systems. This must all be accomplished during his training so that it comes as a natural reflex and he will not have to consciously think about such things when he gets into combat. But more than that he needs to be able to think *ahead* of the aircraft's progress so he can cope with changing circumstances rather than let the plane drive him into emergency situations. He might, for example, be leading a flight of anywhere from four to a hundred other planes, and any adjustments he makes must be smooth enough for the other pilots to follow. His training must also include such things as how to manage his fuel consumption and what to do if enemy fire disables his aircraft, as well as rescue procedures, escape and evasion, and other topics. When all of these things are deeply ingrained through training, the pilot is free to focus more of his attention on the briefed mission— target identification, expected enemy opposition, proper radio contacts, and so forth.

Leadership is a difficult concept to define, but I think it is important that a leader try to set a good example for those under him. During the Korean War, for example, when General Partridge asked that VMF-311 lead the flight up to the Yalu River, I quickly assented. And then I led the mission. I never asked any of my pilots to do something that I was not willing to do myself. If one of my pilots complained that his plane was not as combat ready as mine was, I traded planes with him. A leader must be fair in all of his actions and should lead by example.

I have set down a considerable portion of my life in these pages in order to show families of future prisoners of war that a man's life need not end when he enters into an enemy prison compound. He *can* survive, recover, and lead a useful, productive life. He must keep his health, morale, and sense of humor up as best he can, and he must support his fellow prisoners. Thousands of Americans have survived enemy prison camps and have gone on to successful careers.

Notes

CHAPTER ONE

1. Curtiss Aeroplane and Motor Corporation, *The Curtiss Standard JN4-D Military Trainer Hand Book* (Buffalo, N.Y.: Curtiss Aeroplane and Motor Corporation, 1918), pp. 11–12, 54, 48.

2. Jay E. Wright, "Pacific International Air Races," in *The Golden Age of Air Racing: Pre 1940*, ed. S. H. Schmid and Truman C. Weaver (Oshkosh, Wis.: EAA Aviation Foundation, 1991), pp. 452–61.

CHAPTER TWO

1. Thomas B. Buell, et al., *The Second World War: Europe and the Mediterranean* (Wayne, N.Y.: Avery Publishing Group, 1984), p. 2.

2. James I. Killgore, "The Planes That Never Leave the Ground," *American Heritage of Invention and Technology*, Winter 1989, pp. 56–63.

3. Telephone conversation between David Kliewer and James McCaffrey, October 16, 1993.

4. *Medal of Honor* (Washington, D.C.: Government Printing Office, 1968), pp. 505, 492, 559–60.

5. Theodore C. Mason, *Battleship Sailor* (Annapolis: Naval Institute Press, 1982), p. 159.

6. Gwenfread Allen, *Hawaii's War Years: 1941–1945* (Honolulu: University of Hawaii Press, 1950; reprint ed., Westport, Conn.: Greenwood Press, 1971), pp. 69–85.

7. Thomas Edward Blake, "Waves and Thrills at Waikiki," *National Geographic*, May 1935, p. 597.

8. Ed Sheehan, *Days of '41: Pearl Harbor Remembered* (Honolulu: Kapa Associates, Ltd., 1976), p. 36.

9. Gordon W. Prange, *At Dawn We Slept: The Untold Story of Pearl Harbor* (New York: McGraw-Hill, 1981; New York: Penguin Books, 1982), pp. 124, 187.

10. Mason, *Battleship Sailor*, pp. 164, 168.

CHAPTER THREE

1. Gordon W. Prange, *At Dawn We Slept: The Untold Story of Pearl Harbor*

(New York: McGraw-Hill, 1981; New York: Penguin Books, 1982), pp. 400–401.

2. Prange, *At Dawn We Slept*, p. 406.

3. E. B. Potter, *Bull Halsey* (Annapolis: Naval Institute Press, 1985), p. 6.

4. James M. Merrill, *A Sailor's Admiral: A Biography of William F. Halsey* (New York: Thomas Y. Crowell, 1976), p. 2.

5. Potter, *Bull Halsey*, pp. 7–8.

6. Robert D. Heinl, Jr., *The Defense of Wake* (Washington, D.C.: Historical Section, Division of Public Information, Headquarters, U.S. Marine Corps, 1947), p. 9.

7. Heinl, *Defense of Wake*, pp. 65–66.

8. Heinl, *Defense of Wake*, p. 9.

9. Heinl, *Defense of Wake*, pp. 2, 10, 12.

10. Henry Scammell, "Pan Am's Pacific," *Air and Space*, August–September 1989, p. 71.   186

CHAPTER FOUR

1. Arthur A. Poindexter, "Informal Report of Operations of the .30 Caliber MG Battery and the Mobile Reserve During the Defense of Wake Island" (Washington, D.C.: Headquarters, U.S. Marine Corps, 1945).

2. Robert D. Heinl, Jr., *The Defense of Wake* (Washington, D.C.: Historical Section, Division of Public Information, Headquarters, U.S. Marine Corps, 1947), pp. 11–12.

3. Duane Schultz, *Wake Island: The Heroic Gallant Fight* (New York: St. Martin's Press, 1978), p. 63.

4. Schultz, *Wake Island*, pp. 64–65; Heinl, *Defense of Wake*, p. 19.

5. Heinl, *Defense of Wake*, pp. 23–24.

6. Heinl, *Defense of Wake*, pp. 24–26.

7. Woodrow M. Kessler, *To Wake Island and Beyond* (Washington, D.C.: History and Museums Division, Headquarters, U.S. Marine Corps, 1988), pp. 50–52.

8. Heinl, *Defense of Wake*, pp. 27–28. Most other sources agree with this range of numbers for Japanese casualties, for example: Winfield Scott Cunningham and Lydel Sims, *Wake Island Command* (New York: Popular Library, 1962), p. 74; Samuel Eliot Morison, *The Rising Sun in the Pacific: 1931–April 1942*, vol. 3 of *History of the United States Naval Operations in World War II* (Boston: Little Brown, 1948), p. 234. Major Devereux, however, claimed nine Japanese ships sunk and 5,350 Japanese killed: James P. S. Devereux, *The Story of Wake Island* (Philadelphia and New York: J. B. Lippincott, 1947), p. 90.

9. David Kliewer to James McCaffrey, September 5, 1993.

10. Paul A. Putnam, "Report of Lieutenant Colonel Paul A. Putnam, USMC," (Washington, D.C.: Headquarters, U.S. Marine Corps), p. 12.

11. The "Send us more Japs" line has been repeated so often that it is taken as fact. The truth is it was very likely the figment of some stateside newsman's imagination. Major Devereux never sent it: James P. S. Devereux, "Fight Left Unfinished," interview with Blaine Taylor, *Military History* (December 1987), p. 38.

12. Heinl, *Defense of Wake*, pp. 37–39; Morison, *Rising Sun in the Pacific*, pp. 235–44.

13. Gordon W. Prange, *At Dawn We Slept: The Untold Story of Pearl Harbor* (New York: McGraw-Hill, 1981), pp. 513, 576.

14. Morison gives the number of Special Naval Landing Force troops at two thousand; others use a figure of one thousand: *Rising Sun in the Pacific*, pp. 244–45.

15. Heinl, *Defense of Wake*, p. 43.

16. Poindexter, "Informal Report," pp. 4–5.

CHAPTER FIVE

1. Duane Schultz, *Wake Island: The Heroic Gallant Fight* (New York: St. Martin's Press, 1978), p. 133; Robert D. Heinl, Jr., *The Defense of Wake* (Washington, D.C.: Historical Section, Division of Public Information, Headquarters, U.S. Marine Corps, 1947), p. 58.

2. These regulations have been reproduced from Kinney's original copy.

3. Woodrow M. Kessler, *To Wake Island and Beyond: Reminiscences* (Washington, D.C.: History and Museums Division, Headquarters, U.S. Marine Corps, 1988), pp. 81–82.

4. These regulations have been reproduced from Kinney's original copy.

CHAPTER SIX

1. Japanese translations courtesy of Michael K. McCaffrey.

2. Lord Russell of Liverpool, *The Knights of Bushido: The Shocking History of Japanese War Atrocities* (New York: E. P. Dutton, 1958), pp. 119–21; Winfield Scott Cunningham and Lydel Sims, *Wake Island Command* (New York: Popular Library, 1962), pp. 121–24.

3. This was probably one of several editions of Oreste Vaccari and Enko Elisa Vaccari, *Complete Course of Japanese Conversation Grammar: A New and Practical Method of Learning the Japanese Language.*

4. Relevant parts of the Geneva agreement are reproduced in Appendix A of E. Bartlett Kerr's *Surrender & Survival: The Experience of American POWs in the Pacific, 1941–1945* (New York: William Morrow, 1985), pp. 329–34.

5. John A. White, *The United States Marines in North China* (Millbrae, Calif.: John A. White, 1974), p. 56.; James P. S. Devereux, *The Story of Wake Island* (Philadelphia and New York: J. B. Lippincott, 1947), p. 223.

6. These regulations have been reproduced from Kinney's original copy.

7. White, *Marines in North China*, pp. 50–51.

8. White, *Marines in North China*, pp. 48–49.

9. White, *Marines in North China*, p. 94.

10. White, *Marines in North China*, p. 95; Woodrow M. Kessler, *To Wake Island and Beyond: Reminiscences* (Washington, D.C.: History and Museums Division, Headquarters, U.S. Marine Corps, 1988), pp. 104–105.

11. Theodore A. Abraham, Jr., *"Do You Understand, Huh?": A POW's Lament, 1941–1945* (Manhattan, Kans.: Sunflower University Press, 1992), p. 77; Kessler, *Wake Island*, pp. 109–110; White, *Marines in North China*, p. 62.

CHAPTER SEVEN

1. There were variations in the contents of these Red Cross boxes. See, for example, John A. White, *The United States Marines in North China* (Millbrae, Calif.: John A. White, 1974), p. 83; Rodney Kephart, *Wake, War and Waiting* (Stanley, N.D.: Rodney Kephart, n.d.), p. 68; James B. Darden, III, *Guests of the Emperor: The Story of Dick Darden* (Clinton, N.C.: The Greenhouse Press, 1990), p. 222.

2. Woodrow M. Kessler, *To Wake Island and Beyond: Reminiscences* (Washington, D.C.: History and Museums Division, Headquarters, U.S. Marine Corps, 1988), pp. 112–13.

3. Kessler, *To Wake Island*, p. 118; White, *Marines in North China*, p. 99.

4. "The Wonders of Diet," *Fortune*, May 1936, pp. 86–91, 120, 123–24, 126.

5. Theodore A. Abraham, Jr., *"Do You Understand, Huh?": A POW's Lament, 1941–1945* (Manhattan, Kans.: Sunflower University Press, 1992), pp. 145–47; James P. S. Devereux, *The Story of Wake Island* (Philadelphia and New York: J. B. Lippincott, 1947), pp. 229–30; Alec Ernest Pay diary, p. 55; White, *Marines in North China*, pp. 97–110.

6. James A. Cox, "'Tokyo Bombed! Doolittle Do'od It,'" *Smithsonian*, June 1992, p. 116.

CHAPTER EIGHT

1. Bill Taylor to John Kinney, December 26, 1992.

CHAPTER NINE

1.   Edward H. Heinemann and Rosario Rausa, *Ed Heinemann: Combat*

Aircraft Designer (Annapolis: Naval Institute Press, 1980), pp. 217, 221.

2. Keith Carey, *The Helicopter* (Blue Ridge Summit, Pa.: TAB Books, 1986), p. 27; Fairchild Hiller Corporation, *Yesterday, Today, Tomorrow: Fifty Years of Fairchild Aviation* (Fairchild Hiller Corporation, 1970), p. 73.

3. Carey, *Helicopter*, p. 33; Walter J. Boyne and Donald S. Lopez, eds., *Vertical Flight: The Age of the Helicopter* (Washington, D.C.: Smithsonian Institute Press, 1984), p. 42.

Bibliography

BOOKS

Abraham, Theodore A., Jr. *"Do You Understand, Huh?": A POW's Lament, 1941–1945*. Manhattan, Kans.: Sunflower University Press.

American Ex-POW, Inc. *The Japanese Story*. Marshfield, Wis.: National Medical Research Committee, 1980.

Astarita, Joseph. *Sketches of P.O.W. Life*. Brooklyn: Rollo Press, 1947.

Bayler, Walter L. J. *Last Man Off Wake Island*. Indianapolis and New York: Bobbs-Merrill, 1943.

Boyne, Walter J., and Lopez, Donald S., eds. *Vertical Flight: The Age of the Helicopter*. Washington, D.C.: Smithsonian Institute Press, 1984.

Caler, John W., and Underwood, John. *The Art Chester Story*. Sun Valley, Calif.: John W. Caler, 1968.

Carey, Keith. *The Helicopter*. Blue Ridge Summit, Pa.: TAB Books, Inc., 1986.

Cohen, Stan. *Enemy on Island. Issue in Doubt: The Capture of Wake Island, December 1941*. Missoula, Mont.: Pictorial Histories Publishing Company, 1983.

Conn, Stetson; Engelman, Rose C.; and Fairchild, Byron. *United States Army in World War II: The Western Hemisphere: Guarding the United States and its Outposts*. Washington, D.C.: Office of the Chief of Military History, Department of the Army, 1964.

Cressman, Robert J. *A Magnificent Fight: Marines in the Battle for Wake Island*. Marines in World War II Commemorative Series. Washington, D.C.: Marine Corps Historical Center, 1992.

Cressman, Robert J., and Wenger, J. Michael. *Steady Nerves and Stout Hearts: The Enterprise (CV-6) Air Group and Pearl Harbor, 7 December 1941*. Missoula, Mont.: Pictorial Histories Publishing Company, 1990.

Cunningham, Winfield Scott, and Sims, Lydel. *Wake Island Command*. New York: Popular Library, 1962.

Curtiss Aeroplane and Tractor Corporation. *The Curtiss Standard JN4-D Military Tractor Hand Book*. Buffalo, N.Y.: Curtiss Aeroplane and Tractor Corporation, 1918.

Darden, James B., III. *Guests of the Emperor: The Story of Dick Darden*. Clinton, N.C.: The Greenhouse Press, 1990.

Devereux, James P. S. *The Story of Wake Island*. Philadelphia and New York: J. B. Lippincott, 1947.

Doll, Thomas E. *USN/USMC Over Korea: US Navy/Marine Corps Air Operations Over Korea 1950–53*. Carrollton, Tex.: Squadron/Signal Publications, 1988.

Fairchild Hiller Corporation. *Yesterday, Today, Tomorrow: Fifty Years of Fairchild Aviation*. Fairchild Hiller Corporation, 1970.

Francillon, R. J. *Japanese Aircraft of the Pacific War*. New York: Funk and Wagnalls, 1970.

Frank, Benis, and Shaw, Henry I., Jr. *Victory and Occupation: History of U.S. Marine Corps Operations in World War II: Victory and Occupation*, vol. 5. Washington: Historical Branch, G-3 Division, Headquarters, U.S. Marine Corps, 1968.

Grover, David H., and Grover, Gretchen G. *Captives of Shanghai: The Story of the* President Harrison. Napa, Calif.: Western Maritime Press, 1989.

Hallion, Richard P. *The Naval Air War in Korea*. Baltimore: Nautical and Aviation Publishing Company of America, 1986.

Heinemann, Edward H., and Rausa, Rosario. *Ed Heinemann: Combat Aircraft Designer*. Annapolis: Naval Institute Press, 1980.

Heinl, Robert D., Jr. *The Defense of Wake*. Washington, D.C.: Historical Section, Division of Public Information, Headquarters, U.S. Marine Corps, 1947.

Hill, Joe. *Some Early Birds: The Memoirs of a Naval Aviation Cadet, 1935–1945*. Manhattan, Kans.: Sunflower University Press, 1983.

Hill, Richard Vernon. *My War with Imperial Japan: Escape and Evasion*. New York, Los Angeles, and Chicago: Vantage Press, 1990.

Isely, Jeter A., and Crowl, Philip A. *The U.S. Marines and Amphibious War: Its Theory, and Its Practice in the Pacific*. Princeton, N.J.: Princeton University Press, 1951.

James, Joe. *Teacher Wore a Parachute*. New York: A.S. Barnes, 1966.

Johnson, Edward C. *Marine Corps Aviation: The Early Years, 1912–1940*. Edited by Graham Cosmas. Washington, D.C.: History and Museums Division, Headquarters, U.S. Marine Corps, 1977.

Kephart, Rodney. *Wake, War and Waiting*. Stanley, N.D.: Rodney Kephart, n.d.

Kerr, E. Bartlett. *Surrender and Survival*. New York: William Morrow, 1985.

Kessler, Woodrow M. *To Wake Island and Beyond: Reminiscences*. Washington, D.C.: History and Museums Division, Headquarters, U.S. Marine Corps, 1988.

Layton, Edwin T.; Pineau, Roger; and Costello, John. *"And I Was There."* New York: William Morrow, 1985.

LeVier, Anthony. *Pilot*. New York: Harper, 1954.

Linnekin, Richard. *Eighty Knots to Mach 2: Forty-Five Years in the Cockpit*. Annapolis: Naval Institute Press, 1980.

Mason, Theodore C. *Battleship Sailor*. Annapolis: Naval Institute Press, 1982.

McBrayer, James D., Jr. *Escape! Memoir of a World War II Marine Who Broke Out of a Japanese POW Camp and Linked Up with Chinese Communist Guerrillas*. Jefferson, N.C., and London: McFarland, 1994.

Merrill, James M. *A Sailor's Admiral: A Biography of William F. Halsey*. New York: Thomas Y. Crowell, 1976.

Mersky, Peter B. *U.S. Marine Corps Aviation, 1912 to the Present*. Annapolis: Nautical and Aviation Publishing Co. of America, 1983.

Millett, Allan R. *Semper Fidelis: The History of the United States Marine Corps*. New York: MacMillan, 1980.

Morison, Samuel Eliot. *The Rising Sun in the Pacific: 1931–April 1942*, vol. 3 of *History of United States Naval Operations in World War II*. Boston: Little Brown, 1948.

Polmar, Norman. *Aircraft Carriers: A Graphic History of Carrier Aviation and its Influence on World Events*. Garden City, N.Y.: Doubleday, 1969.

Potter, E. B. *Bull Halsey*. Annapolis: Naval Institute Press, 1985.

Prange, Gordon W. *At Dawn We Slept: The Untold Story of Pearl Harbor*. New York: McGraw-Hill, 1981.

Rea, Robert R. *Wings of Gold: An Account of Naval Aviation Training in World War II: The Correspondence of Aviation Cadet/Ensign Robert R. Rea*. Edited by Wesley Philips Newton and Robert R. Rea. Tuscaloosa and London: University of Alabama Press, 1987.

Reynolds, Quentin. *Officially Dead: The Story of Commander C. D. Smith*. New York: Random House, 1945.

Russel of Liverpool, Lord. *Knights of Bushido: The Shocking History of Japanese War Atrocities*. Liverpool: E. P. Dutton, 1958.

Sambito, William J. *A History of Marine Attack Squadron 311*. Washington, D.C.: History and Museums Division, Headquarters U.S. Marine Corps, 1978.

Schultz, Duane. *Wake Island: The Heroic Gallant Fight*. New York: St. Martin's Press, 1978.

Seventeenth International Red Cross Conference. *Report of the International Committee of the Red Cross on its Activities during the Second World War (September 1, 1939–June 30, 1947)*. 3 vols. Geneva, 1948.

Sheehan, Ed. *Days of '41: Pearl Harbor Remembered*. Honolulu: Kapa Associates, Ltd., 1976.

Sherrod, Robert. *History of Marine Corps Aviation in World War II*. Washington: Combat Forces Press, 1952.

Swanborough, Gordon, and Bowers, Peter M. *United States Navy Aircraft since 1911*. New York: Funk and Wagnalls, 1968.

Tillman, Barrett. *The Wildcat in WWII*. Annapolis: Nautical and Aviation Publishing Company of America, 1983.

Updegraph, Charles L., Jr. *U.S. Marine Corps Special Units of World War II*. Marine Corps Historical Reference Pamphlet. Washington, D.C.: Historical Section, United States Marine Corps, 1972.

Wagner, Ray. *American Combat Planes*. Garden City, N.Y.: Doubleday and Co., 1968.

White, John A. *The United States Marines in North China*. Millbrae, Calif.: John A. White, 1974.

Williams, Robert H. *The Old Corps: A Portrait of the U.S. Marine Corps Between the Wars*. Annapolis: Naval Institute Press, 1982.

ARTICLES

Anderson, Charles R. "The United States Army in Hawaii: Outpost Reinforcement in 1941." *Army History*, Fall 1991, pp. 1–8.

Andrews, Peter. "The Defense of Wake." *American Heritage*, July/August 1987, pp. 65–80.

Baldwin, Hanson W. "The Saga of Wake." *Virginia Quarterly Review*, Summer 1942, pp. 321–35.

Blake, Thomas Edward. "Waves and Thrills at Waikiki." *National Geographic*, May 1935, pp. 597–604.

Burroughs, John R. "The Siege of Wake Island." *American Heritage*, June 1959, pp. 65–76.

Castle, William R. "Hawaii, Then and Now." *National Geographic*, October 1938, pp. 419–21, 423–27, 432–34, 443–44, 451–53, 455–57, 460–62.

Cox, James A. "'Tokyo Bombed! Doolittle Do'od It.'" *Smithsonian*, June 1992, pp. 112–14, 116, 118, 120, 122, 124, 126, 128.

Davenport, Walter. "Impregnable Pearl Harbor." *Collier's*, June 14, 1941.

Devereux, James P. S. "Fight Left Unfinished." Interview by Blaine Taylor. *Military History*, December 1987, pp. 34–41.

Elliott, John M. "Wake Island: A Gallant Defense." *Naval Aviation News*, January–February 1992, pp. 26–31.

Graybar, Lloyd J. "American Pacific Strategy After Pearl Harbor: The Relief of Wake Island." *Prologue*, Fall 1980, pp. 134–50.

"Hawaii: Sugar Coated Fort." *Fortune*, August 1940, pp. 31–37, 78, 81–82.

Heinl, Robert D., Jr. "'We're Headed for Wake.'" *Marine Corps Gazette*, June 1946, pp. 35–38.

Holmes, Wilfred J. "Pearl Harbor Aftermath." *U.S. Naval Institute Proceedings*, December 1978, pp. 68–75.

"Japs Lie About U.S. Heroes." *Life*, September 14, 1942, pp. 25–29.

Junghans, Earl A. "Wake's POWs." *U.S. Naval Institute Proceedings*, February 1983, pp. 43–50.

Ketcham, Richard M. "Warming Up on the Sidelines for World War II." *Smithsonian*, September 1991, pp. 88–94, 96, 98, 100, 102–103.

Killgore, James I. "The Planes That Never Leave the Ground." *American Heritage of Invention and Technology*, Winter 1989, pp. 56–63.

Kinney, John F. "The Case for Jet Attack Aircraft in Korea." *Foundation*, Fall 1983, pp. 23–29, 61–64.

McPoil, William D. "The Development and Defense of Wake Island, 1934–1941." *Prologue*, Winter 1991, pp. 360–66.

Miller, William Burke. "Flying the Pacific." *National Geographic*, December 1936, pp. 665–707.

"Pan American Airways." *Fortune*, April 1936, pp. 78–93.

Poindexter, Arthur A. "Wake Island: America's First Victory." *Leatherneck*, December 1991, pp. 28–35.

———. "Our Last Hurrah on Wake." *American History Illustrated*, January–February 1992, pp. 64–67, 73–74.

Scammell, Henry. "Pan Am's Pacific." *Air and Space*, August–September 1989, pp. 64–73.

Urwin, Gregory J. W. "The Wildcats of Wake Island." *Air Classics*, September 1977, pp. 76–82; 94–95.

———. "Profile of a Marine Aviator." *Air Combat*, March 1980, pp. 60–65.

———. "The Road Back from Wake Island." *American History Illustrated*, December 1980, pp. 16–23.

———. "The Road Back from Wake Island." *American History Illustrated*, January 1981, pp. 43–49.

———. "The Defenders of Wake Island and Their Two Wars, 1941–1945." *Prologue*, Winter 1991, pp. 368–81.

"The Wonders of Diet." *Fortune*, May 1936, pp. 86–91, 120, 123–24, 126.

Wilson, Kenneth D. "The Story of Roscoe Turner, Someone and 'Something Special.'" *The Golden Age of Air Racing: Pre 1940*. Edited by S. H. Schmid and Truman C. Weaver. Oshkosh, Wis.: EAA Aviation Foundation, 1991, pp. 466–81.

Wright, Jay E. "Pacific International Air Races." *The Golden Age of Air Racing: Pre 1940*. Edited by S. H. Schmid and Truman C. Weaver. Oshkosh, Wis.: EAA Aviation Foundation, 1991, pp. 452–61.

UNPUBLISHED

Devereux, James P. S. "Wake Island Report." Washington, D.C.: Headquarters, U.S. Marine Corps, 1946.

Infusino, Frank J., Jr. "The United States Marine Corps and War Planning (1900–1941)." M.A. thesis, California State University at San Diego, 1973.

Kiangwan Prisoner of War Camp, Record Group 389, National Archives.

David Kliewer to James McCaffrey, September 5, 1993.

David Kliewer to James McCaffrey (telephone conversation), October 16, 1993.

Pay, Alec Ernest. Diary (typescript). December 8, 1941, to September 23, 1945.

Platt, Wesley McC. "Informal Report on the Defense of Wilkes (Island)." Ca. 1945.

Poindexter, Arthur A. "Informal Report of Operations of the .30 Caliber MG Battery and the Mobile Reserve During the Defense of Wake Island." Washington, D.C.: Headquarters, U.S. Marine Corps, 1945.

Putnam, Paul A. "Report of Lieutenant Colonel Paul A. Putnam, USMC." Washington, D.C.: Headquarters, U.S. Marine Corps, 1945.

Records of the Office of the Provost Marshall General, Kiangwan, China; Folders 1 and 2, Record Group 389, National Archives.

Slezak, Rudolph M. Diary (typescript). April 29, 1943, to July 5, 1945.

Index

Biographies

JOHN F. KINNEY was born in Endicott, Washington, in 1914. His love of aviation led him to become a Marine Corps fighter pilot in 1940. Captured during the early weeks of World War II, Kinney survived three and a half years in a Japanese prison camp until his escape in May 1945. He stayed in the service after the war, commanding a Marine fighter squadron in the Korean War, where he flew 125 combat missions, and a helicopter group in the late 1950s. As head of the Operations Requirements Section at Marine Corps Headquarters he drew up the requirements for a jet attack aircraft that led to the adoption of the Douglas A4. Following retirement from the Marine Corps in 1959 with the rank of brigadier general, Kinney spent another twenty years working for various aviation companies. Kinney's awards include the Bronze Star, the Silver Star, two Legions of Merit, the Distinguished Flying Cross, thirteen Air Medals, the POW Medal, the Wake Island Expeditionary Medal, the Pacific Theater Campaign Medal, the World War II Victory Medal, and the Korean Campaign Medal. John is also one of only two hundred members of the Golden Eagles (the Early and Pioneer Naval Aviators Association) and remains active in the Marine Corps Aviation Association, the Naval Aviation Museum Foundation, the Marine Corps Historical Foundation, and Alpha Tau Omega Fraternity. He and his wife, June, reside in Portola Valley, California.

JAMES M. McCAFFREY is an associate professor of history at the University of Houston–Downtown. His previous books include *This Band of Heroes: Granbury's Texas Brigade, C.S.A.* (1985) and *Army of Manifest Destiny: The American Soldier in the Mexican War, 1846–1848* (1992).